THE
GERMAN SOCIAL DEMOCRATS AND
THE FIRST INTERNATIONAL
1864–1872

T0382213

THE GERMAN SOCIAL DEMOCRATS AND THE FIRST INTERNATIONAL 1864–1872

BY

ROGER MORGAN

Lecturer in History in the University of Sussex

CAMBRIDGE

AT THE UNIVERSITY PRESS

1965

CAMBRIDGE UNIVERSITY PRESS
Cambridge, New York, Melbourne, Madrid, Cape Town, Singapore, São Paulo, Delhi

Cambridge University Press
The Edinburgh Building, Cambridge CB2 8RU, UK

Published in the United States of America by Cambridge University Press, New York

www.cambridge.org
Information on this title: www.cambridge.org/9780521057660

© Cambridge University Press 1965

First published 1965
This digitally printed version 2008

A catalogue record for this publication is available from the British Library

ISBN 978-0-521-05766-0 hardback
ISBN 978-0-521-08844-2 paperback

TO MY PARENTS

CONTENTS

CONTENTS

PREFACE

The International Working Men's Association, or First International, lasted as an effective organisation for a mere eight years, from 1864 to 1872, but it left its mark on the labour movement of every European country. While all were influenced, however, some were more influenced than others. 'Germany', as the International's General Council laconically reported to the organisation's Lausanne Congress in 1867, 'is still in an abnormal state, not favourable to the development of our Association'.[1]

The basic abnormality about Germany, of course, was the fact that the country was still not politically united, or rather that it became united, 'by iron and blood' and amid violent political recriminations, precisely at the time when the International was trying to bring together the labour movements of Europe.

As this study seeks to show, Germany's disunity and the disputed predominance of Prussia profoundly affected German reactions to the International. These circumstances help to explain, among other things, why Germany's first socialist party the *Allgemeiner Deutscher Arbeiterverein* founded by Ferdinand Lassalle and led after his premature death by J. B. von Schweitzer, was closely involved in Bismarck's attempts to win working-class support against his domestic and foreign enemies, and had little sympathy with the International; why Marx and Engels, easily the most important exiles of the 1848 revolution, had virtually no following in Germany when the International was founded, and succeeded only partially in expressing its aims in terms relevant to Germany's problems; why another distinguished exile, Johann Philipp Becker of Geneva, though he worked devotedly to spread the Inter-

[1] J. Freymond, ed.: *La Première Internationale. Recueil de Documents* (Geneva, 1962), I, p. 169.

national's message in Germany from 1865 onwards, was unable to give it durable organisational strength; why Marx's somewhat wayward disciple Wilhelm Liebknecht, when he began to organise a democratic labour movement in opposition both to Prussia and to the party of Lassalle, concentrated on these tasks to the virtual exclusion of propaganda for the International; and why, finally, when the International's rising prestige made it a useful asset in the struggle between rival German socialists, Liebknecht reaped where Becker had sown, and affiliated his own faction to the International on terms which implied the minimum of material or ideological dependence on this non-German organisation.

Thus, although by the 1870s the German labour movement was easily the largest and most highly-organised in Europe—in 1878, out of 438,231 votes given to socialist candidates throughout the world, 437,158 were recorded in Germany[1]—the movement's preoccupation with the politics of national unification had precluded any close identification with the International.

The reader of this book, in fact, will gain the impression that the International, for the German labour movement, was something marginal, a factor playing a considerable but still a subsidiary role in struggles that were concerned with essentially German problems. If the International is considered from an organisational point of view, this was certainly the case. However, the very fact that the International's involvement, even marginal, in these German disputes was largely due to its own prestige, indicates that its programme aroused interest and won converts in Germany; and in fact the International did make a specific contribution to the evolution of German socialist thinking.

An attempt to assess this contribution is made in the concluding chapter; the greater part of this book, however, aims not to provide yet another history of socialist ideas, but to

[1] C. Jantke: *Der Vierte Stand. Die Gestaltende Kräfte der deutschen Arbeiterbewegung im 19. Jahrhundert* (Freiburg, 1955), p. 129.

PREFACE

reconstruct the significance of one source of these ideas—the International—and the problems of working with it, as they appeared to a generation of German labour leaders already faced with day-to-day problems of organisation and tactics. The ideas associated with the International are thus considered here in the forms in which the Germans 'received' and acted upon them, and not for their own sake. As Professor H. Stuart Hughes puts it in a slightly different connection: 'on the level of popular acceptance, ideas can scarcely be handled in intrinsic terms: they are not sufficiently explicit for that'.[1] This study of what might be called 'applied' ideas (some of their authors would quite certainly have said 'misapplied') leads us away from what Professor Hughes calls the *via regia* of intellectual history as such, into considering the complex interaction of abstract ideas and living organisations: the proper concern of the historiography of socialist movements, however, perhaps even more than of other political movements, seems to me to lie precisely in this intermediate and somewhat ill-defined field.

As a result of undertaking this study I have incurred numerous debts to other people. First, I would like to express my gratitude to Mr Noël Annan, Provost of King's College, Cambridge, for all his advice and encouragement both during and since the three years of research under his supervision which led to the original version of this book. Dr David Thomson, Master of Sidney Sussex College, first drew my attention to the problem with which I have tried to deal, and both he and Mr James Joll, Sub-Warden of St Antony's College, Oxford, kindly advised me during the early stages of my approach to it. I am deeply indebted to Professor E. H. Carr for much kind encouragement, as well as for reading and commenting on more than one draft of the manuscript; it has also benefited from the critical scrutiny of Mr Bert Andréas, Mr Julius Braunthal, and Dr Susanne Miller.

For various items of information and advice I am indebted to

[1] *Consciousness and Society: the Reorientation of European Social Thought, 1890–1930* (1959), p. 10.

xi

Mr Chimen Abramsky, Dr Rolf Dlubek, Professor Georg Eckert, Professor Ernst Engelberg, Professor Fritz Fischer, Professor Erich Matthias, and Mr Boris Nicolaevsky.

The kindness of other scholars, either in making suggestions for the improvement of my manuscript, or in sharing with me the results of their own research, makes it more than usually necessary for me to stress that my conclusions—with which some, if not all, of them would disagree—are my own responsibility.

My thanks are due to the staffs of the following institutions for helping me to make use of documents and other material in their care: the British Library of Political and Economic Science; the Musée Social and the Institut Français d'Histoire Sociale, Paris; the Deutsches Zentralarchiv, Potsdam and Merseburg; the Landeshauptarchiv Brandenburg, Potsdam; the Institut für Marxismus-Leninismus, Berlin; the Partei-Archiv of the SPD, Bonn; the Schweizerisches Sozialarchiv, Zürich; the Stadtbibliothek, Braunschweig; the Auer-Bibliothek, Hamburg; the Istituto Giangiacomo Feltrinelli, Milan; and the University Libraries of Hamburg, Bonn, and Cologne. I am grateful to the Microfilms Committee of the Cambridge Faculty of History for a grant towards the cost of filming documents, and to the University College of Wales, Aberystwyth, for a research grant from the D. Owen Evans Bequest Fund.

A particular word of thanks is due to the staff of the International Institute for Social History in Amsterdam, for making available first the material without which this study could not have been written, and secondly an ideal environment in which to work on it. I am indebted to Professor A. J. C. Rüter, the Director of the Institute, for permission to publish extracts from documents in its archives, and to Miss Maria Huninck, the Librarian, for much bibliographical and other help. The typing of the final version of the manuscript was carried out by the late Miss J. E. Morris, for many years Secretary of the Department of International Politics at the University College of Wales, Aberystwyth.

My greatest debts, however, are two: first to Herr Werner

Blumenberg, curator of the German department of the International Institute for Social History, for his indispensable help in providing material and advising me on its use; and finally to my wife Annette for all her interest in German Social Democrats (at first perhaps partly a matter of politeness), and for her good sense in advising me how to write about them—as well as for all the hours she spent in typing various drafts of the manuscript and in compiling the index.

R. P. M.

LIST OF ABBREVIATIONS

ADAV.	*Allgemeiner Deutscher Arbeiterverein*
Bebel, *AML.*	August Bebel, *Aus Meinem Leben.*
Chronik.	*Karl Marx; Chronik seines Lebens in Einzeldaten*
Hochverratsprozess.	*Der Hochverraths-prozess wider Liebknecht, Bebel, Hepner, vor dem Schwurgericht zu Leipzig vom 11. bis 26. März 1872. Mit einer Einleitung von W. Liebknecht.* There is a recent reprint of this: *Der Leipziger Hochverratsprozess vom Jahre 1872* (Berlin 1960), but references here are to the edition of 1894.
IISG.	International Institute for Social History (Internationaal Instituut voor sociale Geschiedenis), Amsterdam.
Lassalle-Nachlass.	Ferdinand Lassalle, *Nachgelassene Briefe und Schriften,* ed. Gustav Mayer.
Mayer, *Engels.*	Gustav Mayer, *Friedrich Engels: Eine Biographie.*
Mayer, *Schweitzer.*	Gustav Mayer, *J. B. von Schweitzer und die Sozialdemokratie.*
MEB.	Marx, Engels, *Briefwechsel.*
MEGA.	*Karl Marx-Friedrich Engels: Historisch-Kritische Gesamtausgabe.*
Mühlbradt, *Liebknecht.*	Werner Mühlbradt, *Wilhelm Liebknecht und die Gründung der deutschen Sozialdemokratie, 1862–1875.*
SAR.	J. B. von Schweitzer, *Politische Aufsätze und Reden,* ed. F. Mehring.
SPD.	Sozialdemokratische Partei Deutschlands.

xv

AUTHOR'S NOTE

I have not attempted to challenge the anarchy which prevails in the rendering of German place-names into English, but have employed in each case the version which seemed to me most natural. Thus I have written 'Braunschweig' not 'Brunswick', 'Cologne' not 'Köln', 'Hanover' not 'Hannover' and 'Leipzig' not 'Leipsic'.

CHAPTER I

THE GERMAN SOCIALIST PARTIES,
1864 TO 1872

INTRODUCTION

In January 1871 the King of Prussia was proclaimed Emperor
of a Germany very different from that in which he had made
Bismarck his chief minister nine years earlier. In a spate of
industrial expansion, Germany had doubled her coal output,
almost quadrupled her production of iron, and herded together a discontented new population of factory-workers with
a rapidity of which the trebling of Krupps' labour-force during
the sixties was merely one typical example;[1] geographically
and constitutionally, the country which had seemed condemned
to permanent partition between almost forty sovereignties had
now become a united and powerful empire; and lastly—most
important of all since it reflected both the economic and the
constitutional revolutions—the balance of Germany's political
forces had totally changed.

In 1862 the central political conflict had resembled that of
the 1848 revolution: on one side stood the forces of monarchical
absolutism and particularist reaction, and on the other the
protagonists of parliamentary government and a Germany
united under the rule of law, who by 1862 had somewhat
revived after their defeat of 1848–9 in the atmosphere of the
Liberal 'New Era' of the later 1850s. By 1871, in contrast, the
Liberal spirit of 1848 or of the 'New Era' seemed dead:
Bismarck and his Progressive enemies of 1862 (now re-named
'National Liberals') stood together to defend the new *Reich*
against its enemies the South German Catholics, and against
another enemy ultimately more dangerous—the party of

[1] Cf. H. Lademacher, *International Review of Social History*, IV (1959), p. 240.

Socialist democracy. In 1848 this party, in a relatively un-industrialised Germany, had been insignificant; in 1862 it had been non-existent; by 1871, however, Bismarck was writing that 'socialistic theories and assumptions are already so widespread among the masses that any attempt to ignore them ... would be in vain'; he saw them as a threat to the whole 'existing order of state and society', and within a few decades the new party's dramatic rise to power was to prove him, in a sense, right.[1]

Bismarck's forebodings might, indeed, have been justified rather earlier if the industrial revolution had been the only process at work, with its tendency to spread 'socialistic theories' among 'the masses'. However, Germany's industrialisation occurred in the same period as the most acute tensions arising from the country's political division, and these tensions helped to split the young social-democratic movement into two bitterly hostile factions whose disputes severely blunted the early impact of socialism on German political life. It was not until 1875 that these factions united to form a single party, and their differences —at least until 1871—appeared to many observers irreconcilable.

The first party was the General German Workers' Union (*Allgemeiner Deutscher Arbeiterverein*), founded by Ferdinand Lassalle in 1863, and usually known as 'the Lassallean party'; its rival, the Social Democratic Workers' Party (*Sozialdemokratische Arbeiterpartei*) led by Wilhelm Liebknecht and August Bebel, was formally founded at a congress at Eisenach in 1869 (though an important nucleus had existed earlier), and thus came to be known as 'the Eisenach party'.

'Lassalleans' and 'Eisenachers' were divided not only by the personal rivalries of their leaders and by disagreements over tactics, but also by authentic differences of principle, which were reflected in the fact that the leaders of the two parties took opposite sides on the question of how Germany was to be united. Lassalle and his successor Schweitzer lived in Berlin,

---

[1] Bismarck to Itzenplitz (Prussian Minister of Commerce), 17 Nov. 1871 *Ministerium für Handel und Gewerbe*. BB *VII*, 1, 2. Bd. 1, Bl. 76 (See Bibliography II).

admired Bismarck, and took it for granted that Germany should be unified by the armed might of Prussia; Liebknecht and Bebel, heirs to the 1848 tradition of 'greater-German' democracy (called by its critics 'South German' to stress its particularist and Austrophil tendencies), based their movement in Saxony, South-West Germany and to some extent Bavaria, preached a democratic unification which would check or destroy 'Bismarckian Caesarism', and regarded Prussian hegemony as the worst thinkable catastrophe.

These geographical and national-political differences between the two socialist parties, as will be seen, helped to produce somewhat paradoxical contrasts in the social composition of their respective memberships, and in the degree of socialism which they actually advocated: Lassalle and Schweitzer, taking for granted a 'Prussian solution' to the problem of German unification, and also carrying on their propaganda mainly on Prussian territory (particularly in the industrial Rhineland), were able to preach fairly full-blooded socialism, in the sense of state intervention and ultimate public ownership, and their party was largely working-class in membership; Liebknecht and Bebel, on the other hand, appealed in Saxony and the South to all democrats and Prussian-haters whether they were manual workers, lawyers, teachers, or merchants, so that even though by 1870 or 1871 the Eisenach Party was predominantly working-class and clearly socialistic, its social composition, even in 1869, was much more varied, and in the public speeches of Liebknecht and Bebel the economics of socialism took second place to the politics of anti-Prussianism.

In talking of 'the working class', incidentally, it should be noted that the main active support of the German labour movement, until about 1880 at least, came not from the new factory-proletariat, the 'masses' of whom Bismarck spoke so apprehensively, but rather from the still-independent artisans fighting a grim and hopeless struggle against forced incorporation in this urban class: in the textile-industry area of Saxony, for instance, August Bebel won an election-campaign in

February 1867 'not in the economically much more highly-developed Chemnitz, the German Manchester', but in a semi-rural constituency 'still dominated by household manufacture';[1] and in the following year seven out of every nine of the Lassallean party's members in Hamburg were either tailors, shoemakers, joiners, or cigar-makers—the politically-active trades of the 1848 revolution or even earlier.[2] There appears to have been little difference between the parties led respectively by Bebel and Schweitzer as regards the occupational status of the manual workers they recruited in industrial or semi-industrial areas: they differed sharply, however, as has been noted, in that the former party also sought support among other classes and in other areas.

Tactically, the dispute between Lassalleans and Eisenachers was on the question of whether socialists should side with Bismarck or with his Liberal-democratic opponents. In Prussia, at least until 1866, Lassalle and his successor Schweitzer took sides with Bismarck; outside Prussia, at least until 1870, Liebknecht and Bebel sided firmly with his opponents. This disagreement, however, was much more than an ephemeral question of tactics; it reflected a deep conflict between the principles of the two parties, which in turn arose from the fundamental fact of Germany's division.

LASSALLE AND HIS SUCCESSORS, 1863–6

The first German socialist party was founded in Leipzig, but Lassalle was able to bring it into existence because of Bismarck's activities in Berlin. The Liberal opposition in the Prussian Diet, where Bismarck had become Prime Minister in September 1862, consisted of the Progressive Party (*Fortschrittspartei*) founded in 1861 as the parliamentary expression of the National Association (*Nationalverein*) started two years earlier. Both these Liberal organisations, although they stood out against Bismarck

[1] G. Benser, *Zur Herausbildung der Eisenacher Partei* (Berlin, 1956), p. 62.
[2] H. Laufenberg, 'Die Politik J. B. von Schweitzers und die Sozialdemokratie', *Neue Zeit*, XXX (1911–12), p. 693 *et seq.*

for the principle of ministerial responsibility, shared his view that the 'German question' should be solved by extending the power of Prussia (a solution which its opponents stigmatised as 'greater-Prussian'), and on the other vital contemporary problem, the 'social question', they accepted the *laissez-faire* doctrine which befitted a class of prosperous manufacturers. Finally, they refused to give way to popular demands for a Parliament elected by universal suffrage in place of that where they sat, elected by the three-class voting system imposed after the Revolution of 1848, and they emphasised this refusal in January 1863. The occasion was a request by the chairman of the Leipzig Workers' Educational Club that manual workers should be admitted to full membership of the *Nationalverein*, 'as they desired to take a more active part in politics'; he got the discouraging reply that workers might become 'honorary members' without voting-rights, but no more.[1] As for the question of universal suffrage itself, it was not until the autumn of 1865 that the Prussian Liberals, resigning themselves to the inevitable, joined the movement for electoral reform, and by this time their conversion was too late to win them any organised working-class support.

The Leipzig workers' leaders, indeed, after their negative reception at the Liberal headquarters, had turned to Ferdinand Lassalle, the arrogant and brilliant author of two tracts on the constitutional crisis; and the result of this approach was that the General German Workers' Union (*Allgemeiner Deutscher Arbeiterverein*) was founded at Leipzig on 23 May 1863. It was a socialist party independent of both government and Liberals, its first aim being to achieve universal suffrage, and its first President, elected for life, being Lassalle. His life, in fact, continued for little more than another year, but the nationalistic outlook and dictatorial constitution which he imposed on the ADAV[2] during this time formed an enduring legacy for his successors.

[1] *Die Gründung der deutschen Sozialdemokratie: Eine Festschrift der Leipziger Arbeiter*, pp. 20–5.

[2] The Lassallean party will henceforth be referred to by its German initials: ADAV.

5

Lassalle, born into a Jewish merchant-family in Breslau in 1825, was thirty-eight years old when his party was founded. His ambitions as a progressive political leader had developed from a boyhood vow to free the Jewish people from legal discrimination, and in the revolution of 1848–9 he had played a prominent enough part to be put on trial for high treason. An impressive conduct of his own defence (he had trained as a lawyer) secured his acquittal, and he avoided both imprisonment and the decade of exile in England or Switzerland which was the fate of most German revolutionaries of his generation. The fact that he remained in Germany made him, on the one hand, a useful source of information for Marx and Engels (though he concealed his contact with them from the German public and in any case it ceased, thanks to insurmountable mutual distrust, in 1862); on the other hand, Lassalle's continued residence in Germany certainly contributed to his high regard for Bismarck and for Prussia, which was reinforced by his study of the political philosophy of Hegel. As a labour leader, Lassalle was a somewhat incongruous figure; but despite his elegant clothing and his paternalistic proclamations (one of which opened: 'Workingmen! Before I leave for the spas of Switzerland . . .') the devoted loyalty which he inspired among his followers made the ADAV a force with which both rivals and opponents had to reckon.

The essence of Lassalle's propaganda, repeated in spectacular mass-meetings throughout Germany, was its simplicity. Hoping for massive support and quick results, he concentrated on two demands only: that universal suffrage should be introduced at once, to bring about 'the representation of the working class in the legislative assemblies of Germany', and that the State should finance co-operative factories so that the workers could become 'their own employers' and at last overcome the 'iron law of wages' which impoverished them under capitalism.

Lassalle's hostility to Liberalism had already brought him into private contact with Bismarck shortly before the ADAV was founded, and they continued to meet occasionally for some months, thanks to Bismarck's preoccupation with the politics of the 'social question', and with the prospect of reinforcing the workers' loyalty to the state by the grant of universal suffrage. Lassalle's public speeches of 1863, however, continued to be thoroughly radical, blaming both 'government and bourgeoisie' for the condition of the working class, and calling for a democratic socialist state. Only in the last months of his life, when he despaired of quickly founding a mass party, did he give the impression that the State, whose function, like a true Hegelian, he described as 'the elevation and development of the human race into freedom', and from which more immediately he expected help for co-operative factories, was after all the Prussian State of Bismarck and not the socialist State of the future. He now seemed, as one eminent critic has put it, to have abandoned socialism by revolution for 'the simpler and rapider method of converting Bismarck and the Prussian Ministry'.[1]

The ADAV's tactical alignment with Bismarck against the Liberal Progressive Party, which now became more pronounced, was deplored by many of its more militant members, among whom was Wilhelm Liebknecht.

Liebknecht (1825–1900) was almost the same age as Lassalle, but his experiences since the 1848 revolution (in which, as a student, he had participated at the cost of forgoing his degree and a hoped-for academic career) had been very different, and had only confirmed his early revolutionary faith. After joining the distinguished band of German political refugees in Switzerland in 1849, he had spent over twelve years in London, much of the time in almost daily contact with Marx. Liebknecht certainly failed to grasp the more intricate doctrines of Marx and Engels (who were unsparing in their private criticism of his mental capacities), but his personal loyalty to them was unshakable; he developed during this time a profound conviction that a new revolutionary movement must arise in Germany

---

[1] Bertrand Russell, *German Social Democracy*, p. 56. The quotations from Lassalle are taken from W. Mommsen (ed.), *Deutsche Parteiprogramme: eine Auswahl vom Vormärz bis zur Gegenwart*, pp. 95–6. The standard biography is H. Oncken's *Ferdinand Lassalle*.

to reverse the disaster of 1849, and in particular to destroy the power of Prussia. This hatred of Prussia dominated his political views after his return to Germany in 1862 (at first to occupy a series of journalistic posts with Liberal or democratic newspapers), and he joined Lassalle's new party only after some hesitation.

When Lassalle, addressing a private meeting before he left Berlin for the last time in June 1864, said that the party must regard the bourgeoisie as 'the only enemy', and if necessary ally itself with the monarchy, Liebknecht jumped up to protest that they could 'of course never take sides with Bismarck against the bourgeoisie'. According to Liebknecht, 'a scene was avoided' on this occasion, but he continued to disagree with the pro-governmental tactics of Lassalle and his successors, and led the opposition to them among party-members in Berlin until the Prussian government expelled him a year later.[1]

In the meantime, the constitutional struggle between Bismarck and the opposition dominated the political life of Prussia, and (owing to the state of passive apprehension to which Bismarck's advent had reduced Austria and the smaller states) that of all Germany. To Marx and Engels, contemplating the situation from England, the deadlock between Bismarck and the Liberals was an outward expression of the conflict between the historic forces of aristocratic feudalism and bourgeois capitalism. They therefore urged the ADAV to drive the 'revolutionary' Liberals forward against the government, preparing at the same time to lead the proletariat in its turn against the victorious forces of the bourgeoisie once the feudal system had succumbed to their onslaught.[2]

No such clear pattern of the situation, however, presented itself to Lassalle and his followers on the spot. Their close observation of Prussian Liberalism convinced them that Marx

[1] Cf. K.-H. Leidigkeit, *Wilhelm Liebknecht und August Bebel in der deutschen Arbeiterbewegung 1862–1869*, p. 39.

[2] For the attitude of Marx and Engels see Chapter II; the fullest statement of their own case, Engels' pamphlet *Die preussische Militärfrage und die deutsche Arbeiterpartei* (*1865*), is summarised by Leidigkeit, *op cit.*, pp. 88–90.

and Engels greatly exaggerated its revolutionary propensities, and they decided that the quickest way for the ADAV to increase its influence was to join Bismarck's campaign against its old liberal opponents. In return for this support they expected the government to grant certain socialist demands, including freedom of the press and freedom of association, credits for co-operative factories, and above all manhood suffrage, which Lassalle and his successors regarded as the key to any futher advance. At the beginning of 1864, indeed, inspired rumours were circulating that Bismarck's government planned to make concessions of this kind to its new allies.[1]

Lassalle was killed in a duel in August 1864, and in the next few months his party, exposed to violent dissension over policy, organisation, and leadership, almost disintegrated. It survived, however, and its internal development, from mid-1865 to the general political upheaval of 1866, demonstrated three things: first, that the ADAV was after all an extremely tightly centralised and well-disciplined organisation, which would accept without much question the tactical line laid down by those who commanded it; secondly, that by far its most capable leader was J. B. von Schweitzer (1833–75), a gifted and unscrupulous lawyer, son of a minor nobleman in Frankfurt, who had been appointed by Lassalle as a newspaper-editor and who by 1866 was in virtually complete control of a party more obedient and centralised than ever; and thirdly, that the economic aims of the party (though its leaders sometimes shared the views of Bismarck, and its members were not in any sense Marxists) were unequivocally and outspokenly socialist.

Was the ADAV in fact obedient and well-disciplined? It may seem paradoxical to assert this, in view of the violent disputes which broke out after Lassalle's death. Bernhard Becker, the party's nominal president, and J. B. von Schweitzer, the editor of its paper *Der Social-Demokrat*, repeatedly denounced threats to their authority organised by Lassalle's former secretaries

[1] Gustav Mayer, *Bismarck und Lassalle: Ihr Briefwechsel und Ihre Gespräche*, pp. 39–55.

9

Vahlteich and Willms, his long-standing friend and idolatress (and probably mistress) the Countess Hatzfeldt, and what Schweitzer (after the short-lived collaboration of Marx, Engels and Liebknecht on his newspaper) described as 'the antiquated coterie of Marx';[1] local party branches, indeed, were passing votes of censure on Becker as 'an infamous libeller and irrecoverable idiot', and members were resigning in protest against 'the party letting itself be led around by the nose by that accursed Schweitzer'.[2] These disputes were partly personal, but there were also tactical disagreements: Schweitzer, like Lassalle, supported the Prussian government against the Liberals, and his leading articles in the *Social-Demokrat* urged Bismarck to go forward on the German question 'if necessary with blood and iron' (17 February 1865); the organ of the Lassallean opposition, the Hamburg weekly *Nordstern*, answered with a denunciation of all such 'jesuitical intrigues by the lackeys of Bismarck' (25 February), and urged the socialists 'to reject any compromise with the privileged parties now dominant in Prussia' (11 March).

The opposition, however, was gradually overcome: in July 1865, the Prussian government expelled Liebknecht, the main opposition leader, from Berlin (Schweitzer has been accused of complicity in this expulsion, though there seems to be no proof); the Hamburg *Nordstern* went bankrupt a few months later; and throughout Germany, for instance in Leipzig, Stuttgart, and Cologne, the official leadership's active opponents were abandoning the ADAV to Schweitzer, and joining the International Working Men's Association, particularly when, as will be seen, this became better known in 1866. The ADAV's losses outside Prussian territory, however, were more

---

[1] Schweitzer in *Reform* (Berlin), 21 March 1865, quoted by Gustav Mayer, *J. B. von Schweitzer und die Sozialdemokratie*, p. 120 fn.

[2] Unpublished letter of 26 July 1866 from Heinrichs (Cologne) to Johann Philipp Becker (Geneva), typical of several in the latter's *Nachlass* (IISG). On the Berlin resolution of 30 March 1865 against Bernhard Becker, cf. *Nordstern* 15 April 1865, quoted in C. Schilling, *Die Ausstossung des Präsidenten Bernhard Beckers aus dem Allgemeinen deutschen Arbeiterverein*, and E. Bernstein, *Geschichte der Berliner Arbeiter-Bewegung*, Vol. I, pp. 132–4.

than made good by new recruitment, largely in the industrial Ruhr, so that the membership in November 1865 was twice that of a year earlier—9,421 instead of 4,610.[1] The party's extremely centralised administrative and financial structure contributed to strong discipline, and this was made acceptable by the skill with which Schweitzer's articles in the *Social-Demokrat* exploited working-class contempt for Liberalism and the widespread popular sympathy—at least in Prussia—with the German policy of Bismarck.

The increasing central control of the party was related to the growing ascendency of Schweitzer, in December 1864 a newly-appointed newspaper-editor and by June 1866 virtual ruler of the movement. Lassalle's immediate successor as President, the ineffectual journalist Bernhard Becker, was formally installed at a congress in Düsseldorf in November 1864, but the party's disunity was too much for him (in July 1865 he was also, like Liebknecht, expelled from Berlin), and he was removed after a year in office. The ADAV's condition was by now critically weak, but Becker's successor, Carl Wilhelm Tölcke, a socialist from Westphalia and a crude but effective orator, began to rebuild its unity and make it, as it had been under Lassalle, a serious political force; in this he was helped by Schweitzer's skilled editing of the *Social-Demokrat* and by the progressive weakening of the opposition. Early in 1866, however, a new opposition developed, in the form of an attempt by the Countess Hatzfeldt to replace Tölcke by Hugo Hillmann, a Solingen engineering-worker completely subservient to herself. At the ADAV's Leipzig Congress of June 1866, when the issue was decided, the Countess's attempt was warded off, but the real victor was Schweitzer; the new President, elected against Hillmann by a large majority, was the Hamburg socialist August Perl, who was nominated (and dominated) by Schweitzer. His own accession to the presidency was to wait for another year, but the election of his protégé

[1] Figures from H. Müller, *Die Geschichte der Lithographen, Steindrücker und verwandten Berufe*, Vol. I, p. 279.

Perl marked his attainment of a position of power in the party which corresponded to his outstanding gifts as a political leader. His tactical line remained, with nuances, the same as Lassalle's —that the workers could hope for nothing from the Liberals, and should therefore concentrate on demanding universal suffrage from the government—and it was only after the events of 1866 that a significant change occurred in the tactics of the ADAV.

There could be no doubt, finally, about the socialistic character of the party's economic policy. The *Social-Demokrat* echoed Lassalle's attacks on the 'iron law of wages', and his demand for producers' co-operatives to replace capitalist industry; Schweitzer poured scorn on the idea that democracy could mean anything unless it was 'based on a social idea'; and he welcomed industrial strikes which would arouse the revolutionary class-consciousness of the workers. Schweitzer's socialism was indeed related to his general antipathy to the Liberals and support for Bismarck: for the working class to bring the Liberal bourgeoisie to power, he argued, would mean 'to let the dreadful social conditions of today develop to their furthest extreme', while to prevent this class getting power (i.e. to support Bismarck) would allow 'a gradual change in the basis of modern society'. Despite these reminders of Lassalle's sympathy with Bismarck, however, there was no doubt that the ADAV was a distinctively socialist party.[1]

THE ORIGINS OF THE EISENACH PARTY, 1863–8

How and why did the Eisenach Party, the rival organisation led by Wilhelm Liebknecht and August Bebel, differ from the ADAV of Lassalle and Schweitzer?[2]

The Lassallean party was centrally-controlled, dominated by a single outstanding leader, and unmistakably socialist in

[1] Quotations from Schweitzer's articles of 1865–6 in *Politische Aufsätze und Reden von J. B. von Schweitzer*, ed. by F. Mehring, pp. 76, 107, 110.

[2] Cf. on this Gustav Mayer, 'Die Trennung der proletarischen von der bürgerlichen Demokratie in Deutschland' in *Grünbergs Archiv* . . . Vol. II, pp. 1–67, and Leidigkeit, *Wilhelm Liebknecht und August Bebel*, Chapter IV.

outlook; its rival, which was called after 1863 *Verband Deutscher Arbeitervereine* (League of German Workers' Clubs), and was in 1869 to become the Eisenach Party, was in each respect its opposite.

Where the ADAV was a single centralised party, the *Verband* was a loose federation of local clubs, whose central administration had only a minimum of authority; its leaders even ran, in conjunction with the *Verband*, two separate political organisations with aims related only loosely to its own, the bourgeois-democratic German People's Party (which led a vocal but ineffective existence from 1865 onwards) and the largely proletarian Saxon People's Party (which was founded by Liebknecht and Bebel in 1866).

Where the ADAV was under the personal domination of Lassalle, and later of Schweitzer, authority in the *Verband Deutscher Arbeitervereine* and its associated People's Parties was amicably divided between Liberal philanthropists like Leopold Sonnemann, Ludwig Büchner and Ludwig Eckardt, socialist veterans like Wilhelm Liebknecht and Robert Schweichel, and young workers, generally but at first unexplicitly progressive in outlook, like August Bebel; this meant that the achievement of Liebknecht and Bebel in getting the *Verband* to adopt socialist programmes in 1868–9 involved significant concessions on all sides.

Where the largely working-class ADAV, finally, left no doubt about its commitment to socialism, the socially-diversified *Verband* remained doctrinally confused; it was originally founded as an anti-socialist answer to Lassalle's ADAV, and although Liebknecht imparted some uncertain notions of socialism to his colleagues, the tradition of 'pure' democracy was strong enough to leave considerable doubt, even after the *Verband Deutscher Arbeitervereine* had become the Eisenach Party in 1869, whether it was really a socialist movement at all, or still merely a broad alliance of enemies of Prussia.

These characteristics must be borne in mind when the *Verband*'s history is considered.

Workers' clubs, educational and social, were by now established throughout Germany, some with a history going back several decades, others dating only from about 1860, and the *Verband*, a federation in which most of them were represented, was founded at a congress in Frankfurt in June 1863. A month earlier, Lassalle had started his ADAV, and the Liberal sponsors of the rival organisation were making a double answer to his challenge. The *Verband* was intended both to safeguard Liberal political interests against the Lassallean threat, and also to show its founders' recognition that Lassalle's concern with 'the social question' and his call for political democracy were perfectly justified, provided they were not carried—as he threatened to carry them—to their respective extremes of socialism and an independent working-class party. The Liberals also had a purely economic motive for encouraging workers' educational clubs: the need for technical training to keep pace with advancing methods in industry.[1]

These men (for instance Leopold Sonnemann, the director of the later world-famous *Frankfurter Zeitung*) were not only, like the Prussian Progressive Party, concerned to use the new crop of workers' clubs as a barrier against socialism; they were also, as the Prussian Liberals were not, democrats, which meant that they wanted a future German government to be responsible to a Parliament elected not merely by the three-class voting system in force in Prussia since 1850, but by equal manhood suffrage.

The task which the Liberal-democrats set themselves was to interest the clubs represented in the *Verband Deutscher Arbeitervereine* in the idea of democratic progress, and to use its annual congresses for constructive debates on 'the social question', while discouraging its more radical members from founding a separate working-class party. Until 1868, these Liberals had very little difficulty in keeping the *Verband* away from socialism, partly because the workers were in any case unreceptive to socialist ideas (except in parts of industrial Saxony, where Lassalle had found some response), but mainly because the

---

[1] Leidigkeit, *op. cit.*, p. 12; G. Benser, *Zur Herausbildung der Eisenacher Partei*, p. 34.

chief political preoccupation of these years was not with 'the social question' but with the efforts of Bismarck to extend the power of Prussia. These efforts created an alliance between all Bismarck's opponents—middle-class Liberals as well as potential socialists—and this alliance began to break down only after 1867, when they all found social and economic problems replacing opposition to Bismarck as their main political preoccupation.

Although the split between Bismarck's Liberal and socialist opponents outside Prussia was still in the future, it was fore-shadowed at the *Verband*'s second congress in 1864, when some opposition to the *laissez-faire* doctrines of the Liberal leaders was expressed, and one delegate made Lassallean proposals for the replacement of capitalist industry by producers' co-operatives.[1]

The Liberal leaders, among them Sonnemann, the physicist Büchner, and the Mannheim publicist Ludwig Eckardt (whose *Deutsches Wochenblatt* soon became the mouthpiece of the move-ment), tried to restrain their protégés from speculating along lines which questioned the foundations of capitalism in this way. When they attempted, moreover, to mobilise the political opposition to Prussia in 1865, entitling the new organisation created for this purpose the 'German People's Party' (*Deutsche Volkspartei*), they clearly hoped to keep the whole movement true to the ideals of 'pure' (i.e. non-socialist) democracy. The party's main organiser was Eckardt, who tried to exclude any hint of socialism from its programme, and wanted it to work closely with the *Verband Deutscher Arbeitervereine*.

With a policy-statement innocent of any precise proposals on 'the social question', Eckardt turned for support to the *Verband*'s third congress, which met at Stuttgart in August 1865. (He had tried without success to incorporate in his party the remains of Lassalle's ADAV; it was certainly weak, but Eckardt exaggerated its weakness, as well as its readiness to

[1] Erich Eyck, *Der Verband deutscher Arbeitervereine, Ein Beitrag zur Geschichte der deutschen Arbeiterbewegung*, pp. 25–34.

15

join a campaign which was essentially anti-Prussian).[1] The delegates at the *Verband*'s congress represented 106 workers' clubs with a total membership of 23,000, more than twice that of the ADAV; they knew already that the Liberal leaders believed in democracy, but Eckardt's demand that the *Verband* as such should join the People's Party (which had well-defined views on the vital question of Germany's political future) was something quite new. The *Verband* had still not begun to take sides on current problems of this kind, but its members were keenly interested in political, as well as purely educational and 'self-helping' solutions to working-class problems, as the Lassallean ideas expressed at the previous year's congress had shown.

There were thus at the Stuttgart congress two conflicting currents tending to induce the *Verband* to take sides in politics: the efforts of Eckardt to get the League's support for the anti-Prussian and non-socialist programme of the 'pure democratic' German People's Party, and also a much less articulate feeling that the situation of the working class demanded a political force which should also oppose the workings of the capitalist system. The first step, of inducing the *Verband* to abandon its non-political standpoint, was taken by the 'pure democratic' movement, which brought it into the opposition to Bismarck, but the organisation ultimately adopted a more socialistic kind of democracy, once the effects of Bismarck's war in 1866 had been overcome.

The potential leaders of this leftward move were Wilhelm Liebknecht, who settled in Leipzig after Prussia expelled him in 1865, and August Bebel, a carpenter who was considerably his junior, being at this time only twenty-five. Bebel, who had left school at the age of fourteen, and whose apprenticeship had included the customary tour of Germany (and also Austria), had been at the founding-congress of the *Verband* in 1863, and had been elected to its committee a year later. By the time he met Liebknecht in the summer of 1865, Bebel was an influential

---

[1] Mayer, 'Die Trennung', pp. 18–19.

figure, being president not only of the Leipzig Workers' Educational Club itself, but also of the League of Workers' Clubs for the whole of Saxony, which had a total membership of over 4,500. He made up for his lack of formal education by a gift for organisation, a shrewd sense of political tactics, and a capacity for hard and systematic work—qualities which formed the perfect complement to Liebknecht's talents as a persuasive journalist and orator, and to which the social-democratic movement owed a great deal, right up to Bebel's death in 1913.[1]

In the autumn of this year, 1865, there was a general feeling that 'the German problem' was moving towards a crisis, and the idea of general suffrage, previously put forward only by the ADAV and the liberal democrats outside Prussia, was suddenly accepted by the most varied political organisations, hastening to adjust themselves to the new political current: by the Stuttgart congress of the *Verband Deutscher Arbeitervereine*; by Eckardt's new German People's Party (though practically this still existed only on paper); by the tiny group of democrats in Prussia, who had been led into revolt against the Progressive Party by the individualist radical Johann Jacoby; and finally even by Lassalle's old antagonist Schulze-Delitzsch on behalf of the Progressive Party itself.

Only the lack of these groups, however, represented a serious political force, and it was clear that by 'universal suffrage' they meant something along the lines envisaged by Bismarck, which implied a Germany dominated by Prussia; this was more important in deciding the alignment of these various groups than their disagreements on social policy, which would in any case have prevented their unexpected concord on the suffrage question from developing into a permanent alliance. The tension between Austria and Prussia, rising throughout the winter and spring of 1865–6, dwarfed all other political issues; determining for a time the process of German political

---

[1] On Liebknecht and Bebel cf. Leidigkeit, *Wilhelm Liebknecht und August Bebel*, and the unpublished dissertations by W. Mühlbradt, H. Löschner, and M. Sauerbrey, cited in the bibliography.

alignments, it divided all parties into those who supported Prussia and those who opposed her.

On the opposition side, it also had the natural effect of solidifying the alliance between all the 'greater-German' democrats opposed to Bismarck, whether they were socialistically-inclined like Liebknecht (and Bebel, whom the old 'forty-eighter' was beginning, in his confused way, to convert to Marxism), or inspired by 'pure-democratic' ideals like Eckardt and his friends in the German People's Party. In April 1866 a mass-meeting in Frankfurt (held to protest against Bismarck's threatening moves against Austria) set up a propaganda-committee with representatives of both the People's Party and the *Verband Deutscher Arbeitervereine*, including Bebel.

It was hostility to Bismarck which made the *Verband* at last accept the need to engage in political activity; during the critical months before war came in June, and during the war itself, mass-meetings in Frankfurt and Mannheim (organised by Bebel) and throughout Saxony (organised by Liebknecht) demonstrated the unpopularity of Prussia. Military power, however, prevailed; by July the war was over, the forcible union to Prussia of Saxony and all North Germany was certain, and Bebel and Liebknecht had to revise their tactics.

Their previous aim had been a united democratic Germany (preferably a republic) with whatever social reforms could be secured from a State which would certainly not be socialistic; after Sadowa, they had the choice of either recognising the *fait accompli* in the national field, and continuing a socialist campaign adapted to the new political arrangements (this was the course chosen by the ADAV) or of striving to undo 'the work of 1866', which meant making Germany more democratic and less 'Prussian', at the same time as carrying on specifically socialist propaganda.

Unlike the Lassalleans, Bebel and Liebknecht chose the latter course: not only were they driven instinctively into total opposition to what Bismarck had done, but their whole political activity so far had been based on a wide coalition of anti-

Bismarckian forces rather than on any idea of a purely working-class party. Bebel proudly wrote to Sonnemann in January 1868 of the respect he and Liebknecht had won from 'many of these bourgeois, who are good Prussian-Bismarckians to a man', for their far-sighted criticism of the North German Confederation; and Liebknecht summed up his policy—anti-Prussian, not anti-capitalist—by telling Engels bluntly 'I start from the viewpoint that the fall of Prussia equals the victory of the German revolution'.[1]

Their activities after the disaster of 1866 were first, to keep alive the political consciousness which had been aroused in the *Verband Deutscher Arbeitervereine* by opposition to Bismarck, and secondly, to create the Saxon People's Party, whose programme was drawn up at Chemnitz in August 1866.

The Saxon People's Party was much less dependent on the German People's Party than might have been expected, partly because of the latter's organisational weakness and partly because of Bebel's great personal influence in Saxony; on the other hand, Bebel and Liebknecht were not in a position to press the new party, despite its largely working-class membership to adopt a socialist programme, and the social and economic demands of the Chemnitz programme scarcely go further than the vague references to 'improving the Lot of the Labouring Classes' which had been current in the German People's Party since its foundation. The real *raison d'être* of the Saxon People's Party became clear during the two general election campaigns of 1867: to protest against the incorporation of Saxony into the North German Confederation. (The Chemnitz Programme had been adopted five days before the treaty accepting this incorporation, at a time when Saxony was still occupied by the troops of Prussia—regarded by Liebknecht as the arch-enemy.)

In February the party won two seats in the Confederation's Constituent Assembly, and later in the year, when its first and

---

[1] Bebel to Sonnemann 9 January 1868, in Leidigkeit, *op. cit.*, p. 201; Liebknecht to Engels 11 December 1867, in G. Mayer, *Friedrich Engels, Eine Biographie*, Vol. II, p. 161.

only *Reichstag* was elected, four seats went to the Saxon People's Party and four to the ADAV.

Bebel and Liebknecht now played leading roles both in the Saxon People's Party (though this had largely served its purpose when the elections were over) and in the *Verband Deutscher Arbeitervereine*, a much more permanent organisation, of which Bebel became President late in 1867.

The main question which the *Verband* now faced was no longer whether it should play an active part in politics at all—the events of 1866 had decided that it could 'henceforth withdraw from politics as little as a fish can from the water';[1] the question now was what should be the actual contents of the programme which the organisation must adopt. Should its policy-statement be drafted by Sonnemann, the Liberal newspaper-owner who had replaced Eckardt as leader of the German People's Party and was as anti-socialist as ever, or should the *Verband* entrust the task to its new President Bebel, who was likely to offer it something more radical?

In the event, the programme which Bebel and Liebknecht successfully proposed to the *Verband*'s Nürnberg Congress in September 1868 was that of the International Working Men's Association. One reason why (after much hesitation) their choice fell on this programme is to be found in their relations with the rival party led by Schweitzer, in the new situation created by the war of 1866.

THE TWO PARTIES IN RIVALRY, 1866–9

Bismarck's victory of 1866 transformed the state of affairs in Germany, and the Berlin *Landtag*'s vote of September of that year changed the situation in Prussia; the majority of the Progressives now condoned Bismarck's violation of the constitution since 1862, and conclusively proved Marx's error in thinking that they might undertake any sort of revolution against the governing aristocracy. The vote showed that the rising forces of German industrialism, whose political representatives

[1] Article in *Deutsche Arbeiterhalle*, 1866, quoted by Mayer, 'Die Trennung', p. 24.

soon took the name of National Liberal Party, preferred to come to terms with the existing state-power, rather than to continue their struggle for representative government. The ADAV, virtually controlled by Schweitzer, gradually adapted its tactics to the new situation.

The ADAV was now faced no longer by a struggle between government and opposition (in which concessions might be won by lending support to the former), but by an apparently solid front of ruling-class and Liberals, united against all working-class demands—with the single exception of the demand for universal suffrage, which was now granted.

The political line which the party now adopted was influenced by events at its congress at Erfurt in December 1866, when the Countess Hatzfeldt again attempted to remove Schweitzer's ally Perl from the presidency. Schweitzer prevented this, but had to submit to the passing of policy-resolutions which recalled the most nationalistic slogans of Lassalle. The ADAV's manifesto for the forthcoming elections demanded 'the unification of the whole German race into a unitary State...which alone can give the German people a glorious national future', and it concluded with the cry: 'through unity to freedom!', which was one of the slogans of the National Liberals. Schweitzer adopted this phraseology partly to catch the prevailing wind of public opinion and partly to appease the supporters of the Countess, but at the same time the signs that he was considering less conventional Lassallean tactics— in particular, more open opposition to the government—still aroused her suspicions.[1]

When Schweitzer contested Wuppertal at the February election, standing against a government candidate and a National Liberal, the Countess financed the additional candidature of her protégé Hillmann, making Schweitzer's chances hopeless. In May 1867, when the ADAV's Braunschweig Congress elected him as President, about one-fifth of the members, encouraged by the Countess and representing chiefly

---

[1] G. Mayer, *Schweitzer*, pp. 187–9.

the party's sections in Saxony, Schleswig-Holstein and Bremen, broke away to form a separate party, which they emphatically entitled '*Lassall'scher Allgemeiner Deutscher Arbeiterverein*'. (This organisation was also known, on account of the personal and financial domination of the Countess, as the 'female line' of the Lassallean movement. Its internal development, during its separate life of a little over two years, is without significance; its existence, however, was a vital element in determining the tactics later followed by Schweitzer, and thus—as will be seen —in enabling Liebknecht and Bebel to found the Eisenach Party in 1869.)

Schweitzer's political pronouncements of the summer of 1867, particularly in his campaign for the *Reichstag* elections, showed how the Liberals' action in coming to terms with the government had affected his ideas on working-class tactics. Now that the government had given up its hints of solicitude for the workers (which had served their turn in the struggle against the Liberals) and the Liberals had given up the fight for political liberty, Schweitzer began to criticise both sides with a violence he had not previously shown.

His first line of attack was to champion political liberty in matters which no longer seemed to interest the Liberals— freedom of the press and freedom of association (soon to be essential, as the founding of Trade Unions became economically practicable); then, extending political freedom further, Schweitzer argued that the creation of a 'politically free State' in the sense of 1848—a nationalist sense—was insufficient, and that the ADAV should aim to create an international community of 'free people's States'.[1]

Schweitzer's ascendency in the ADAV, and the revival of its traditional discipline, ensured that the resolution on these lines, which he proposed at the party's Berlin Congress in December 1867, was overwhelmingly accepted.

Despite these changes of line in the Lassallean party, however, there remained a fundamental hostility between Schweit-

[1] G. Mayer, *Schweitzer*, p. 214.

zer and the *Verband* led by Liebknecht and Bebel, arising mainly from Schweitzer's readiness—which his rivals totally rejected—to regard the Prussian-dominated North German Confederation as an improvement on the previous situation, and its *Reichstag* in Berlin as a useful forum for the raising of such issues as labour legislation and possible Factory Acts.

The new tone of Schweitzer's propaganda, together with his capable and laudatory analysis of *Das Kapital* in the *Social-Demokrat*, not unnaturally resulted, early in 1868, in an improvement in his relations with Marx. These had been unfriendly (non-existent, even) since the breakdown of Schweitzer's attempt in 1864–5 to get Marx, Engels and Liebknecht to write for the *Social-Demokrat*. When Schweitzer wrote again to Marx after this interval of three years, using Marx's friendly reaction to his review as an excuse to ask politely for his opinion on the topical question of tariff reform, Liebknecht sent a warning to London that the motives behind the ADAV's new left-wing policy were opportunistic, and that Schweitzer could not be trusted. (Liebknecht, indeed, was convinced that Schweitzer's previous sympathy for Bismarck—which he regarded as surpassed in baseness, if possible, by the Lassalleans' readiness to accept the *fait accompli* of 1866—could be explained only by bribery.) Despite this warning, however, Marx, as the International's 'Corresponding Secretary for Germany' sent a full reply to Schweitzer's enquiry.

In the spring of 1868, in Berlin, Schweitzer met Liebknecht (now in a dominant position in the Saxon People's Party and in the *Verband Deutscher Arbeitervereine*) to discuss how the relations between the International and the German labour movement could be improved, and how at the same time the ADAV and the *Verband*, despite their differences, could demonstrate their good faith and their lack of hostility to each other; the two leaders suggested that both these organisations, at their respective congresses at Hamburg and Nürnberg, should formally declare their loyalty to the International, as a symbol both of socialism and of unity.

The *rapprochement* between Marx and the Lassalleans soon reached the point where Marx was invited to attend the Hamburg Congress in person, and in excusing himself (on the grounds of his preliminary work for the Brussels Congress of the International), complimented Schweitzer again on the ADAV's achievement (though, as he told Engels, he felt that Schweitzer had really 'given up Lassalle's programme'); the Hamburg Congress passed a resolution proclaiming in enthusiastic terms its solidarity with the International; and Schweitzer, responding to an unprecedented wave of industrial strikes and lock-outs in 1867–8, abandoned the traditional Lassallean hostility to Trade Unions (which had been regarded as ineffective because of the doctrine of the 'Iron Law of Wages'), and called a new congress to meet in Berlin in September, at which a Lassallean Trade Union movement would be founded.[1] Schweitzer's attitude to the problems of the Trade Union movement later contributed to a new breakdown of his relations with Marx, but before this happened their apparent *rapprochement* had helped to decide Bebel and Liebknecht to bring their own organisation, the *Verband Deutscher Arbeitervereine*, closer to the International.

Relations between Schweitzer's ADAV and the *Verband* under Liebknecht and Bebel had for months been extremely strained, as has been seen, despite the 'armistice' concluded in the spring. Liebknecht and Bebel, whose dominant political sentiment was hatred of Prussia, utterly condemned Schweitzer's readiness to base his socialist campaign on acceptance of the *fait accompli* of 1866. The animosity between the rival leaders came into the open during a tumultuous debate in the *Reichstag* in October 1867, when Schweitzer attacked Liebknecht's Austrophile sympathies and pledged the ADAV to defend 'the powerful Prussian heart of our German fatherland'; Liebknecht, who violently deprecated Schweitzer's attempts to get factory legislation passed by the *Reichstag*—in his view a mere 'fig-leaf of absolutism'—

---

[1] G. Mayer, *Schweitzer*, pp. 225–53; the episode is discussed in more detail in Chapter V below.

replied by denouncing Schweitzer as an agent of the Government.[1] Liebknecht and Bebel were also irked by Schweitzer's perpetual claim that his movement was purely socialist, whereas theirs was an incongruous alliance cemented only by anti-Prussianism—an accusation which was all the more annoying because it was so largely true; and they renewed, both in their speeches and after January 1868 in their new *Demokratisches Wochenblatt*, strong attacks on Schweitzer as a traitor both to socialism and to democracy.

The prestige of the International among German socialists was now so great that loyalty to its principles could be regarded as a test for any organisation claiming to be truly socialist. This had been indicated by Schweitzer's public demonstration of his new-found harmony with Marx, and by the understanding reached between Schweitzer and Liebknecht; the only possible next step was for Liebknecht and Bebel, who intended in any case to give the *Verband Deutscher Arbeitervereine* a precise programme of some kind, to make this programme the prestige-bearing one of the International.

The *Verband*'s Nürnberg Congress, in September 1868, was accordingly invited to declare its agreement with this programme, and despite the misgivings of several delegates (who in fact withdrew from the whole organisation) it did so. The *Verband* now stood committed to the International's principle that 'the emancipation of the working class must be the task of the working class itself', and as far as its co-operation with bourgeois democrats was concerned, this marked the beginning of the end.

Only the beginning, however: the International itself was only just starting at its Brussels Congress taking place at the same time, to include 'public ownership' or 'socialism' in its aims (it had always been explicitly working-class—voting in favour of trade unionism, the eight-hour day, public education,

[1] *Stenographische Berichte über die Verhandlungen des Reichstages im Norddeutschen Bunde. I. Legislatur-Periode 1867*, pp. 452, 470–1.

and co-operative production—but scarcely socialistic); this meant that non-socialist democrats such as Sonnemann could still stand by the *Verband* without any feeling of incongruity, even after it had recognised its affinity with the International. Thus the adoption by the *Verband Deutscher Arbeitvereine* of the principles of the International signified in itself neither its severance from the anti-socialist German People's Party, nor its establishment as an independent political force; these developments followed in the twenty months which elapsed between the Nürnberg Congress and the war of 1870, and they were occasioned (like the *Verband*'s initial adoption of the International's programme) by further developments in the ADAV.

THE EISENACH CONGRESS, 1869

Schweitzer's 'left-wing' policy of attacking both government and Liberals, adopted in 1867, had resulted in the ADAV's tactical alignment with the forces already in opposition to 'the work of 1866': the *Verband Deutscher Arbeitervereine*, the Saxon People's Party and other South German democrats, and in Prussia the dissident democratic minority of the old Progressive Party, led by Johann Jacoby.

Jacoby, wishing to make this alliance permanent, called for unity between all democrats and socialists for 'a remodelling of existing political and social conditions, towards freedom founded on equality'.[1] Early in 1868 his proposal for a closer alliance between the Lassalleans and these other groups found a response among leading members of the ADAV, notably its treasurer Wilhelm Bracke (a young Braunschweig business-man who was one of Germany's outstanding socialist leaders and publicists in the 1860s and '70s); in order to combat this threat to his authority (the more dangerous as it was keenly encouraged by Liebknecht) Schweitzer turned the party's course even further to the left, proclaiming that no alliance with non-

---

[1] Quoted in Leidigkeit, *Wilhelm Liebknecht und August Bebel*, pp. 122-3.

socialist parties could be other than temporary and tactical. Schweitzer obviously hoped by this leftward move to preserve his authority in the ADAV, and his attempts to make use of Marx and the International were by now clearly dictated by the same considerations of personal prestige and of the out-manoeuvring of Liebknecht.

Relations between Schweitzer and Marx, however, had once again deteriorated by October 1868, partly because Marx strongly disapproved of the centralised organisation of Schweitzer's new Trade Unions, and Bebel and Liebknecht were thus free to reopen the campaign against the ADAV whose volume and violence they had considerably reduced during the Congresses at Nürnberg and Hamburg that summer. Two blows by the public authorities helped them: in mid-September the Leipzig headquarters of the ADAV were closed by the police, and it was only after a month of disorganisation that the party-machine was again functioning, henceforth in Berlin; and then Schweitzer was in prison for several weeks, starting early in December.

Bebel and Liebknecht tried to use his absence to induce lead-ing members of the ADAV to desert him, and Schweitzer realised that his position might be threatened at the next party congress, due to take place at Barmen-Elberfeld in March 1869. He decided that he could only rally enough support to reassert his authority by again protesting his loyalty to the International; the prestige of this organisation was higher than ever, and an assertion of his loyalty to it might shield him from the attacks of Bebel and Liebknecht, who had actually been invited during his imprisonment to present their case against him at the ADAV's congress.

At the end of March Bebel and Liebknecht duly appeared at the Lassallean congress, and attempted to prove the accusation made in the *Demokratisches Wochenblatt* of 20 February, that 'Schweitzer, whether for money or by inclination, had system-atically tried to hold back the organisation of the labour party since the end of 1864, and played the game of Bismarck'.

27

Although the North German audience disagreed with their version of the events of 1866, and Schweitzer succeeded in his plan of silencing his critics by promising to affiliate the ADAV to the International 'as soon as the laws allowed it', they won a clear moral victory; this was clear when Schweitzer asked the Congress for a vote of confidence, and nearly a third of the delegates pointedly abstained from voting. They included the influential men who had been attracted by Jacoby's call for unity the previous year, and who now confirmed their distrust of Schweitzer by amending the ADAV's constitution so as to reduce his powers.

Bebel and Liebknecht waited until June before taking advantage of the situation, and then a series of indirect attacks which they made on Schweitzer had the effect of making him panic; the one quarter from which he could still expect support was the Countess Hatzfeldt's rival Lassallean party which had seceded from the ADAV two years earlier. On 18 June Schweitzer and the Hatzfeldtian president Fritz Mende announced, without any warning, the reunion of their two parties. There was to be no congress to debate the fusion; the local branches were simply to say, within three days, whether they approved or not.

Schweitzer's opponents acted with equal speed: a number of prominent Lassalleans left the party, including the treasurer Bracke of Braunschweig, his colleague Spier from Wolfenbüttel, and the Hamburg leaders York, Perl, and Geib. They had already decided that there were other socialist allies preferable to Schweitzer, and four days after Schweitzer's *coup d'état* a number of them met Bebel and Liebknecht in a small hotel in Magdeburg.

Two 'appeals to the German working class', the first drafted that night and the second published in mid-July (and signed by 66 leading members of the ADAV and 114 of the *Verband Deutscher Arbeitervereine*) denounced Schweitzer as a traitor to the socialist movement and summoned 'all the social-demo-cratic workers of Germany' to send delegates to a congress in

Eisenach in August, where a new united party would be founded.[1]

Schweitzer (whose main concern was now to preserve his position, whatever means might be necessary) sent more than 100 emissaries to the Eisenach Congress, with orders to interrupt its proceedings; they succeeded in doing this on the first day, but were then excluded, leaving 262 delegates (who claimed to represent over 150,000 workers) to their deliberations. These resulted in the founding of the 'Social Democratic Workers' Party' with a new programme derived partly from Marx and partly from Lassalle, and immediately afterwards in the formal dissolution of the *Verband*.

'LASSALLEANS' AND 'EISENACHERS' AFTER 1869

Liebknecht and Bebel, thanks to the deserters from the ADAV, had transformed the Liberal *Verband* of six years earlier—a non-political federation of workers' clubs—into a socialist party whose programme contained more Marxist ideas than any yet adopted in Germany. The Eisenach Party's final separation from those middle-class democrats who had remained in contact with the *Verband*, after 1868, was only a question of time. The International, at its Brussels Congress of 1868, had at last adopted unequivocally the idea of nationalisation, and just after the triumph of Bebel and Liebknecht at Eisenach, it proceeded, at its Basle Congress, to apply the principle explicitly to the land.

Liebknecht represented the new Eisenach Party at Basle, and argued against the resolution on land nationalisation, explaining privately that he 'wanted to avoid premature trouble' with his non-socialist allies in Germany, and realising that these allies would desert the party at once if the International, with which it was clearly associated, accepted anything so radical as this.[2]

Despite his opposition, the resolution was passed, and this

[1] These two appeals, and other documents concerning the Eisenach Congress, are reprinted in Benser, *Zur Herausbildung der Eisenacher Partei*, pp. 102–13.

[2] Liebknecht to Bonhorst, October 1869, quoted in *Der Hoch-Verrathsprozess wider Liebknecht, Bebel, Hepner . . .*, p. 195. The significance of the land-nationalisation issue is discussed in detail in Chapter VI below.

meant growing tension between the partners in the old alliance between socialist and non-socialist democrats which had originated in shared hostility to Bismarck in 1865–6. Bebel and Liebknecht were under pressure to clarify the situation from two sides: the Liberal democrats wanted them to deny that the Eisenach Party agreed with the Basle resolution, and various left-wing socialist groups (including the committee of their own Eisenach Party, situated in Braunschweig and dominated by the powerful figure of Bracke) insisted that they should unambiguously declare the opposite.

After a period of hesitation, Liebknecht made his choice, and the Basle resolution was formally ratified at the Eisenach Party's Stuttgart Congress of June 1870. This immediately ended the socialist movement's connection with the bourgeois democrats, and established the Eisenach Party as an independent organisation.

As for the Lassallean party, the re-entry of the Hatzfeldtian element, and significant gains in Berlin, almost made up for the defection of members to the Eisenachers. Schweitzer had to pay a price for the Countess' support (even though he lost this again in 1870): his speeches and articles came to contain increasingly unctuous praise for 'our titanic teacher and master Ferdinand Lassalle', which increased the animosity felt for him by the leaders of the Eisenach Party, though it consolidated his position at the head of his own considerable following.

The basic difference between the two parties was still geographical and ideological: the ADAV, based in Prussia and having accepted or even welcomed Bismarck's 'work of 1866', was in a position, as Bebel put it, 'to deflect the workers from the political struggle into a one-sided social struggle',[1] whereas the Eisenach Party, issuing from a broad political movement directed against Prussia, was often reluctant (as the land-nationalisation episode indicated) to admit that it was socialist at all.

This contrast, and the personal antipathy between the rival

[1] Bebel to Siegfried Meyer 8 February 1870, in Leidigkeit, *op. cit.*, p. 203.

leaders, were quite enough to keep the two parties uncompromisingly hostile to each other until the Franco-Prussian war of
1870. The war at first only emphasised their divisions, but in
the end it set their feet on the road which was to lead them to
unity at the Gotha Congress of 1875.

When France declared war on Prussia on 19 July 1870 the
decisive fact facing German socialist leaders was that virtually
all Germany regarded Napoleon III as the aggressor, and
demanded that France be punished. When the *Reichstag* met to
vote the war credits, the ADAV members Schweitzer and Hasenclever, as well as the former Lassallean Fritzsche (now a member
of the Eisenach group), voted for the government. Liebknecht
at first intended to vote against the credits, but Bebel persuaded
him that such a step would imply not only condemnation of
Bismarck, but also approval of Napoleon, so the two finally
abstained from voting.

The war let loose a wild confusion of aims inside the German
social-democratic movement; and the confusion only began to
be resolved after the battle of Sedan and the fall of Napoleon,
when it became clear that Prussia was henceforth fighting not
in self-defence, but to annex Alsace-Lorraine from the new
French Republic. The realisation of this reunited Schweitzer
and the Braunschweig committee of the Eisenach Party (who,
like him, had welcomed a war to defeat Napoleon) with those,
such as Liebknecht and Bebel, who had condemned the war
from the start.

Marx and Engels, for their part, were convinced that Bismarck's victory in the war would serve their ends not only by
creating a united Germany in which socialist propaganda and
organising would be simplified, but also by ensuring the predominance of the German socialist movement over the French
on the international level; at this, however, they refrained from
doing more than hinting in the manifestos which Marx wrote
in the name of the International, or in the letters with which he
tried to reconcile the Braunschweig committee and the *Reichstag* deputies Bebel and Liebknecht.

After the annexation-question became dominant in September, Marx's mediation was no longer necessary; all the Eisenachers and most of the Lassalleans joined in protesting against a forcible annexation of Alsace-Lorraine, and Schweitzer himself insisted that Prussia would only be justified in taking over these areas if their populations voted for it in a plebiscite. However, the jubilation with which the whole of German public opinion greeted the victory of Bismarck, the annexation of Alsace-Lorraine, and above all the establishment of the German Reich in January 1871, brought all forms of socialism into disrepute.

The two main socialist papers, Schweitzer's *Social-Demokrat* and the Eisenachers' *Volksstaat*, had already lost most of their subscribers during the war, and the government did not hesitate to use the new climate of opinion to begin repressive measures against the socialists in general. At the elections of March 1871 (two weeks before the proclamation of the Paris Commune) all the social-democratic deputies of both parties lost their seats, with the one exception of Bebel, who was already in prison; at the end of the month Schweitzer announced his resignation from the ADAV's presidency, and two days later the *Social-Demokrat* ceased publication. Although the growth of the social-democratic movement could not be checked for long (the circulation of its revived newspapers began to rise again by the end of 1871), the war came as a very serious blow.

The sympathy which both Lassalleans and Eisenachers declared for the Commune, and their condemnation of the new Imperial Constitution as illiberal, coming after their attacks on the policy of annexation, earned them widespread fear and denunciation. The persecution at first concentrated on the Eisenach Party was soon extended to the Lassalleans, and after the beginning of 1874 the new Public Prosecutor in Berlin, Tessendorf, succeeded in obtaining mass-sentences against members of both parties, which culminated in a ban of the ADAV as a whole.

It was under these circumstances that the two parties overcame their mutual distrust to the extent of supporting each other at the *Reichstag* elections of January 1874, and that the small groups of socialists then elected (three Lassalleans and four Eisenachers, not counting the imprisoned Bebel and Liebknecht) tentatively began to co-operate in parliamentary activities.

The Gotha Congress of May 1875, when this co-operation finally led to the unification of the two parties, marked the end of a long period of fratricidal strife: a period in which differing interpretations of the political situation (and above all of the problems caused by Germany's own belated and forcible unification) had made hostility between two rival organisations the main characteristic of the German labour movement.[1]

[1] These developments are summarised in F. Mehring, *Karl Marx*, pp. 507–10. For the Gotha Congress, cf. the various editions of Marx's *Critique of the Gotha Programme*, the discussion of the theoretical issues in K. Brandis, *Die deutsche Sozialdemokratie bis zum Falle des Sozialistengesetzes*, pp. 25–48, and Chapter VII below.

CHAPTER II

THE LASSALLEAN PARTY AND THE INTERNATIONAL, 1864 TO 1865

INTRODUCTION

The International Working Men's Association attempted from its foundation, in September 1864, to establish contact with working-class organisations on the continent of Europe.

In Germany, the only labour organisation existing in 1864 was the ADAV started by Lassalle. This gave the International's early relations with Germany a character different from that of later years, when they were to be modified—and in fact intensified—by the ADAV's struggle against a rival German party.

Another circumstance which affected these relations in 1864–5 was that neither the ADAV nor the International was very highly organised, so that personal relations between individuals counted for even more at this stage than they did later. The main protagonists—Marx, Engels, Liebknecht, Schweitzer and Johann Philipp Becker (in fact all the actors of the story's later stages, except for Bebel)—appeared in 1864–5 as individuals, rather than as representatives of the bodies which they later rallied in support of their various viewpoints. The events of 1864–5 may be regarded almost as a rehearsal —with some changes in the players' roles—for the large-scale battle of 1868–9.

What was the situation in 1864–5, and how did it affect the International's first contacts with Germany? The outlook for the labour movement in the autumn of 1864 was extremely uncertain; this was true both for the ADAV, suddenly bereft of the founder-president to whom all had turned for leadership, and for the new International Working Men's Association, brought into existence in a mood of tentative optimism but

34

endowed for some weeks neither with a precise statement of aims nor with a settled form of organisation.

When the International's statutes did finally receive the approval of its Central Council (soon to be called 'General Council'), at the beginning of November, they were very cautiously worded in order not to offend any organisation which might be persuaded to affiliate.[1]

As for the ADAV, it suffered until the end of 1865 (i.e. during the presidency of Bernhard Becker, Lassalle's immediate successor) from dissensions which hindered all its activities and at times threatened its very existence. In December 1865 Becker was replaced by Tölcke, a man of firmer character and greater authority, whose few months as president, combined with Schweitzer's lively editing of the *Social-Demokrat*, revived the party's self-confidence.

About the same length of time was necessary before the International, strengthened by its first representative conference (London, September 1865) and the increasing number of newspapers at its disposal, overcame its original indecision and took up a more self-assertive attitude. In the course of the year 1865, as the post-Lassallean ADAV and the new International felt their respective ways forward, it became increasingly obvious that their paths lay in different directions, and by the the summer of 1866 this was quite certain. By this time, the International's needs—for ideological flexibility and a decentralised structure—were being clearly indicated by the varied composition of its first full congress at Geneva; while the ADAV, proffering to Bismarck its relatively unguarded support against Austria and the Liberals, seemed under Schweitzer's leadership to be conclusively reverting to the centralised organisation, nationalistic outlook, and pro-governmental tactics of Lassalle.

By 1866, in fact, both the International and the ADAV had proved their ability to live, to flourish, and to defy each other; but the situation had at first been very different. In 1864 and

---

[1] Marx to Engels 4 November 1864, *MEB*, III, pp. 237–8; provisional statutes in Stekloff, *History of the First International*, pp. 446–8.

1865 Marx and Engels, who took charge of the International's relations with Germany, believed that they could turn the ADAV into its German branch or even destroy it altogether; and the ADAV's demoralised state, in the first few months after Lassalle's death, offered such hopes the prospect of success.

<h2 style="text-align:center">THE ADAV'S PROBLEMS IN 1864-5</h2>

There were three main reasons for the babel of dispute which arose in the ADAV when Lassalle was killed.

First, his successors were agreed on only part of their programme: the reiteration of Lassalle's demands for general suffrage and social reform. When it came to the party's attitude towards political developments in Germany, their disagreements were numerous and acute.

Secondly, many members were very critical of the centralised organisation bequeathed by Lassalle, and the amendment of the party's constitution was a permanent subject of debate.

Finally, the sudden removal of Lassalle left a power-vacuum which none of his successors, owing to their differing views and relatively limited capacities, was able to fill unchallenged.

The ADAV was thus exposed to dissension over policy, organisation and leadership; and as the chiefs of the International could only influence the party when one German leader or another, for tactical reasons, invited their help, some attention must be given to these leaders and to the causes of their disputes.

Of the various feuds among Lassalle's successors, there was only one in which the theoretical and tactical issues were relatively clearly-defined, and in which the element of personal division could be said not to go beyond a strong mutual antipathy; this was between Bernhard Becker, the new President (supported by Schweitzer as editor of the *Social-Demokrat*) and the anti-Prussian, anti-centralising forces dominant in certain local party-sections, whose views were expressed in the weekly paper *Nordstern*, edited by Karl Bruhn in Altona. This struggle, fed by disputes on policy, disagreement on organisation and personal rivalry for power, lasted until July 1865; at this point it was interrupted by the expulsion from Prussia both of Bernhard Becker and of Wilhelm Liebknecht, the main leader of opposition to him in Berlin. What were the issues involved? Politically, the ADAV's dilemma was this: faced by a situation in which the only two real political forces in Prussia, Bismarck's government and the Liberal opposition, were locked in a struggle apparently likely to last for years, would the workers' party do better to throw its small weight on the side of the government or that of the opposition? Bernhard Becker and Schweitzer, like Lassalle before them, sided with Bismarck. Only the government, they argued, could grant universal suffrage; and as only representation in Parliament could bring strength to the ADAV, the advantages to be expected from alliance with the government were greater than any offered by co-operation with the somewhat forlorn Liberal opposition. The Liberals, indeed, opposed universal suffrage, and this provoked Becker and Schweitzer to deride their pious invocations of 'parliamentarism' against the 'Caesarism' of Bismarck. 'Parliamentarism' wrote Schweitzer in the *Social-Demokrat* of 27 January 1865, 'means empty wordiness... the rule of mediocrities, whereas Caesarism at least means masterful initiative, *überwältigende Tat*': this sentence occurred in the first of Schweitzer's articles on Bismarck's government, which as described below, played a part in the decision of Marx and Engels to break with the *Social-Demokrat*.[1]

As far as 'the German question' was concerned, Schweitzer urged Bismarck to go forward 'if necessary, with blood and iron' (*Social-Demokrat*, 17 February 1865), thus again siding pointedly with the government against the Liberals.

The opposite view expressed by the *Nordstern* was, not surprisingly, held mainly by Lassalleans outside Prussia.[2] The

[1] On Schweitzer's tactics cf. further Mehring's notes on Schweitzer's *Aufsätze und Reden*, pp. 41–80, and Mayer, *Schweitzer*, pp. 110–17, 132.

[2] Johann Philipp Becker's *Nachlass* (IISG) includes letters indicating the extent of this opposition, for instance from Bruhn (Altona), Arndt and Schilling (Berlin), and Lange (Leipzig). Bruhn's *Nordstern* published resolutions and complaints against Bernhard Becker in almost every number during the first half of 1865.

opposition was handicapped by its ignorance of how far Lassalle had already committed the party to supporting the government, and honestly believed that in denouncing Schweitzer's tactics as 'jesuitical intrigues by the lackeys of Bismarck' they were remaining true to the doctrines of their "irreplaceable teacher and master Ferdinand Lassalle".[1]

While Schweitzer angled for the sympathy of the government by declaring (in the *Social-Demokrat* of 30 December 1864) that 'not everything that appears reactionary to the Progressive Party appears so to us', the Lassallean opposition answered (in the words of Wilhelm Liebknecht addressing a Berlin meeting in February 1865): 'the fact that the Progressive Party has failed in its duty is no reason for the workers to throw themselves into the arms of those who offer even less, and are even more backward, than the Progressive Party'.[2]

The Lassallean opposition inside Germany was largely inspired by simple hostility to Prussia. A more sophisticated argument for their views (and one which was scarcely heeded in Germany) came from Marx and Engels in England. They totally rejected Schweitzer's view that a workers' party could prosper under general suffrage granted by Bismarck in return for joining his campaign against Liberal politicians, however 'bourgeois'. In the purest traditions of the *Communist Manifesto* they warned the German labour movement that its historical duty was to support any 'progressive' forces, even if, as in the case of the Prussian Liberals, their 'progressiveness' consisted in their representing bourgeois capitalism against aristocratic feudalism.[3] Marx urged Schweitzer to reflect on the way in which general suffrage in Germany, as in France under the Second Empire, would either be perverted by governmental trickery or else produce huge conservative majorities owing to the stupidity

---

[1] *Nordstern* 25 February, 11 March, 1 April 1865, articles by J. Ph. Becker.

[2] *Die Geschichte der Social-Demokratischen Partei in Deutschland seit dem Tode Ferdinand Lassalles* (anonymous—perhaps Bernhard Becker), p. 30.

[3] 'In Germany, as soon as the bourgeoisie rise in revolution, the communist party struggles jointly with the bourgeoisie against the absolute monarchy, feudal landed property, and the petit-bourgeois spirit' (*Communist Manifesto*, new German ed. 1949, p. 102).

of the rural electorate; and Engels, in a pamphlet originally written as an article for the *Social-Demokrat*, but separately published after he and Marx had ended their connection with Schweitzer, summed up their argument thus:

Each victory of the forces of reaction obstructs the development of society, and infallibly postpones the moment of victory for the workers. Each victory of the bourgeoisie, on the other hand, is in a way a working-class victory too; it contributes to the final collapse of the capitalist system, and brings nearer the moment when the workers will win victory over the bourgeoisie.[1]

Arguments of this kind made sense to few people in the Germany of 1865, and within a short time Schweitzer's calculated nationalism and anti-liberalism had enabled him to rally the majority of active German socialists under his Lassallean banner. For a few months in 1864–5, however, his opponents in the party (despite their failure to compete in profundity with Marx and Engels) were strong enough to create acute dissension which might have been expected to lay the ADAV open to the influence of the International.

There was also the question of organisation.

As well as attacking the pro-governmental tactics bequeathed by Lassalle, the opposition criticised the ADAV's dictatorial constitution. Arguments about this were less heated than on questions of policy, partly because the opposition realised that a tightly-centralised structure, giving wide powers to the party's President, had been adopted not merely to satisfy the dictatorial wishes of Lassalle, but also to conform with the Prussian Combination Acts.[2]

Despite this, the centralised regime was severely criticised: even though some critics confined themselves to proposing minor, if understandable, constitutional amendments—for instance the Augsburg branch, as recorded in the *Social-Demokrat* of 21 December 1864, proposed 'that the President of

---

[1] Engels, *Die preussische Militärfrage und die deutsche Arbeiterpartei*, pp. 43–4.
[2] W. Schröder, *Geschichte der sozialdemokratischen Parteiorganisation in Deutschland*, pp. 7–8

the *Verein* be prohibited from taking part in duels'—others went much further. Wilhelm Liebknecht, for instance, who had watched Lassalle's career with grave suspicion, came forward immediately after his death with the suggestion that the office of President be abolished in favour of a collective leadership which would 'obliterate the memory of Lassalle'.[1] This idea was taken up and repeated during the next few months by the *Nordstern*, where details even appeared (19 August 1865) of a plan by 'the opposition-party in the ADAV' to replace the President by a directorate consisting of three members of the opposition in Leipzig.

In the end the Lassallean tradition triumphed, in organisation as in policy—Lassalle's prestige had been indicated by the insistence of the rebels, even when they proposed the revolutionary constitutional changes just mentioned, that all they were doing was to 'preserve the pure traditions of Ferdinand Lassalle, and the party-statutes destroyed by the false hands of outsiders'; the opposition, however, was strong and vocal— perhaps because it objected to allowing Bernhard Becker the wide presidential powers which had been tolerated when Lassalle was alive.

Finally, there was the question of leadership.

It was in fact the rivalry for power among Lassalle's successors which inspired certain of them (notably Schweitzer) to try to enlist the support of Marx, thus giving him a chance to make the International known in Germany. A comparison of the various individuals concerned in this struggle for power shows clearly why it was eventually won by Schweitzer.

Bernhard Becker, the president nominated in Lassalle's testament, was in many ways so ill-suited for the post that the news of Lassalle's choice caused considerable surprise.[2] Becker

---

[1] W. Liebknecht, *Karl Marx zum Gedächtnis*, p. 113.

[2] On Bernhard Becker (who played a part in the Austrian labour movement in the later 1860s, and committed suicide in 1882) cf. Gustav Mayer, *Ferdinand Lassalle, Nachgelassene Briefe und Schriften*, Vol. V, pp. 32–3, and *ibid.* Vol. VI, p. 408; Heinrich Oberwinder, *Sozialismus und Sozialpolitik*, pp. 47–71; Gustav Mayer, *Schweitzer*, pp. 90–1; and Wilhelm Blos, *Denkwürdigkeiten eines Sozialdemokraten* Vol. I, pp. 127–30.

had indeed participated as a young man in the Revolution of 1848, and had in consequence spent twelve years in exile (when he had written a history of the Revolution notable for its criticism of his older namesake, Johann Philipp Becker). Returning to Germany in 1861, he had been present at the ADAV's foundation and had been prominent in its activities in Frankfurt-am-Main. He was, however, of weak character and mediocre intellect, and during a year as president of the ADAV (November 1864 to December 1865) he seems to have been too overwhelmed by personal problems (particularly, at first, his financial dependence on Lassalle's ex-mistress the Countess Hatzfeldt) to offer the party any effective leadership.

Becker was overshadowed from the start by Johann Baptist von Schweitzer, an aristocrat with a Jesuit education and a training in law, who had won the favour of Lassalle by dedicating to him a socialistic three-volume novel (*Lucinda: or, Capital and Labour*) and by undertaking to edit a Lassallean newspaper. Money for this had been promised by Schweitzer's friend Hofstetten (an ungifted though well-endowed lieutenant in the Bavarian army), but it had not yet begun publication by the time of Lassalle's fatal duel.[1] Schweitzer regarded the newspaper-project as a possible way to power in the party; he was not yet popular enough to think of becoming its president, but by launching the *Social-Demokrat* as an official party-paper he could strengthen his position at the expense of his nominal superior Becker. Schweitzer was indeed anxious to further the socialist cause, but he wanted to further his own career as well. By the spring of 1865 he was to choose the cultivation of purely Lassallean traditions as a means to this end; for a short period in the winter of 1864–5, however, he made an attempt to secure the support and interest of Marx—an attempt which, as will be seen, had great significance for the International's fortunes in Germany. Schweitzer's biographer describes the

---

[1] Mayer, *Schweitzer* (a fundamental work), pp. 95–109. Hofstetten was present at Lassalle's duel, as recorded in Joh. Phil. Becker, *Die Letzen Tagen von Ferdinand Lassalle* ...(proof-sheets with Becker's corrections in IISG), pp. 8–9.

careful process by which he 'wormed his way in among the various tendencies inside the young German social-democratic movement... the orthodox Lassalleans and the out-and-out revolutionaries of the international school', and concludes that he regarded the 'Lassalle-cult' of many ADAV members as 'simply another factor of which he would have to make use in his calculations at the right moment in the future'.[1]

As for the opponents of the ADAV's official leadership, they included many devoted socialists, but none with the organising ability (or the personal ambition) of Schweitzer. The editor of the Hamburg *Nordstern*, Karl Bruhn, was another veteran of 1848, who had vehemently supported Lassalle but disliked both the policies and the characters of his successors; one reason for his hostility to Schweitzer was that the founding of the *Social-Demokrat* threatened the precarious sales of the *Nordstern*—which was indeed forced to cease publication early in 1866.[2]

The opposition in Berlin was led by Wilhelm Liebknecht, who worked for Schweitzer's *Social-Demokrat* until February 1865, but then broke with him and criticised his policy in trenchant speeches before being expelled by the Prussian government in July. He had already won the majority of the ADAV's Berlin members over to his side, and after his departure for Leipzig their opposition to Schweitzer continued, led by Siegfried Meyer, Theodor Metzner, and August Vogt—all of whom later joined the International.[3]

With the possible exception of Liebknecht, none of the rebels was of a stature to challenge Bernhard Becker (let alone Schweitzer) for the presidency of the party. There were in fact no well-qualified challengers, though several of the 'opposition-party', including Luscher of Leipzig and the very active Karl Klings of Solingen (who had been in contact with Marx since 1863), were at different times mentioned as potential presidents.[4]

---

[1] Mayer, *op. cit.*, p. 107.
[2] See Chapter III below.
[3] See Chapter IV below, and Appendix IV.
[4] Letters in Becker *Nachlass*, already mentioned (and letter from Heinrichs, Cologne, 19 March 1865); *Nordstern*, 19 August 1865.

Mention should also be made, among those prominent in the ADAV's divided counsels, of the Countess Hatzfeldt, who had been an intimate friend of Lassalle for twenty years, and 'a mother to him in every sense, including the sense in which Madame de Warens was a mother to Rousseau'.[1] Reference has been made to her financial domination of Lassalle's first successor; but even after he escaped from her power (by the unpopular means of misappropriating the funds bequeathed by Lassalle to pay the party-secretary's salary[2]) her influence over the ADAV, though erratic and unpredictable, was still considerable. Bitterly she accused both leadership and opposition in turn of betraying 'the holy legacy of Lassalle'; and such was her influence (either through the prestige conferred by her association with Lassalle, or through the financial resources which enabled her to keep Bernhard Becker or—later—to pay for pamphlets to be published against his policy) that she contributed much to intensifying both the ADAV's quarrels and its general confusion.[3]

THE INTERNATIONAL'S PROSPECTS IN GERMANY

In 1864 the Lassallean party thus presented a spectacle of dissension and even of disintegration; how could the leaders of the International set about bringing it into their 'fraternal

---

[1] E. H. Carr, *Karl Marx*, p. 157

[2] Bernhard Becker to Bruhn (probably written in November 1865) in *Nordstern*, 29 April 1865. Cf. Oberwinder, *Sozialismus und Sozialpolitik*, p. 108; Mehring, *Geschichte der deutschen Sozialdemokratie*, III, pp. 185, 192, 206, 225; Mayer, *Schweitzer*, p. 108.

[3] The Countess is thought to have financed C. Schilling's pamphlet *Die Ausstossung des Präsidenten Bernhard Beckers aus dem A.D.A.V.* (on this cf. *MEB*, III, p. 337, and also the anonymous work—possibly by Bernhard Becker himself—*Die Geschichte der Social-Demokratischen Partei in Deutschland seit dem Tode Ferdinand Lassalles*), and there is evidence that in May 1865 she gave a subsidy to Bruhn's *Nordstern* (unpublished letter of Bruhn to the Countess copied by Gustav Mayer into his own copy of his *J. B. von Schweitzer*, which was kindly made available to me by Mr C. Abramsky). She also created considerable jealousy and disunity by inviting most of Lassalle's leading associates (Lothar Bucher, Moses Hess, Bernhard Becker, Liebknecht and Marx), either in turn or simultaneously, to write an official memoir of Lassalle.

league of unity between the working class of the countries of the world'?

There were at least three Germans, all veterans of 1848, who might have explained to the faltering Lassalleans the ideas of the International, and pressed them to make the ADAV a part of it: Johann Philipp Becker in Geneva, who within a few days of the International's foundation was recruiting members among his fellow-exiles, and who showed his interest in German labour politics by writing regular weekly articles for the *Nordstern*; Wilhelm Liebknecht, who had returned to Germany in 1862 after years of exile at Marx's side, and who was an active member of the Lassallean opposition in Berlin; and Marx himself, who was the most eminent of half a dozen German exiles on the International's Central Council, and who shortly became its 'Corresponding Secretary for Germany'.

Johann Philipp Becker, however, though he was in constant touch with the more internationally-minded opposition-members in the ADAV, and although his *Nordstern* articles included frequent reports on the International's growth in Switzerland, made no attempt for many months to recruit members for the new organisation inside Germany. He did indeed write a propaganda-leaflet—which, as will be seen, had most important consequences, and which linked his activities in the German labour movement and his efforts for the International—but this was not until November 1865.

As for Wilhelm Liebknecht, he had many preoccupations to distract him from agitation for the International; the need to support his family drove him first to work for the *Social-Demokrat*, then to write a memoir of Lassalle sponsored by the Countess Hatzfeldt; and after he broke with the ADAV's leaders in February 1865 he devoted his energies, until his expulsion from Prussia in July, to organising opposition to them in Berlin. Marx wrote scathingly to Engels in August that during Liebknecht's months in Berlin he had failed to 'found even a six-man branch of the International Association' although he had optimistically told Engels in March that 'if only Marx would

44

come to Berlin just for a few days...we should be absolute masters of the movement'.[1] At the end of August Liebknecht himself wrote to Engels as if he was in terror of Marx, who had left his letters unanswered for weeks: 'Surely Marx won't be cross with me about the International Association? That would be unfair of him. ... How *could* I carry on successful propaganda for the Association...and found branches, with the struggles I had in Berlin?'[2]

The task of spreading the International's message in Germany thus fell mainly to Marx, aided as always by Engels. At this stage—fifteen years after they had last organised anything in Germany—they were in contact with very few potential German members for the International; they accordingly disregarded for a time the idea of enrolling individual members and attempted first to make the International's influence felt on the ADAV as a whole.[3]

Their isolation from German socialists—which had been increased by the final breakdown of their correspondence with Lassalle in 1862[4]—was in some ways an advantage rather than a handicap. It enabled them in particular to co-operate with either the official Lassallean leadership or the opposition, whichever happened at a given moment to invite them to intervene. Their isolation, indeed, made them dependent on such appeals from Germany before they could take any positive steps, but in the autumn months of 1864 these appeals came with a frequency and insistence which surprised them.

Their first reactions to the news of Lassalle's death included no idea that it might open a way for their own influence in

[1] Marx to Engels 5 August 1865, *MEB*, III, p. 337. Liebknecht to Engels 29 March 1865, quoted by Mühlbradt, *Wilhelm Liebknecht und die Gründung der deutschen Sozialdemokratie*, p. 66.

[2] Liebknecht to Engels 30 August 1865, *ibid.*, p. 70.

[3] The International's statutes provided for the adhesion either of individual members or of 'Trade, Friendly, and other Societies': Carr, *Karl Marx*, p. 194. Cf. Braunthal, *Geschichte der Internationale*, Vol. I, p. 123, and L. E. Mins (ed.), *The Founding of the First International*, p. 19.

[4] *MEB*, III, pp. 209, 212. Marx told Liebknecht to remain in the ADAV only 'as long as no errors of principle were committed' (Mayer, *Schweitzer*, pp. 101–3; *Chronik*, p. 209).

THE GERMAN SOCIAL DEMOCRATS

Germany; the foundation of the International was still a month ahead, and Marx and Engels were concerned simply with preventing the publication of their letters to Lassalle and with regretting the disappearance of one who had been, as Marx put it to Engels on 7 September 1864, despite his faults, 'the enemy of our enemies'.

During September, letters from Germany urging them to intervene in the ADAV's affairs were merely a nuisance, since Marx saw as his first task the completion of *Das Kapital*; it was only after the International had been founded at the St Martin's Hall meeting of 28 September that invitations to intervene in Germany became opportunities to be used for propaganda.

These invitations included, chronologically: in September, requests from Liebknecht in Berlin and Klings in Solingen that Marx should become a candidate for the presidency of the ADAV in succession to Lassalle; in October, an invitation from the Countess Hatzfeldt (to whom Marx had sent a note of condolence on Lassalle's death) to write a memoir of Lassalle for publication in Germany; and in November, a proposal from Schweitzer that both Marx and Engels should become contributors to the planned party-newspaper *Der Social-Demokrat*.

The second of these approaches—that of the Countess Hatzfeldt—was not followed up. Marx, not surprisingly, declined to let a tribute to Lassalle appear in his name; he wrote to the Countess commiserating with her on her bereavement, but, as he told Engels, 'warding her diplomatically off'.[1]

It was Liebknecht's idea of Marx's candidature for the presidency of the ADAV, and Schweitzer's suggestion that he and Engels should write for the *Social-Demokrat*, which seemed to offer opportunities for making the International known in Germany. In the event, however, the episode of the presidential candidature was over by the end of December (together with Marx's attempt, to which it had given rise, to induce the ADAV to declare its collective affiliation to the International); and

[1] Marx to Engels 4 November 1864, *MEB*, III, p. 234; *Chronik*, pp. 230–3; *Lassalle-Nachlass*, III, pp. 408–10.

the connection of Marx and Engels with the *Social-Demokrat* lasted only until mid-February. A closer examination will show why all these three hopes of linking the ADAV with the International were so short-lived.

MARX'S PRESIDENTIAL CANDIDATURE; HIS ATTEMPT TO SECURE THE ADAV'S AFFILIATION TO THE INTERNATIONAL

The chaotic condition of the ADAV after Lassalle's death encouraged several of its members to envisage Marx as its next president, though not always for the same reasons. Schweitzer, who suggested the idea to Liebknecht within a few days of Lassalle's death, hoped by making Marx president to safeguard his own party career as newspaper-editor, which had depended on Lassalle's personal favour and which was endangered by his disappearance. Liebknecht, who wrote twice within a few days begging Marx to stand for election (and even suggesting that Bernhard Becker would have no objection to making way for him—which was not the case), hoped to see as Lassalle's successor a man to whom he was devoted, and whose presence and leadership in Germany he urgently needed. Karl Klings, who wrote independently at the end of September to ask Marx his advice on Lassalle's succession (with the strong implication that he might take it over himself), was simply one of the very few German socialists to whom in 1864 Marx's name meant anything, and who attached much value to his views.[1]

Marx himself never seriously considered returning to Germany in response to these appeals. When Liebknecht first raised the idea, the International, which was to give Marx a political task in London, was not yet founded; from the start, however, he preferred the idea of staying in England and working on *Das Kapital* to that of returning to Berlin to lead a party dominated by the Countess Hatzfeldt, under the eyes of the Prussian police.

[1] *Chronik*, pp. 230–1, summarises the letters of Liebknecht and Klings; cf. Mayer, *Schweitzer*, p. 103.

THE GERMAN SOCIAL DEMOCRATS

The foundation of the International on 28 September apparently decided Marx to stand for election after all, and on 4 October he urged Klings to nominate him when the election took place—which was then expected to be at the party-congress planned for November. Marx even supposed that he might be elected; at this, he said, he would decline the office of president, but the congress's vote would be 'a great party-demonstration against the Prussian government and bourgeoisie, and at the same time a demonstration of solidarity with the International committee elected at the London meeting of 28 September'.[1]

Such demonstrations of solidarity with the International, however, could not be so easily obtained from the ADAV. Shortly before the vote took place on 3 November (in fact in the local party-sections, not at the congress, which was now postponed until 17 December) Lassalle's will was made public, with its 'recommendation' to the party to confirm his own choice of Bernhard Becker. Lassalle's prestige naturally assured Becker of an overwhelming victory, and turned Marx's attempt at propaganda into a grievous failure.[2] Becker himself, writing to Moses Hess on 4 November, described the election result as: 'unanimously in my favour, so far as I am aware. The attempt of Klings in Solingen to put up a gentleman from London as candidate in Wermelskirchen failed completely and even in Solingen itself I received a unanimous vote.'[3]

The 'gentleman from London' was made to realise that the failings of Bernhard Becker by no means implied widespread support for himself, and that the prestige of Lassalle swayed German socialists more than that of half-forgotten exiles, however distinguished their past role.

His second attempt to link the ADAV with the International

---

[1] Marx to Klings 4 October 1864, summarised in *Chronik*, p. 231, and partly reprinted in Marx & Engels, *Briefe über Das Kapital*, p. 124; extract in English in *The Founding of the First International*, p. 45.

[2] Bernhard Becker, *Geschichte der Arbeiter-Agitation Ferdinand Lassalle's*, p. 305. Lassalle's testament in his *Reden und Schriften*, III, p. 956.

[3] *Moses Hess—Briefwechsel*, E. Silberner & W. Blumenberg, eds., p. 485.

envisaged nothing so ambitious as his own election to its presidency, but merely the securing of a declaration on its part of affiliation to the London organisation. This attempt was a further response by Marx to the letter he had received from Klings at the end of September. On 22 December, a few days before the ADAV's Düsseldorf congress, he wrote a long letter to Karl Siebel, a cousin of Engels' in Barmen, asking him to work through Klings for the ADAV's affiliation to the International.

'It is important,' [wrote Marx,] 'that the German workers' organisations should affiliate to our central committee, on account of the movement *here*. (Numerous affiliations already here from Italy and France.) Liebknecht writes that the Berlin Compositors' Association will join, but that the ADAV's adhesion is very doubtful because of the machinations of Herr Bernhard Becker....It would be very desirable for you to go briefly to Solingen, and explain in my name to the knife-smith Klings the extreme importance of the ADAV's voting its adhesion to the International at its General Assembly, to be held at Düsseldorf on the 27th of this month.' Marx went on to tell Siebel that he might in this connection freely disparage 'such nullities as B. Becker, etc.', though without involving his (Marx's) name in such attacks, and explained further: 'You understand that the ADAV's adhesion is necessary only for the beginning, against our enemies here. Later on this organisation must be completely destroyed, because the foundations on which it rests are false.'[1]

This letter is extremely important for the picture it gives of Marx's personal views and aims, his determination to win German affiliations to the International, his sanguine expectations of Liebknecht and Klings, his conviction that rival parties like the ADAV could be simply 'destroyed' when the time came, and finally his motives for wanting German support in

---

[1] Marx to Siebel 22 December 1864, reprinted almost in full in *Marx-Engels-Lenin-Stalin zur deutschen Geschichte*, Vol. II, p. 1241. Marx had already sent the International's *Inaugural Address* to Siebel, as well as to Kugelmann in Hanover (cf. *Briefe an Kugelmann*, p. 20).

the International—to strengthen his own position in the General Council—even though it is not clear which particular 'enemies' he had in mind at this point. In Germany, however, the letter had no effect whatever.

Siebel passed on none of Marx's elaborate instructions to Klings, as he did not even meet him until the congress was over;[1] and although he promised vaguely to get the International's *Inaugural Address* published in the democratic *Düsseldorfer Zeitung*, nothing ever came of it, and all Marx got from him and from Klings was news of the ADAV's internal rivalries.[2]

Another optimistic attempt to further the International's cause in Germany had failed, and Marx and Engels were left only with the opportunities offered by Schweitzer's new *Social-Demokrat*.

MARX'S AND ENGELS' COLLABORATION WITH
THE *Social-Demokrat*

The suggestion that Marx and Engels should write for the *Social-Demokrat*, like the idea that Marx should become President of the party, was a by-product of Schweitzer's preoccupation with his career.

It became clear early in November that not Marx but Bernhard Becker would be the new President, and Schweitzer—still hoping to use Marx's prestige among party-leaders to strengthen his own position—hit on the idea of asking him and Engels to write for the new paper, together with other prominent political exiles including Moses Hess, Johann Philipp Becker, Georg Herwegh and Leopold Rüstow. Liebknecht, who was himself accepting a post on the paper (largely for financial reasons) eagerly passed Schweitzer's invitation on to London, and Marx and Engels, delighted at the prospect of having a new organ for their views in Germany, accepted almost without hesitation.[3]

[1] Siebel to Marx 25 December 1864 (unpublished original, IISG), '... Den Mann in Solingen habe ich nicht gesehen. . . .'
[2] Siebel to Marx 25 December 1864, 19 January, 1 February 1865 (IISG).
[3] Liebknecht to Marx 4 November 1864 (*Chronik*, p. 233); *MEB*, III, p. 243.

Predominant in their minds was the hope that the *Social-Demokrat* would spread the ideas of the International in Germany. Marx's comment on passing Schweitzer's first letter on to Engels was 'it is important for us to have an organ in Berlin, mainly because of the Association that I have helped to start in London', and when he wrote to tell Liebknecht of his agreement to write for the paper, he sent the International's *Inaugural Address* as his first contribution.[1]

The apparent compliance of Schweitzer's letters made the *Social-Demokrat* seem a more promising channel for the International's message than any Marx and Engels had yet tried. The official invitation (though it did contain a statement that the paper would be the official organ of the Lassallean party) flatteringly addressed Marx as 'the founder of the German workers' party, and its predominant representative', and was accompanied by a prospectus mentioning 'the solidarity of interests of all peoples' as the *Social-Demokrat*'s first principle. Schweitzer obligingly promised to publish the *Inaugural Address* even before he had seen it, and when it arrived he wrote to confirm this, even though the 'extremely valuable manuscript' was too long to be printed in a single number of the *Social-Demokrat*.[2]

Engels was shocked to hear that the future collaborators of the paper included Georg Herwegh and Moses Hess, but Marx calmed him by repeating (on 24 November 1864) what he had told Liebknecht already—that they both disliked their new colleagues, and would 'disavow them at once, as soon as they started any nonsense'.

Neither Marx nor Engels did anything further about the *Social-Demokrat* until the first and second trial-numbers, distributed free in 50,000 copies, had appeared on 15 and 21 December, but they found the contents of these so distasteful that smooth co-operation with the paper already began to seem much less likely. Publication of the *Inaugural Address*

[1] Marx to Engels 14 & 18 November 1864, *MEB*, III, pp. 242, 245.
[2] *MEB*, III, p. 245; *SAR*, pp. 25–8.

did indeed begin in the second number, but Marx was so infuriated to see a leading article on Lassalle headed by an extract from his own personal letter of sympathy to the Countess as well as a general tendency towards the 'apotheosis' of Lassalle, that he talked already of carrying out his threat to resign. Schweitzer and Liebknecht replied to his protests with a promise to do better in future,[1] and several days went by before Marx had fresh cause for complaint.

The *Social-Demokrat* then published on 13 January an article from Moses Hess in Paris, alleging that Tolain, the chosen representative of the International in France, was a Bonapartist agent, and that the International had so 'compromised itself through its connection with him that the 'real representatives' of the French working class would have nothing to do with it.

Marx at once accused Schweitzer of deliberate 'provocation', described the article by Hess as 'a declaration of war', and refused to be pacified even by Schweitzer's polite explanation that it was Liebknecht who had been responsible for the article's publication.[2] Schweitzer's letter of apology (18 January) continued: 'I have spoken to Becker about effecting the affiliation of the ADAV to the Association (i.e. the International), and it may be that he will do it'; mollified—significantly—by this, Marx sent the *Social-Demokrat* a long obituary-article on Proudhon (who had died on 19 January) which appeared in the first three numbers in February.

He included in this article, however, several passages criticising Proudhon's sympathy for Napoleon III in terms so general that they could be applied (as indeed they were meant to be) to the ADAV's tendency to side with Bismarck against the Liberals; and the same line was emphasised in a contribution by Engels.[3]

Since the *Social-Demokrat*, on the other hand, had already given a clear indication of its support for the government in the

[1] *Chronik*, p. 238; *SAR*, p. 40
[2] *MEB*, III, p. 258; *Chronik*, p. 238; *SAR*, pp. 60–1; Zlocisti, *Moses Hess*, pp. 344–5.
[3] *Social-Demokrat*, 1, 3, 5 February 1865; *MEB*, III, p. 261

constitutional conflict by a declaration, published on 30 December 1864 that 'not everything which seems reactionary to the Progressive Party seems so to us', the tension between the paper and its contributors in England remained high.

When another article by Hess, published on 1 February, again referred to the International in terms ambiguous enough for Marx to feel slighted, he wrote, as he told Engels two days later, 'a furious letter to Liebknecht, telling him that this is the *very last* warning he will get; that I don't care a farthing for "good will" that has the same results as bad will; that I can't make the members of the International Committee here believe that things like this can happen in *bonne foi*, through simple stupidity'; and he followed this with a biting declaration to the *Social-Demokrat* condemning Hess's remarks as 'libellous insinuations'.[1]

There is no reason to disbelieve Schweitzer's claim that Marx's letter to Liebknecht filled him 'with astonishment', since Hess had merely expressed his regret that there should be a small number of doubtful elements in the International 'which otherwise consists only of the best-tried and most influential friends of Labour'.[2] Schweitzer formally declared that 'nothing concerning the International Working Men's Association shall be published in the paper which has not been approved by Liebknecht expressly and in writing',[3] and must have been amazed to receive in reply the scathing 'Declaration' written by Marx.

This document was answered by the *Social-Demokrat*'s publication on 12 February 1865 of a soothing explanation by Hess, and by another letter—less patient this time—from Schweitzer. Besides giving fresh assurances that Liebknecht had the right at any time of vetoing any questionable reference to the International, Schweitzer hinted clearly (as Marx and

---

[1] *MEB*, III, pp. 267–8; declaration, *ibid.*, p. 272; cf. *Chronik*, pp. 238–9.
[2] *Social-Demokrat*, 1 February 1865; *SAR*, p. 61; *Chronik*, p. 238.
[3] *SAR*, p. 62. It is not surprising that Schweitzer's letter of 4 February 'does not mention the declaration' (Mehring in *ibid.*, p. 62), as it only reached him about the 9th (*Chronik*, p. 238).

Engels had done privately from the beginning) that a break between the *Social-Demokrat* and its contributors in England would be the best solution, if they refused to be satisfied with this arrangement, and with Hess's explanation. Referring to his previous hints about the ADAV's affiliation to the International, Schweitzer went on:

I am losing all inclination to bother about this Association any further, to try as I planned to bring about the ADAV's adhesion; for it seems that at every step one takes in connection with this Association, one 'offends' somebody. For this reason . . . I pray you to consider the newspaper, as far as the International Association is concerned, as though Liebknecht alone is responsible. This is in fact the case.[1]

Schweitzer (a trained lawyer) had carefully confined his letter to the formal grounds of Marx's first protests—the *Social-Demokrat*'s unfriendly attitude to the International, and the publication of the ambiguous articles by Hess; his offer to give Marx complete satisfaction on these points, and his pretence that *this* might be the cause of a break, prompted a full reply which made it clear beyond all doubt that the real causes of division lay deeper, and in which, indeed, the International received no mention at all.

Marx now repeated in greater detail his insistence that 'the paper must be at least as hostile in tone to the government and the feudal-aristocratic party as it is to the progressives'— an insistence which seemed particularly necessary after the publication of Schweitzer's first two articles on the rise of Bismarck, making Prussian domination of Germany seem not only inevitable but also desirable—and also that the ADAV should agitate more vigorously for the abolition of the legal ban on strikes and Trade Unions. Summing up his and Engels' objections to the *Social-Demokrat*'s one-sided anti-Liberal propaganda and its appeasement of the government, Marx rousingly concluded 'the working class is revolutionary or it is nothing!'[2]

[1] Schweitzer to Marx 11 February 1865, in *MEB*, III, p. 283.
[2] *Ibid.*, pp. 285-7.

Two days later, Schweitzer answered by confirming his readiness, already expressed in his letter of 4 February, to listen to Marx's advice on 'theoretical questions', but insisting that he alone, as the man 'in the middle-point of the movement', could decide on the tactical line to be taken by the party. He explained the ADAV's pro-governmental tactics further by the strength of the Lassallean tradition—'things *in concreto* always tend to drag a ball and chain with them'—and concluded with a rather obvious attempt to win back Marx's sympathies by a further promise to work for the International:

... as the Federal Laws (*Bundesgesetze*—i.e. the German Combination Acts of 1854) make our affiliation impossible, I intend to propose the following resolution to Becker for the ADAV: (1) The ADAV declares its total concurrence with the basis and aims (*Grundsätzen und Streben*) of the International Working Men's Association; (2) If it does not affiliate to this Association, the only reason for this is that the Combination Acts forbid such adhesion; (3) The ADAV will be represented at the Congress. I think this formula protects the interests of both sides. Are you in agreement with it?[1]

For Marx, however, Schweitzer's promises were worthless compared with his conviction of the man's duplicity, and of the impossibility of further co-operation with the *Social-Demokrat*. While Schweitzer's letter was still in the post, Liebknecht—whose disillusion had been accumulating since the start—resigned in protest against Schweitzer's article on Bismarck; Marx and Engels in their turn (the former declaring Schweitzer for 'incorrigible—probably in secret agreement with Bismarck', and the latter concluding that Schweitzer had 'the task of discrediting us') despatched a letter of resignation to the *Social-Demokrat*, sending it simultaneously for publication in other German papers.[2]

After the letter had appeared in two Liberal papers, the *Elberfelder Zeitung* and the Berlin *Reform*, the *Social-Demokrat*

---

[1] Schweitzer to Marx 15 February 1865, *SAR*, pp. 63–4. The first Congress of the International was then expected to take place later in 1865 in Belgium.
[2] *MEB*, III, pp. 284, 288; *Chronik*, pp. 240–1.

reprinted it, together with a general attack on Marx and Engels by their long-standing critic Karl Blind. To this Marx replied by a further long attempt to prove Schweitzer's perfidy by contrasting his flattering correspondence of the previous November with the 'servile praise-singing' of Lassalle subsequently carried on by the *Social-Demokrat*. After one more public declaration on each side, both published in the *Reform*, the unedifying polemic came to an end, and it seemed to exclude any chance of Marx's and Engels' ever co-operating with the Lassalleans again.[1]

One of the striking things about the public declarations which followed the break between Marx and Engels and the *Social-Demokrat* was that none of them made any reference whatever to the International, which had played such a large role in the private correspondence leading up to it. If the only reason for this large role had been, as Marx said, Schweitzer's determination to make him appear to have broken with the paper on the ridiculous grounds that Hess had insulted the International, the sudden silence about this organisation after the break would be neither surprising nor significant. In fact, however, Schweitzer's alternate offers to affiliate the ADAV to the International, and half-threats *not* to do so, had been based on a quite justified assumption that the International was so important to Marx that his continued tolerance could be assured, if at all, only by hints of this kind.

Daily contact with Liebknecht, as well as the immediate arrival of the *Inaugural Address* as Marx's response to the invitation to write for the paper, must have shown Schweitzer that propaganda for the International was a major concern for Marx; the rightness of this conclusion is confirmed by Marx's own communications to Engels, Siebel, Klings, Kugelmann, and Liebknecht.

---

[1] Marx's declaration of 19 March in Schilling's pamphlet, *Die Ausstossung des Präsidenten Bernhard Beckers*, pp. 58–61; Schweitzer's reply of 21 March in Mayer, *Schweitzer*, pp. 120–1 fn. Marx and Engels were followed in their resignation from the *Social-Demokrat* by all the paper's other distinguished émigré correspondents, except Moses Hess.

The very importance of the International for Marx had been behind his violent protests against the articles by Hess; and his irritation with Schweitzer for trying to hold him to the text of his original protest—'posing the question of confidence in this impudent way', Marx called it in a letter of 18 February to Engels—reflected his frustration when he realised that his great hopes for the International in Germany were illusory.

THE REASONS FOR THE INTERNATIONAL'S FAILURE IN 1864-5

One after another, Marx's attempts to influence the ADAV in the interests of the International had failed; the attempted demonstration over the presidential election had passed unnoticed; the ADAV's possible affiliation had come to nothing; and now the attempt to use Liebknecht's position on the *Social-Demokrat* had failed too.

'In the spring of 1865 it became conclusively obvious that Lassalleanism was the main obstacle to the development of a workers' party based on the revolutionary principles of the First International':[1] this is one way of summarising the situation as Marx and Engels now saw it.

Nothing more could be done with the ADAV, and all that the organisers of the International could do was to 'let that pack fight it out among themselves', and hope that the resulting disintegrations of the Lassallean party would leave the way clear for the International. Marx's joy at the 'lovely mess' into which the ADAV seemed to be collapsing was perhaps justified by the reports he got from Liebknecht and Klings.[2] On the other hand, 'the development of a workers' party based on the revolutionary principles of the First International' was in 1865 still impossible; all that the Corresponding Secretary for Germany could do was to instruct Liebknecht to enrol individual

---

[1] Professor Engelberg in *Zeitschrift für Geschichtswissenschaft*, 1954, p. 638; cf. Marx to Engels 13 February 1865, *MEB*, III, p. 281.

[2] *MEB*, III, pp. 255, 272, 326; Liebknecht to Engels 29 March 1865 (printed in *Hamburger Echo*, 29 March 1926); *Chronik*, p. 242.

members in the International[1]—a slow and wearisome business, and quite without the spectacular prospects held out by a 'capture' of the whole ADAV.

Even this modest demand, however, was bound to remain without effect, partly because Liebknecht, until his expulsion from Prussia at the end of July, was wholly absorbed in the internal struggles of the ADAV, and partly for the same deeper reasons which had obstructed the earlier attempts at propaganda for the International of Marx and Engels themselves.

It is too simple to ascribe the break between the International and the ADAV, symbolised by the rancorous departure of Marx and Engels from the *Social-Demokrat*, to the 'treasonable opportunism' of Schweitzer's policy, or to his having tried to bring the German proletariat into 'an impossible and intolerable dependence on the feudal-aristocratic reaction, on Bismarck, and on the Prussian crown';[2] nor, on the other hand, is it enough to say that Marx and Engels were 'a positive menace with their ignorance of the Prussian situation', and their suggestions 'a string of political naïveties', or that the break's 'real cause was the prejudice of Marx and Engels against everything Lassallean'.[3]

What serious hopes could Marx and Engels have of overcoming 'Lassalleanism' and 'developing a workers' party based on the revolutionary principles of the First International' in the Germany of 1864–5? They had been in exile for fifteen years, during which political conditions in Germany, as well as their own reluctance to spread their views through such organs as a newspaper edited by Lassalle, had made it inevitable that they should be little known to the German public.

The distance separating 1848 (or the Communist League) from 1865 (or the ADAV) inevitably seemed far shorter to the two exiles than it did to socialists inside Germany. These had experienced the long years of reaction in the 1850s, then the

[1] *Chronik*, p. 243; Liebknecht to Engels 30 August 1865, quoted p. 45 above.
[2] Engelberg, *loc. cit.*, p. 535; E. Fuchs in Mehring, *Karl Marx* (5th edition, Berlin, 1933), *Nachwort*, p. 609.
[3] Zlocisti, *Moses Hess*, p. 348; Mehring in *SAR*, p. 64.

apparent rebirth of Liberalism in the 'New Era' under the Crown Prince, and finally the revival of the labour movement in its distinctive Lassallean form; and even those members of the old Communist League who remained active in the movement turned for inspiration to Schweitzer rather than to Marx. In March 1865, at a meeting in Barmen, the cigar-maker Röser (one of the defendants in the Cologne Communist trial of 1852, but now in the pay of the police) asserted that even in 1849 Marx and Engels had done the Socialist cause more harm than good, and that the movement could have no further use for them.[1]

When this kind of attack, and Schweitzer's contemptuous dismissal of the 'antiquated Marxian coterie', could pass without any contradiction in the German labour movement, it was clear that Marx had virtually no influence; Bernhard Becker's taunt that the 'Marxian party' consisted only of 'the master Marx, his secretary Engels, and his agent Liebknecht' was at this stage only a slight exaggeration.[2] A few Berlin workers influenced by Liebknecht; Engels' cousin Siebel; isolated and uninfluential admirers like Klings in Solingen or Kugelmann in Hanover: these were virtually Marx's only supporters in Germany in 1865.

It would be wrong to depict the ADAV in 1864–5 as a solidly-organised party, united in a conscious resolve to resist any permeation by Marxism or other extraneous doctrines. Enough has been said of the jealousies and divisions in the party to show that Schweitzer was seriously exaggerating when he told Marx 'the ADAV is a consolidated entity, which is

---

[1] On the Barmen meeting of 12 March 1865, cf. *Social-Demokrat* 25 March; *Nordstern* 19 March; Mehring, Vol. III, p. 212; Mayer, *Schweitzer*, p. 124. It has been established that Röser himself was in the pay of the police (cf. O. Mänchen-Helfen and B. Nikolajewsky, *Karl und Jenny Marx: Ein Lebensweg* (Berlin, 1933), p. 149, and more recently L. Stern, ed., *Archivalische Forschungen zur Geschichte der deutschen Arbeiterbewegung*, Vol. I, pp. 133–6); but this fact is surely less important than the total absence of any dissension from his attack on Marx.

[2] Schweitzer and Becker quoted respectively in Mayer, *Schweitzer*, p. 120 fn., and (anon.) *Die Geschichte der Social-Demokratischen Partei in Deutschland...*, p. 35. Cf. General Council *Minutes* (ms., IISG), Vol. I, p. 43 (1 April 1865).

bound to remain tied to its traditions'.[1] The ADAV, on the contrary, was at this time a demoralised, disintegrating party, in which the ideas of Marx and Engels struggled for influence against the modified Lassalleanism of Schweitzer and Bernhard Becker. If 'propaganda for Karl Marx was carried on in certain local sections',[2] it remained without success even in the ADAV's most vulnerable period, and was soon overcome by the Lassallean traditions encouraged by Schweitzer, and by the consolidation of the party through his surely-calculated tactics.[3]

The ADAV's consolidation as an independent party, which had seemed so unlikely in the first months after Lassalle's death, ended all hopes of what Liebknecht later called 're-placing it by the International Working Men's Association as the framework of the German labour movement';[4] it meant the end of the International's prospects of overcoming the ADAV by a direct assault.

Even the *Social-Demokrat*'s limited interest in the International during the period of Marx's and Engels' collaboration had been questioned by certain members of the ADAV. The Frankfurt cigar-maker Fritzsche (an exceptionally open-minded Lassallean, among the first to challenge Lassalle's 'iron law of wages' by founding a Trade Union) sent a querulous letter to the *Social-Demokrat* asking what was the *raison d'être* of the International, whose programme was 'so much less precise than that of the ADAV'. Schweitzer explained that the demands of the

---

[1] Letter of 15 February 1865, in *SAR*, p. 63.

[2] Bernhard Becker, *Geschichte der Arbeiter-Agitation Ferdinand Lassalle's*, p. 304.

[3] The motives for Schweitzer's pro-Bismarckian tactics have been the subject of much controversy, including the accusations of Bebel and others that he accepted bribes from the government. However, the evidence for this (discussed by Gustav Mayer in *Archiv für Sozialwissenschaft und Sozialpolitik*, Vol. 57, pp. 167–75, and enlarged by Engelberg, *Zeitschrift für Geschichtswissenschaft*, 1954, pp. 536–7 fn.) suggests rather that Bismarck found it useful to support Schweitzer—thus tacitly confirming the latter's influence and hence the effectiveness of his tactical line since 1864—than that Schweitzer was bribed into departing from the line he would in any case have pursued.

[4] W. Liebknecht, *Karl Marx zum Gedächtnis*, p. 114. Cf. Mehring, *Geschichte*, III, p. 189, and *SAR*, p. 65.

International, being general formulae applicable to all European countries, were necessarily 'vaguer' than the ADAV's specific demands for Germany, and continued: 'The aim of the International is surely less to further social-democratic agitation *directly* in the different civilised countries than to allow effective and integrated co-operation in suitable cases, by creating informal multilateral unity between social-democratic elements in the various countries'.[1]

In Germany, where Lassalle's creation of the ADAV had brought into being a centralised national organisation for all 'social-democratic elements', it was possible, and perhaps necessary for the International to be regarded in this way—as a *liaison* bureau linking the separate and autonomous national movements; though for a long time this was true of Germany alone. It was not surprising that the French workers, whose Unions had only recently received a limited degree of toleration through the Imperial Government's Law of 25 May 1864, should have no centralised organisation beside the Paris office of the International, and should regard the General Council (as Marx triumphantly reported to Engels on 4 March 1865), as the 'government of labour'; as Liebknecht was to remind Engels six years later: 'the French have no organisation apart from the International'.[2] In Germany, however, the attitude to the International could only be that sketched in Schweitzer's reply to Fritzsche, and the International's organisers, after their break with the ADAV, could do nothing but attempt to enrol individual members. This admission of defeat, though perhaps temporary, was for the time being conclusive.

Marx and Engels had indeed been able to use the *Social-Demokrat* 'to speak to the most progressive workers in Germany, and make the programme of the First International known to them',[3] but despite all their efforts, the International was still virtually unknown in Germany at the end of the year 1865,

---

[1] Schweitzer's (anonymous) reply to Fritzsche's letter, in *Social-Demokrat*, 3 February 1865.
[2] Letter of late 1871 in Mayer, *Schweitzer*, pp. 439–40.
[3] Engelberg, *loc. cit.*, p. 536.

as was shown by the letters of reply to Johann Philipp Becker's circular sent out in the month of November.

During 1865 'the International was gathering strength; and it was for the national organisations on the Continent to come to it, not for it to go to them'.[1] The French, Belgians, and later Swiss, did 'come to it', but the German Lassalleans eluded the determined attempts its leaders had made to 'go to them'. The ADAV under Schweitzer, shaking off without difficulty any attempt by Marx and Engels to exert their influence, continued on the tactical course which brought it in 1866 even closer to Bismarck than it had been during Lassalle's lifetime, while the leaders of the International, resentful at the defeat they had suffered, made no more ambitious attempts to win power in Germany until the situation was more propitious.

They had to wait, first, until Marx's name had acquired such a public reputation in Germany that it would benefit a socialist leader to make use of it; and secondly, until laborious preparatory work had been undertaken by others.

This work, which was to lead within a few years to a—superficially—complete reversal of the defeat of 1865, was carried out by Liebknecht in Leipzig, very hesitantly and ineffectively, and with astonishing energy and enthusiasm by Johann Philipp Becker in Geneva.

---

[1] Carr, *Karl Marx*, p. 208.

CHAPTER III

JOHANN PHILIPP BECKER AND THE INTERNATIONAL IN GERMANY, 1864 TO 1868

INTRODUCTION

It is worth recalling that the story of the International's relations with Germany, as usually interpreted, runs roughly as follows:

During the confused period after Ferdinand Lassalle's death the International failed to influence his disintegrating party; and its missed opportunity was prevented from recurring by J. B. von Schweitzer's reinvigoration of the Lassallean tradition, and by his tactical *rapprochement* with Bismarck in 1866. It was only after the Austro-Prussian war that Marx's disciple Wilhelm Liebknecht successfully propagated internationalist ideas in Germany, and transformed the Liberal-democratic League of Workers' Clubs (*Verband Deutscher Arbeitervereine*), under the impact of South German hostility to Prussia, into a non-Lassallean socialist party which adopted a partly Marxist programme and a sympathetic attitude towards the International. The propaganda of Liebknecht and of August Bebel among the Saxon and South German Workers' Clubs led first to a collective declaration of sympathy with the International (at the Nürnberg congress of September 1868), then to the foundation, at Eisenach in August 1869, of the *Sozialdemokratische Arbeiterpartei*, which regarded itself, in the words of the new Eisenach Programme, 'in so far as the Combination Laws allow, as a branch of the International Working Men's Association'. Even though Marx regarded the German contacts made by the International in 1868–9 as still unsatisfactory, he saw the attitude of the 'Eisenachers' as representing a distinct advance on the Lassalleans' indifference to the International in 1864–5.

After 1869 the Eisenach Party, separated finally from its Liberal-democratic associates in the *Deutsche Volkspartei* by its acceptance of the Basle resolution calling for land-nationalisation, played a modest but positive part in the life of the International, carrying on propaganda according to its congress-resolutions and making its war-aims known to the German public in 1870–1. In the International's great internal struggle, finally, the German party gave what support it could to the Marxists, and in September 1872 sent a valuable delegation to the Hague Congress which saw the expulsion of Bakunin, the removal of the General Council to New York, and the virtual extinction of the International in Europe.

Such an account of the story's outlines contains nothing positively untrue, but it directly encourages false interpretations by omitting one vital link. This link is the campaign of propaganda carried on by Johann Philipp Becker, a German emigrant living in Geneva, and the omission has led many authorities to conclude that local Sections of the International in Germany dated only from the Eisenach Congress of 1869;[1] in fact, Becker had by then been founding and sustaining such Sections for nearly four years.

This was the foundation on which Liebknecht built when he assumed the nominal leadership of the International in Germany after 1868, and so the failure to recognise Becker's importance leads also to a misleading exaggeration of Liebknecht's role and of his achievement.

One reason why Becker's vital contribution to the International's growth in Germany is easily overlooked is that it came second, both chronologically and in importance, to his propaganda inside Switzerland. In 1864–5, the first year of the International's existence, Becker was so pessimistic about his chances of spreading its ideas in Germany that he addressed

---

[1] This is implied, for instance, in Boris Nicolaevsky's article 'Karl Marx und die Berliner Sektion der I. Internationale' in *Die Gesellschaft*, X. Jrg. Nr. 3 (1933), p. 256. Mr. Nicolaevsky has very kindly communicated to the present writer (in a letter dated 23 December 1957) subsequently-discovered evidence that the Berlin Section was in fact founded in 1866. Cf. Appendix IV, pp. 253-4.

his propaganda only to his fellow-exiles in Switzerland, and to the few native Swiss who were prepared to listen; and his subsequent influence in Germany, considerable though it was in 1866 and the three following years, was fragile enough for the German party-leaders to destroy it in 1869, while his prestige in Switzerland remained undamaged.

Another reason why Becker is commonly allowed no greater role than that of 'one of the organisers of the First International's German Section in Switzerland'[1] is that historiography in the SPD was for generations a weapon in the party's internal and external controversies, and that no party historian had any motive for seriously defending Becker's achievement against writers whose version of the past implicitly minimised it. By about 1900, the memory of the 'old International' was a glorious element in the party-mythology, an element whose prestige was transferred to anyone who could claim to have spread the International's ideas in Germany. It was thus natural that Liebknecht and Bebel should be tempted to exaggerate their own work for the International in the 1860s, and to overlook that of the obscure, and meanwhile deceased, exile Becker. Thus Liebknecht, for instance, republished in 1894 the full proceedings of the trial of 1872 in which he and other alleged agents of the International had been arraigned for high treason.[2] In this Liebknecht and Bebel are seen arguing for page after page that their relations with Becker were non-political (at times even that they were non-existent), and that his influence in Germany was negligible. Although they knew in 1872 that this was merely prevarication designed to establish their innocence, they may by 1894 have come to believe it.

Becker's place in the hagiology of the International thus became that of the organisation's 'chief representative in

---

[1] This entry, in the *Namenverzeichnis* of the anthology *Karl Marx und Friedrich Engels über die Gewerkschaften* (1953), p. 238, is typical of many, up to and including that in H. H. Gerth, *The First International: Minutes of the Hague Congress of 1872, with Related Documents* (1958), p. 298.

[2] *Der Hochverraths-Prozess wider Liebknecht, Bebel, Hepner*, 944 pp., here cited as *Hochverratsprozess*.

Romance Switzerland',[1] and this over-modest assessment, persisting until the present day, has provoked no reasoned contradiction. The only historians who knew enough about Becker to acknowledge his work in Germany have been led to make such wildly-exaggerated claims as Gustav Jaeckh's (in 1865): 'Becker's outstanding skill in organising succeeded in attracting to the International, in serried ranks, all the existing workers' clubs and other workers' organisations in German Switzerland, Germany, and Austria';[2] and the version generally accepted, partly in reaction to such absurd claims, has been that of the men whose destruction of Becker's German organisation in 1869 naturally inclined them in later years to pretend that its importance had always been small. Bebel's memoirs present Becker's attempt in 1868–9 to hold this organisation together as a kind of usurpation, and there has been no criticism of Marx's claim that its only justification in 1869 was that 'we allowed him (Becker) *provisionally*, until the International's strength in Germany *grew*, to remain as centre for the correspondents he already had'.[3]

An unprejudiced estimate of the International's debt to Becker, however, written when his activity was at its height, shows neither the calculated disparagement of Marx and Bebel, nor the immoderate exaggeration of Jaeckh: Wilhelm Eichhoff, one of the International's ablest members in Germany, writing a pamphlet on its history and aims in the summer of 1868, called Becker 'the soul of the international labour movement in Switzerland', and added in parentheses: 'it is he, in fact, who has recruited all the German elements which have joined the Association in Germany itself'.[4] Eichhoff (whose estimate of Becker was almost certainly provided by Marx, an indication

[1] Marx-Engels, *Briefwechsel*, Vol. III (Stuttgart, 1913), p. xxiv.
[2] Gustav Jaeckh, *Die Internationale*, p. 20, followed by G. M. Stekloff, *History of the First International*, p. 58.
[3] August Bebel, *AML*, Vol. I, p. 182; Vol. II, p. 82, etc.; Marx to Engels 27 July 1869, *MEGA*, III/4, p. 214.
[4] Wilhelm Eichhoff, *Die Internationale Arbeiter-Association: Ihre Gründung, politisch-sociale Thätigkeit und Ausbreitung*, p. 35 fn. On Marx's contribution, cf. *Chronik*, pp. 268–70.

that the latter's opinion of Becker was higher in 1868 than a year later), was not only right in putting Becker's role as leader of the International in Switzerland first; he was very nearly accurate in attributing to him a virtual monopoly of its effective propaganda in Germany as well.

Who then was this man, to whose efforts the First International owed what little success it had in Germany? The story of how Becker transformed the International's 'German Section in Geneva' into the centre of a far-flung 'Group of German-speaking Sections', whose propaganda deeply influenced the German labour movement, forms one of the most striking chapters in a remarkable life-story.[1]

In length alone, to take the obvious starting-point, few revolutionary careers of the nineteenth century can compare with that of Johann Philipp Becker, who was born in 1809 at Frankenthal in the Palatinate and died in 1886 in Geneva. According to one story, Becker remembered seeing, in 1819, the execution of Kotzebue's assassin, Sand. It is certain that by 1830, as well as learning the trade of a broom-maker, he had developed a firm attachment to the 'pre-March' ideals of democratic freedom and German unity; at the celebrated Hambach demonstration of 1832, as he was to recall fifty years later, his was among the most radical speeches.

After the German democratic clubs of the 1830s came the beginnings of socialism in Switzerland (whence Becker emigrated in 1838), and then the revolution of 1848–9, when, returning to Germany, he commanded one of the few revolutionary armies to have any military success. In the 1850s he retired reluctantly to what he called 'everyday life', becoming successively innkeeper, gardener, photographer and journalist

---

[1] The following account is based mainly on Becker's own *Curriculum vitae*, reprinted with notes by N. Riazanov in *Grünbergs Archiv für die Geschichte des Sozialismus and der Arbeiterbewegung*, Vol. IV, pp. 313–29. See also Riazanov's articles in *Vorwärts*, 6 & 7 June, 1914 (Nos. 151, 152); Gustav Mayer's introduction to *Ferdinand Lassalle, Nachgelassene Briefe und Schriften*, Vol. V, pp. 37–8; E. Schneider, 'J. Ph. Becker', in *Das Hambacher Fest*, ed. J. Baumann, pp. 205–37; and G. Trübner, 'Der deutsche Republikaner Johann Philipp Becker... in der Schweiz' in *International Review of Social History*, Vol. VI, pp. 256–76.

in Switzerland, and in 1856 metallurgist in Paris. When the 1860s brought a new wave of revolutionary movements in Europe, the volatile Becker became in turn an enthusiastic disciple of figures as diverse as Garibaldi, Lassalle, Marx, and Bakunin, and the 1870s saw him engaged in vigorous attempts to hold up the ebb of the revolutionary tide which followed the extinction of the Paris Commune. In 1881 he presided over a congress in Chur where a little-known attempt was made to revive the International; and in 1886, shortly before his death at the age of seventy-seven, he journeyed to London, Paris, and various parts of Germany, discussing plans for the future and memories of the past with revolutionaries ranging in age from Engels, his junior by only ten years, to Marx's young son-in-law Lafargue, a leader of the rising *Parti Ouvrier Français*.

BECKER, LASSALLE, AND THE FOUNDING
OF THE INTERNATIONAL

A closer survey of Becker's career from 1860 onwards suggests that he was a natural revolutionary, tending to throw himself without much reflection into any movement, whatever its aims and leadership, which offered a challenge to the political, social and international order established after the abortive revolutions of 1848.

By 1860, for instance, the movement for Italian unity had become a symbol of revolt against the *status quo*, and Becker hastened to Genoa to raise a German volunteer brigade in support of Garibaldi. He arrived too late to help, however, and found in any case that his enthusiasm for Italy was shared by disappointingly few of his compatriots;[1] yet the example of Italy seemed to Becker to offer hope for the democratic unification of Germany, and he spent the first part of 1861, before leaving Italy, in writing a fiery book on this theme (*Wie und Wann: Ein Ernstes Wort über die Fragen und Aufgaben der Zeit*) which was published at Geneva in the following year.

[1] On Becker's unsuccessful efforts to recruit German volunteers in London through Sigismund Borkheim and Lothar Bucher, cf. Moritz Busch, *Tagebuch-blätter*, Vol. III, pp. 104–5.

The only potential leader of a German revolution at this time was Lassalle, and by 1863, after the launching of his sensational campaign to revive the German labour movement, Becker was in eager correspondence with him. Their motives were as different as their characters: where Lassalle coldly calculated that Becker would be a more effective Swiss agent than Georg Herwegh (who was nominally the Lassallean party's 'plenipotentiary' for Switzerland, but whose activities seem to have been limited to the composition of its battle-hymn), the unreflecting Becker—whom Engels later described as 'the perfect type of a man of action'—was merely overjoyed at the prospect of a new upsurge of German radicalism, and in this exalted mood promised to serve Lassalle 'with all my strength and the whole fire of my heart'.[1]

In August 1863 he wrote a forty-four-page contribution to Lassalle's current polemic, supporting every Lassallean tenet from 'state help' to the need for a strongly centralised labour party. It is curious, in view of Becker's later disagreements with the successors of Lassalle, to find him urging the German workers 'above all to build a tightly-knit, well-organised, strongly-centralised social-democratic party', and to 'join the *Allgemeiner Deutscher Arbeiterverein* without delay and *en masse*'. Perhaps he was not, however, concerned with the details of what he was saying; his joy at finding himself once more with a German public which he could harangue in the style of 1848, whatever its basic doctrines, can be clearly read in the tone of his peroration: 'Forward then, you men of Labour! . . . Workers, the Cause depends on you!'[2]

Becker was naturally offended when Lassalle neglected to thank him for this pamphlet, but he received due acknowledgment in April 1864 when his leader, addressing one of his last mass-meetings, expressed his thanks to 'the doyen of all German

[1] *Chronik*, p. 212; Lassalle, *Nachgelassene Briefe & Schriften*, Vol. III, pp. 384–6, Vol. V, introduction, pp. 36–7, text, pp. 208–9.

[2] Johann Philipp Becker, *Offener Brief an die Arbeiter über Schulze-Delitzsch und Lassalle, die Bourgeoisie und das Proletariat, der deutschen und Schweizerischen Jugend gewidmet*, pp. 10–11, 41, 44.

democratic exiles'; and in Lassalle's fatal last days in Geneva, it was to this 'doyen' that he turned for help—to Becker's mixed gratification and embarrassment.[1] Even before the death of Lassalle, which fundamentally altered the prospects for socialism in Germany, Becker had twice demonstrated his optimistic faith that all revolutionary movements were one, however differently they labelled themselves: in July 1863 he had invited all the regional representatives of the Lassallean party in Germany (about forty in number) to an international conference in La Chaux-de-Fonds —at which none of them appeared; and five months later he had tried unsuccessfully to interest them in two meetings (held in Geneva) of a 'German Republican People's League' presided over by himself, whose programme included a unified German republic, independence for Poland and Hungary, a people's militia, and other unseasonable and impracticable echoes of 1848.[2]

The not unnatural failure of the German Lassalleans to respond to these overtures forced Becker for a time to aim more carefully, and reminded him that not all revolutionary movements would automatically share each others' aspirations— though in 1869 the same assumption was to take hold of him again, leading him to attempt whole-hearted co-operation with both Marx and Bakunin.

For the moment, once the international labour movement had begun to recover from the shock of Lassalle's duel and death, Becker was more careful to adjust his propaganda to his audience. The 'German Republican People's League' of Geneva was by October 1864 thrust into the background by the

---

[1] Lassalle, *Nachgelassene Briefe . . .*, Vol. V, pp. 35, 265, 294; *Gesammelte Reden und Schriften*, IV, pp. 224–5. For Becker's mixed reactions to Lassalle's duel (which he regarded as a frivolous enterprise unworthy of a revolutionary leader) cf. his anonymous pamphlet *Die Letzten Tagen von Ferdinand Lassalle: Ein Wahrheitsgetreuer Bericht von Einem Augenzeugen*, proof-sheets in IISG, Amsterdam); Lassalle's *Nachgelassene Briefe . . .*, Vol. V, p. 356 fn. 4; *Neue Zeit* 1888, pp. 518, 558; and David Footman, *The Primrose Path*, p. 282.

[2] Max Nettlau, *Der Anarchismus von Proudhon zu Kropotkin*, p. 75 fn.; Lassalle, *Nachgelassene Briefe. . .*, Vol. V, pp. 210–13; pamphlet containing resolutions of December meetings, bound with Lessner's copy of *Der Vorbote*, IISG, Amsterdam.

newly-founded International Working Men's Association, so that the League's affiliation to the Lassallean party, which Becker had reported to Lassalle on 2 August 1864 (a few days before his dramatic arrival in Geneva), passed unnoticed; and for a time Becker resisted the temptation to reattempt any such fusion of incompatible organisations. He threw himself into recruiting members for the new International, but in Switzerland only, among his fellow-émigrés and the workmen of Geneva; in his public appeals to Germany he scarcely ever referred to the International, and virtually confined himself to supporting one of the rival factions in the complicated and at times multilateral strife which Lassalle's removal let loose in the *Allgemeiner Deutscher Arbeiterverein.*

This reticence is all the more striking as it was Bruhn's weekly paper *Nordstern* in Hamburg which gave Becker the opportunity for publicly testifying both (explicitly) to his energy on behalf of the International in Switzerland and (implicitly) to his relative reluctance to do anything for it in Germany. This was the paper of the opposition in the Lassallean party, which attacked Lassalle's presidential successor Bernhard Becker as dictatorial, incompetent, and a 'lackey of Bismarck'; the official organ of the party, which took a different line, was the new *Social-Demokrat* edited by J. B. von Schweitzer. Johann Philipp Becker, whose connection with the *Nordstern* dated back to Lassalle's lifetime, at first agreed to Schweitzer's request that he should contribute to the *Social-Demokrat* as well (being reluctant, as usual, to admit that any discord could divide the camp of progress); in a letter of November 1864 to the Countess Hatzfeldt he expressed a hope that the *Social-Demokrat* would not become the official organ of the party 'without an amicable agreement with the *Nordstern*'.[1] This hope, however, could not be realised; after attempting for a few weeks to bridge the gap of mistrust and rivalry between Schweitzer and the *Nordstern*, Becker saw that the task was im-

[1] Unpublished letter of 25 November 1864, copied by Gustav Mayer into his own copy of *J. B. von Schweitzer*, which was kindly made available by Mr C. Abramsky of London.

possible, and chose in March 1865 to come down on the side of the *Nordstern*. It seems likely that the *Social-Demokrat*'s relative indifference to the International was one reason for this decision, but the main reason was the paper's obvious sympathy with Bismarck, and indeed Becker himself had no serious hopes at this stage of raising support for the International in Germany.[1]

Becker realised, in fact, that his common interest with Bruhn and the other dissident Lassalleans lay in the party's internal struggle inside Germany, and that any attempt to recruit support for the new and unknown International would inevitably be unsuccessful—at least for a time. This conclusion must have been confirmed by the letters he got from Bruhn: in twenty letters written between Lassalle's death (August 1864) and the final disappearance of the *Nordstern* (announced by Bruhn to Becker, 10 May 1866), the International is mentioned only twice.[2]

Virtually every number of the *Nordstern* during 1865 contained an article by Becker (the paper appeared almost every week until September, when it lapsed before producing a few more issues early in 1866); but he made no direct attempt to arouse support for the International among his readers in Germany. On the one hand he made regular contributions to

[1] Dr Rolf Dlubek of Berlin has kindly drawn the writer's attention to a letter written to Becker by one of the editors of the *Social-Demokrat*, Hofstetten (13 March 1865, original in IISG) which suggests that Becker had unsuccessfully asked the paper to publish an 'Aufforderung zum Eintritt in die internationale Arbeiter-Association'—probably Becker's *Aufruf an alle Arbeiter, Arbeitervereine, und Arbeiterassociationen in der Schweiz* dated 5 February 1865, which was published in the *Nordstern* of 11 March. This certainly seems to be a case when Becker positively intended to enrol German workers in the International, but if so, it represents an exception to his normal practice during most of the year 1865; his failure to add to this Swiss proclamation any appeal to the Germans to join the International, even when it appeared in the *Nordstern*, surely suggests that he did not expect any practical results from its publication in Germany. The recent work by H. Hümmler, *Opposition gegen Lassalle* (Berlin, 1963), although it gives a detailed and extremely well-documented account of Becker's activities in 1865-6, provides no reason to modify the general conclusions set out here.

[2] These letters (IISG) deal mainly with Bruhn's attempts to keep alive the *Nordstern*; the only concrete reference to the International occurs in the letter of 12 January 1866, in which Bruhn promises to act on Becker's circular of November 1865.

Bruhn's struggle against Bernhard Becker and Schweitzer (a struggle supported by the Countess Hatzfeldt), denouncing them as traitors, government agents, and unworthy successors of the man whom he called 'our unforgettable pioneer Ferdinand Lassalle'; on the other hand he sent long reports of labour conditions and political demonstrations in Geneva, often including accounts of the International's progress, which was now clearly his main interest.

Becker's unwillingness to combine his two roles, and to try to enlist his German public in the International, was most strikingly shown in the occasional articles—for instance on 22 April 1865—in which he attacked the 'perfidious' attitude towards it of Schweitzer and his consorts. While hotly defending the International against Schweitzer's implied criticism (or, on 23 September, the scepticism of Moses Hess), Becker never suggested to German workers that they should actually join it; not even on 15 April 1865, when he announced the forthcoming publication of the International's statutes in the *Nordstern*, did he recommend the Germans to join it, and in fact the promised publication did not take place.

It was only at the end of 1865 that Becker stopped trying to keep the International and the Lassallean party in separate compartments of his mind, and began at last a campaign—determined, prolonged, and increasingly successful—to enrol members for the International in Germany.

There seem to have been four reasons why he had delayed this step for over a year since the International's foundation: first, although he was clearly not the man to regard the apparent doctrinal gap between Marx's *Inaugural Address* and German Lassalleanism as insuperable, it had seemed better during 1865 to fight simply for decentralisation in the Lassallean party, rather than to introduce the International as an additional complicating factor; secondly, Bruhn's evident lack of interest in the International was a clear warning that any attempt to link it with the fight inside Germany might lead to a new fiasco like the unanswered invitations to La Chaux-de-

Fonds in 1863; thirdly, the expanding International in Switzerland was keeping Becker too busy to think at present of pioneering new territory for it in Germany; and finally, he had not been authorised to take such a step by the International's authorities in London.

1865-6: THE GROUP OF GERMAN-SPEAKING SECTIONS

When the International's first anniversary arrived in September 1865, none of these four considerations seemed so potent: Bruhn's *Nordstern* was doomed to disappearance, and despite the embarrassment caused to the Lassallean leadership by Bernhard Becker's expulsion from Berlin, the party looked so strong that its dissenters had a case for using against it the authority of a distinctive new creed, for instance that of the International; the organisation in Switzerland was now vigorous enough for Becker to leave part of its administration to others, and turn unencumbered to Germany; and finally he was officially entrusted by the International's London leaders, including Marx, with responsibility for its affairs in Germany.

The Geneva Section of the International, started by Becker in October 1864, had, like many in Switzerland, a membership including several nationalities; in February 1865 it had grown large enough to be divided into two, one each for French and Germans, and Becker was able to use the separate German Section as a nucleus for spreading the International's message in Germany when he was asked—at its London Conference of September 1865—to do so. While he was in London for this conference Becker saw Marx at least twice, and was apparently asked either by him or by Jung (the Secretary for Switzerland), to extend his attention to Germany.[1]

Becker was preparing to publish the first number of his monthly review *Der Vorbote* in January 1866, and although in a

[1] *Nordstern*, 31 December 1864, *Vorbote*, August 1866; two separate meetings between Marx and Becker are mentioned in *Chronik*, p. 246, and in Borkheim's letter to Marx of 29 September 1865 (IISG). Becker, incidentally, had not been present (as stated by some authorities) at the St Martin's Hall meeting of September 1864.

preliminary notice sent out in November he still seemed uncertain of reaching a public outside Switzerland (the notice did not actually mention Germany, though it was widely publicised there), by January he was certainly prepared to regard himself as the International's agent for Germany as well. In this he was encouraged both by the number of replies from Germany to his circular of November, and by further explicit support from Marx. Although, as we have seen, Marx and his supporters later disputed Becker's claim to speak for the International in Germany (for instance Engels told Liebknecht in July 1872 that Becker's claims rested only on his own 'desire to grant himself Germany'),[1] their attitude in 1865–6 was quite different; Marx observed to Engels on 26 December that the labour movement in Germany was reduced to a 'fiasco' and that Becker's *Vorbote* 'has some prospects because of the death of the *Nordstern* and the discrediting of the *Social-Demokrat*', and continued: 'old Becker is begging for articles, and has asked me to write to you about this, as so far he has no contributors'. As neither the *Nordstern* nor the *Social-Demokrat* had ever pretended to any influence in Switzerland, Marx clearly wanted to improve the 'prospects' of Becker's paper inside Germany; this is confirmed by his (unsuccessful) hint that Kugelmann, who lived in Hanover, might also write for the *Vorbote*.[2] To Becker himself Marx wrote in January 1866: 'the best thing the German Sections can do is to get themselves enrolled in Geneva for the moment, and to remain in contact with you in future. As soon as anything like this happens, let me know, so that I can at last announce here some progress in Germany.'[3]

[1] Marx & Engels, *Briefe an A. Bebel, W. Liebknecht, K. Kautsky und Andere*, Vol. I, ed. W. Adoratski, p. 64.

[2] Marx, *Briefe an Kugelmann*, pp. 26–7. Marx was optimistic in thinking the *Social-Demokrat* discredited, and wrong in thinking the *Nordstern* dead.

[3] Marx to Becker *c.* 15 January 1866 (original in IISG, published only in Russian translation in *Sochineniya*, Vol. XXV, pp. 460–2). The sense of this passage of Marx's letter is inexcusably distorted by the compilers of the *Chronik* (p. 447) to make it seem that he was referring only to Sections of the International in Switzerland. An extract from Becker's enquiry, to which Marx was replying, is printed in *Wilhelm Liebknecht: Briefwechsel mit Karl Marx und Friedrich Engels*, p. 71.

As for the response from Germany itself, Becker's circular of November 1865 brought an immediate increase in his correspondence, which was very large from this time until the International's end in 1872, reaching its greatest extent in 1868–9.[1] In 1864 and 1865 his only correspondents in Germany had been Bruhn and a few others involved in the internal struggles of the Lassallean party; henceforth he ignored the party as such, and corresponded with men occupied in founding and leading local Sections of the International.

The circular of November 1865, as Becker proudly pointed out in the *Vorbote*, was reprinted in several workers' newspapers in Germany and Switzerland (it appeared, for instance, in the *Nordstern* of 13 January); late in January the first number of the *Vorbote* called for the foundation of local Sections wherever three new members were willing to join; and by April enquiries or declarations of adhesion had reached Geneva from Leipzig, Stuttgart, Solingen, Cologne, Berlin, Peterswaldau (Silesia), Magdeburg, Coburg, Hamburg, and Pinneberg, as well as various parts of Switzerland.[2]

In many of these towns Sections were quickly founded, and although their composition and activities varied from place to place, their reports to Becker show that at this stage they all had the common feature of providing centres for the German workers who were attracted to socialism but not to the Lassallean *Allgemeiner Deutscher Arbeiterverein*. Marx's attempts in 1865 to eradicate Lassalleanism 'from above', by writing in the *Social-Demokrat*, had failed; but the International's network of local Sections established by Becker seemed to be the answer to this problem. In 1865 the Lassallean party was the only socialist force in Germany, and socialism was excluded from the league of Workers' Clubs (*Verband Deutscher Arbeitervereine*) set up by the

[1] Between November 1865 and February 1866, Becker received 103 letters (*Vorbote* 1866, p. 25); the surviving letters from Germany alone (IISG) number 29 from 1865, 60 from 1866, 73 from 1867, 100 each from 1868 and 1869, 60 from 1870, and 41 from 1871.

[2] *Vorbote* 1866, pp. 25, 41, 74; letters to Becker from Lange (Leipzig) 26 November 1865, Heyn (Coburg) 5 March 1866, Meincke (Hamburg) 1 January, 20 February 1866, Vogt (Berlin) 29 January 1866; etc.

Liberals; by 1868, partly thanks to Becker's campaign, the prestige of the International was strong enough to induce this same *Verband* (pressed by Bebel and Liebknecht) to adopt its programme at the Nürnberg Congress, and for the Lassallean party also to pass resolutions of sympathy for it at a Congress in Hamburg.

Few of Becker's early agents had the perspicacity of Florian Paul, formerly a prominent Lassallean, who organised eleven small Sections in the Silesian weaving villages around Peterswaldau, and who saw that the International's principles might theoretically be in 'contradiction to the national aims of our *Allgemeiner Deutscher Arbeiterverein*', or of Urbach in Cologne, who came to see that Lassalle was after all no more than 'a pupil of Karl Marx';[1] they founded Sections without considering such doctrinal issues, being attracted by the new workers' organisation mainly because it would be free from the personally-disliked and politically-distrusted leaders of the ADAV. In Cologne, for instance, the founding of a Section was first discussed in the local branch of the ADAV, and police suspicions were deflected by the Section's organisation being camouflaged under that of the officially-tolerated Lassallean party, but all its members (seventeen in March 1866) were opponents of the ADAV leadership, deploring in common the sight of 'the party, misled by Bernhard Becker, letting that accursed Schweitzer lead it round by the nose'.[2] In Solingen, too, the representatives of the International, Karl Klein and Fritz Moll, were experienced but partially disillusioned members of the ADAV.[3]

In Berlin, a Section was formed by the dissident Lassalleans Meyer, Metzner and Vogt, who in November 1865 had urged

[1] Urbach to Becker 10 March 1866; F. Paul to Becker 20 January 1866 (on Paul see further E. Eyck, *Bismarck*, Vol. II, p. 35).

[2] Heinrichs to Becker 26 July 1866, and other letters from Cologne and Bayenthal.

[3] Extensive correspondence from Klein & Moll, IISG; Klein, despite his interest in the International, remained loyal enough to Schweitzer to defend him against Liebknecht at the Lassalleans' Elberfeld Congress of 1869.

Marx to return to Germany and had been advised in reply to join the International.[1] The report sent by Becker's Berlin correspondent on 29 January 1866 was typical (except for its mention of Marx and its optimistic hope of making the whole ADAV 'international') of many others:

A Section of the International Association, with six members at the moment, has been formed here from L. by M. (wrote the shoemaker August Vogt, using only the initial letters of 'London' and 'Marx' because of the police censorship) . . . we have already received several copies of your *Vorbote*, and look forward to great results here from the whole thing, as we have already pushed the whole Berlin A.D.A.V. in this direction. . . . The difficulty will of course be that we shall be unable to agitate publicly for the Association in Prussia because the Combination Acts make centralisation [i.e. joining with other organisations] illegal. . . . It would therefore be desirable for us to consult as to a common propaganda method in Prussia, as the A.D.A.V. is indeed becoming gradually international'. By April 8, Vogt felt able to report to Becker that 'our cause is making progress here, particularly in educated circles; only people are too feeble to come out into the open.[2]

Throughout Germany the workers who now joined the International often visualised it in mainly negative terms, as a working-class organisation which was not Lassallean; for instance, Becker's correspondent in Stuttgart, Kochendörfer, told him on 12 February 1866, that two potential members were less interested in the programme of the International than in being reassured that he was not his namesake Bernhard Becker!

Early in 1866 the Sections in Stuttgart and Magdeburg were already beginning the campaign of propaganda inside the local Workers' Educational Clubs which was to enable Bebel and Liebknecht, in 1868, to get the International's programme adopted by the *Verband Deutscher Arbeitervereine*. The Stuttgart

---

[1] The Berliners' letter of 13 November 1865 (original in IISG) is printed in *Beiträge zur Geschichte der deutschen Arbeiterbewegung*, Vol. I (1959), pp. 530–1; cf. Marx's report to the General Council, in its *Minutes* (IISG), Vol. I, pp. 83–4, and Appendix IV below.

[2] Unpublished originals, IISG.

JOHANN PHILIPP BECKER

Section, consisting of nine members in February 1866, was distributing eighty copies of Becker's *Vorbote* in the local *Bildungsverein* within a month,[1] and in the Magdeburg *Verein* the members of the International fought a long campaign of meetings and debates against an anti-socialist majority led by the Liberal politician David Hirsch and the local pastor Uhlich. Hirsch's influence (so Becker was informed on 27 April 1866 by the Magdeburg socialist Münze, a former Lassallean) long prevented any discussion in the club of 'either the political or the social question', but by 30 August Münze and his colleagues were insisting in the club's meetings, as he told Becker, that it should 'make up its mind about the principles of the International'—whose publications were henceforth spread among the club's members.[2]

The Austro-Prussian War of 1866 placed serious obstacles in Becker's way, as far as the development of his organisation was concerned.[3] In Prussia the state of war brought active persecution by the police authorities, as well as other difficulties, including conscription of the International's members. 'It is lamentable,' wrote Becker's correspondent Heinrichs from Cologne on 26 July 1866 'that in a town as big as Cologne there is so little interest in such a great cause, yet everything has its reasons: on the one hand we cannot discuss international affairs here without being set upon by the police, and on the other hand the present state of war has destroyed family life altogether. Thousands of married men have been killed...and all

[1] Four letters to Becker from Kochendörfer (Stuttgart), Jan.–March 1866, IISG.

[2] Julius Bremer, later described as 'the father of Magdeburg Social Democracy', seems to have played a role subsidiary to that of Münze, who only converted Bremer to socialism during 1866; although he was by then helping Münze to enrol members for the International (Jung's papers, IISG, include an *Aufnahmesgesuch* signed by both of them), a fellow-member described him as 'very passive' about the cause in May 1868, when Münze was dying (Wellner to Becker 19 May 1868). His great activity from 1868 onwards, however, is documented by a mass of letters to Becker, and has recently been studied by R. Dlubek and U. Herrmann: 'Die Magdeburger Sektion der I. Internationale', in *Beiträge*, 4. Jrg. 1962. Sonderheft, esp. pp. 202–4.

[3] On Becker's political judgments on the crisis of 1866, cf. Gustav Mayer, 'Die Lösung der deutschen Frage im Jahre 1866 und die Arbeiterbewegung,' in *Festgabe für Wilhelm Lexis*, pp. 262–7, and Karl Kautsky, *Sozialisten und Krieg*, pp. 172–8.

that is precious in life is near to collapsing.' Heinrichs concluded sarcastically that those who remained went not to political meetings but to church, to 'console themselves with the dead idols'. Elsewhere, difficulties were caused by poverty due to the economic dislocation of war,[1] or by the interruption of postal communication with Geneva: this meant, for instance, that Karl Klein, Becker's correspondent in Solingen, wrote instead to Marx with various enquiries about the International, 'because postal communications with the south are broken off by the present state of war'. (Marx, incidentally, at once confirmed Becker's authority to act as the International's agent in Germany by having the letter forwarded to Geneva by Hermann Jung, who added a note: 'Cher ami Becker, voici ce que Marx vient de me transmettre.... Marx m'a dit de vous dire de lui répondre sur tous les points, tant à lui [i.e. Klein] qu'à Marx.')[2]

Despite these difficulties, Becker's organisation held together: he continued to receive letters and even money from several of the International's Sections and individual members in Germany, as well as letters from new correspondents in parts of South Germany unaffected by the war;[3] and the International's first Congress, held at Geneva in September, made it clear that although Marx was slowly becoming better known in Germany,

[1] Kallen (Bayenthal) to Becker 14 July 1866 reports that all local factories are closed by the war. Münze (Magdeburg) to Becker 30 August 1866 complains of poverty caused by the war—'a crusade against democracy'. Moll (Solingen) to Becker 6 November 1866 laments that the war has sunk the working class—except the Lassalleans—into indifference.

[2] Klein to Marx 27 July 1866 (Marx-*Nachlass*, IISG). Marx's friend Kugelmann further confirmed that Geneva was, as he put it, 'the German headquarters', in a letter of 27 November 1866, in which he explained his preference for paying his subscription to Geneva rather than to London (Becker-*Nachlass*, IISG).

[3] As well as the letters from Cologne and Bayenthal, cited above, cf. Vogt (Berlin) to Becker, August 1866. *Vorbote*, August 1866 also acknowledges an anonymous gift of 100 Francs 'from the German Rhine' towards the Congress expenses. Becker's new correspondents, who enquired about the International, included Heyringer (München) and Schmiedrich (Augsburg)—both letters of August 1866, latter printed in *Vorbote*, August 1867. From Göppingen (Württemberg) the Secretary of the *Bildungsverein*, Bronnenmayer, wrote to Becker on 14 October 1866, welcoming the International as a force which would help the world's workers 'to count for more and to achieve a better position in human society', and announcing the affiliation of the local weavers' co-operative.

and although Liebknecht was known as a radical propagandist, neither of them possessed anything like Becker's authority as a leader of the International.

The Geneva Congress enabled the International to clarify its policy and strengthen its organisation;[1] and Becker's Group of German-speaking Sections, which by now formed a coherent and vigorous entity within the International, carried out both these processes on its own account as well. As far as policy was concerned, the German-speaking Sections aligned themselves with the majority decisions of the Congress as a whole—in favour of Trade Unions and Producers' Co-operatives, legislation for the eight-hour day, and public education—but their concern with the political future of Germany forced them in addition to declare their specific wish for the democratic unification of the *Reich*. (This special problem of the International's German members, confronted simultaneously with patriotic and socialistic tasks, had already been mentioned in Becker's articles in the *Vorbote*; in April 1866, for instance, he summarised the problem thus: 'Shaking off the political yoke, fulfilling the national task, means establishing the unity of the German *Reich* in freedom. Shaking off the social yoke, fulfilling the international task, means setting up socialist states, founded on labour, and a confederation of free Europe.' As usual Becker was unable to envisage a conflict between the different aims—national and social—of progressive thought, and despite his contact with Lassalle he failed to sense that the 'national task' might be accomplished in such a way as to make efforts to deal with the 'social task' the responsibility of nationally-organised parties.)

As for organisation, the Geneva Congress gave Becker the chance to hold a series of meetings of the German and German-Swiss delegates (the latter being naturally the overwhelming majority), at which 'rules for the Group of German-speaking

---

[1] On the Geneva Congress, see the official report, the accounts by Guillaume, Cole, Babel, etc., and Becker's full reports serialised in *Vorbote*, October 1866 to February 1867.

Sections' were discussed.[1] The Geneva Section's committee was unanimously invited to act as the Group's Central Committee, and to draft 'Central Rules defining the relations to the Sections on one hand and to the General Council on the other', which were to be 'circulated to the Sections for confirmation'.

In May 1867 the Geneva committee accordingly published the 'Rules and Central Statute of the Group of German-speaking Sections', together with the International's General Statutes, drawn up after the St Martin's Hall meeting of September 1864 and revised by the Geneva Congress.[2] Possibly foreseeing a future challenge to his authority in Germany, Becker took care to insist that the formation of the Group of German-speaking Sections was authorised by No. 6 of the International's General Statutes, before going on to describe the composition and functions of the Group's Central Committee and slipping in a claim that it should 'conduct all communication between the Sections and the General Council'. (This, more than anything else in Becker's Statutes, was a potential source of conflict with London, since Article 6 of the General Statutes referred explicitly to 'national' workers' societies, not to those based, like Becker's group, on community of language, and it explicitly confirmed the right of all local societies 'to correspond directly with the General Council'.) Finally, the Statutes prescribed a monthly subscription per member for each Section of 15 centimes in Switzerland, 1.5 silver Groschen

[1] On these meetings cf. *Vorbote* 1866, summarised by Jaeckh, *Die Internationale*, pp. 41–2. The German Sections officially represented at Geneva were those of Magdeburg, Stuttgart, Cologne and Solingen, but the delegate mandated by Magdeburg was a teacher, Bütter, who already lived in Switzerland (at Brussels in 1868 he represented Nürnberg: Guillaume, Vol. I, p. 109), and Cologne and Solingen were both represented by Moll, whose main reason for coming to Geneva was to look for work (Klein to Becker 2 August 1866). The presence of only one 'authentic' delegate from Germany (the shoemaker Müller of Stuttgart) did not, however, reflect apathy, but merely the state of war which made the journey to Geneva impossible (cf. Vogt, Berlin, to Becker 18 August 1866); at subsequent congresses Germany was better represented.

[2] *Generalstatuten, zugefugte Reglemente und Zentral-Statuten der Sectionsgruppe deutscher Sprache der Internationalen Arbeiter-Genossenschaft*, 12 pp.; *Vorbote* 1867, pp. 73–7.

in Prussia, or 4.5 Kreuzer elsewhere in Germany; or alternatively, for individual members isolated from local Sections, 3 fr. 75 ct., 1 Thaler, or 1.75 guilders, including a subscription to the *Vorbote*. There was nothing wrong in theory in Becker's laying down such detailed rules, or in stipulating (as did another Article) that workers' clubs in sympathy with the International might adhere only on condition that they took two copies of the *Vorbote*; in practice it was impossible to enforce regulations of this kind, and local Sections of the International in Germany had such difficulty in paying their contributions that Becker had to be grateful for whatever money he received.[1]

In the months following the Geneva Congress, in fact, the *Vorbote* had much to say about donations from Germany, and also announced the founding of new Sections in Barmen, Duisburg, Mainz, Frankfurt, and Darmstadt—a testimony to the success of Becker's propaganda.[2] The Göppingen Section, in Württemberg, was connected with a Co-operative Society producing various woven goods, and as the development of co-operative production was among the main aims of the International, Becker made great efforts to find customers for these products, as well as for those of a steel-workers' co-operative organised by the Section in Solingen.[3]

1867–8: GROWTH AND PROBLEMS OF BECKER'S ORGANISATION

The year 1867 was less dramatic than 1866, which had seen

---

[1] The evidence of Becker's financial receipts from Germany, as recorded monthly in *Vorbote*, suggests that his influence there rose to a maximum in 1868–9, then fairly sharply declined—which confirms the conclusion suggested by his correspondence. Cf. Appendix II, pp. 245-7.

[2] *Vorbote*, November, December 1866; letters to Becker from Krötter (Barmen), Bronnenmayer (Göppingen), Kotter (Duisburg), Stumpf (Mainz), Bonhorst (Wiesbaden: letter of 6 September 1866 on internationalist propaganda in *Bildungsvereine* of Mainz, Offenbach, etc.). There is apparently no evidence that the Frankfurt and Darmstadt Sections lasted for long; although Ludwig Büchner, present at the Lausanne Congress of 1867, lived in Darmstadt, he was not a delegate of the local Section (*pace* Fribourg, *l'Internationale*, p. 205).

[3] *Vorbote*, and copious correspondence from Göppingen & Solingen, IISG. Cf. Becker's report to the Lausanne Congress of 1867 in *La Première Internationale. Receuil de Documents*, Vol. I, p. 185.

Becker's struggle for a foothold in Germany, as well as the Austro-Prussian war and the consequent political upheavals. Becker's correspondence with Germany continued to increase during 1867; so also did contributions to the Geneva Committee's funds, and these came not only from Sections already established, but also from new correspondents, notably in Braunschweig, Dresden, and Leipzig.[1]

In spite of these outward signs of well-being, however, there were hints in 1867 that Becker's Group of German-speaking Sections might not be the best form of organisation for the International in Germany, and that his position might be more fragile than it looked. In the first place, his attempts to provide propaganda, information, and forms of organisation which would interest and satisfy socialists both in Germany and in Switzerland automatically made him concentrate on the common features of the two countries, ignoring their growing differences and particularly the special needs of the movement in Germany. Secondly, he suffered in 1867 a relapse into his habit of trying to co-ordinate the activities and ideologies of basically incompatible movements: he entered into close contact with the League of Peace and Freedom, and although his dealings with this international society of eminent Liberals at first seemed to enhance his general influence, it ultimately weakened his claim to lead the German branch of the International.

Becker's handicap in not being able to concentrate entirely on Germany was reflected in the pages of the *Vorbote*; he had either to give considerable space to news of the International's activities in Switzerland, or to publish theoretical articles which, although they often reached a high level of polemic or even analysis, were inevitably remote from the practical prob-

[1] Details of the Dresden section in *Vorbote*, 1867, p. 143, and in Vahlteich to Metzner 6 September 1866 (IISG); of Leipzig, in Bebel's letters to Becker, published in *Vorwärts*, 1 January 1927; of Braunschweig, in *Vorbote*, May 1867, p. 80. A detailed account of the Braunschweig section, describing its leaders' influence throughout the German labour movement, has been published by Professor Eckert: 'Zur Geschichte der Braunschweiger Sektion der I. Internationale', in *Braunschweigisches Jahrbuch*, 1962, pp. 131–72.

lems of active socialists in Germany.[1] Such people still had no other organisation, apart from the Lassallean ADAV, to which they could turn for leadership—socialist ideas were practically excluded both from the Saxon People's Party which Liebknecht had helped to found at Chemnitz in 1866, and from the *Verband Deutscher Arbeitervereine*, even though its president was now Bebel—but many of them began to ask themselves whether Becker's organisation was after all adequate: indeed, Karl Klein had already suggested to Marx in his letter of July 1866 that it would be 'more efficient' for the International's propaganda in Germany to be carried out from a national centre, and even in March of the same year Becker had been asked by Florian Paul, a correspondent in the Silesian textile area, whether a 'local liaison-committee' should not be set up in Wuste-Giersdorff, since 'from here the ADAV also spread throughout Silesia'.[2]

Becker was the victim of a vicious circle: the *Vorbote* failed to attract a wide German public because its articles often betrayed their authors' ignorance of the situation in Germany;[3] and better-informed writers inside Germany were not to be had because they usually preferred to address themselves to their compatriots directly, not through the *Vorbote*.

Liebknecht, for instance, although he promised Becker at the end of 1867 that he would send articles 'regularly from now on', let it be seen that he was much more enthusiastic about the paper he was himself founding in Leipzig, and in the end wrote nothing for the *Vorbote* at all. Bebel, as usual, was too cautious to make the sweeping promises characteristic of Liebknecht, and simply warned Becker: 'the truth is that the shoulders of those

---

[1] The articles published in 1867 varied from Becker's lively but diffuse series *Zur Weltlage* to extracts from the preface to Marx's *Das Kapital*.

[2] Unpublished originals, IISG.

[3] E.g. Becker's description of the *Verband Deutscher Arbeitervereine* as the 'German workers' Educational Club' (*Vorbote*, January 1866), probably due to an assumption that the *Verband*'s title was similar to that of its Swiss counterpart; also his strange treatment of the Saxon People's Party in *Vorbote* 1867, pp. 47–8, 124, and his attribution of the name *Allgemeiner Deutscher Arbeiterverein* to the dissident sect run by the Countess Hatzfeldt, *ibid.* p. 191.

seriously concerned with the social-democratic movement are already so overburdened that it would hardly be reasonable to take on anything else'.[1]

Marx himself, though he had encouraged Becker to work for the International in Germany, and urged Engels and Kugelmann to send him articles for the *Vorbote*, did nothing to help him, and there were times when the determined but isolated figure in Geneva almost despaired. He wrote in dramatic terms, for instance, to his friend Sorge in America: 'If I withdraw, the whole organisation will fall to pieces, particularly in Germany, so I must keep hauling at the waggon until I collapse under it (*bis ich darunter liegen bleibe*)'[2]. The time had not yet come for Bebel and Liebknecht, acting in the name of a new nationally-organised German movement, to undermine and destroy Becker's authority; but the situation in which this would be possible was coming into being.

Becker's disappointment at the relative lack of response aroused by his efforts in Germany, and by their complete lack of support from London, made him an easy prey to his old temptation to serve more than one revolutionary master at the same time, and he threw himself with great enthusiasm into preparatory work for the Peace Congress held in Geneva in September 1867 by the newly-founded League of Peace and Freedom.[3] At the Lausanne Congress of the International, held immediately before the Peace Congress, Germany had been represented by six delegates as against three the previous year, but Becker's success in Germany, however considerable when measured against his difficulties, still failed to satisfy his impatient spirit, and he forgot his disappointment in working

[1] Liebknecht to Becker, November or December 1867 (undated), in Berlin *Vorwärts*, 27 July 1914; Bebel to Becker 9 October 1867, *AML*, I, p. 169.

[2] Becker to Sorge 26 September 1867, unpublished original in Schweizerisches Sozialarchiv, Zürich. Cf. Marx: *Briefe an Kugelmann* (1952 ed.), pp. 26–7, 45, and Borkheim to Becker 22 June 1867, 16 January, 3 March 1868 (IISG).

[3] *Vorbote*, and Becker to Sorge 26 September 1867. On the Geneva Congress and its background, cf. E. H. Carr: 'The League of Peace and Freedom', in *International Affairs*, Vol. XIV (1935), pp. 837–44, and (on the relations between this Congress and the Lausanne Congress of the International) the accounts by Cole, Guillaume, and Bebel.

to organise the Peace Congress. Its chief promoters, however, were Liberals or at most democrats, whose aims were far removed from those of the International; and even though the process described by Gustav Mayer as 'the separation of proletarian from bourgeois democracy' was not yet completed, it had gone far enough to render illusory Becker's assurances to his socialist friends that he was aiming only to 'use the bourgeois *dilettanti* ('*Schwätzer*')' to stir up the working-class movement.[1]

This pretext was unusually perceptive for Becker, but it played only a small part in his thoughts, since the real width of the gap separating his new associates from the International scarcely struck him. He had some excuse for this: the International was itself represented at the Geneva Peace Congress; Ladendorf and Goegg, two leaders of the League in Switzerland, were connected also with the International; and even in Germany the men who asked Becker for details of the Peace Congress—for instance the democratic lawyer and politician Titus in Bamberg—were interested in the International as well.[2]

Although these factors prevented Becker from realising it, his preoccupation with the Peace Congress removed him even further from the trend of political affairs in Germany (where the Congress was little noticed, particularly among the workers: none of Becker's working-class correspondents referred to it in their letters), and it helped to disqualify him for the leadership of the International's German branch when his authority was

[1] Kugelmann to Becker 8 August 1867 (replying to Becker's invitation to attend both the Lausanne and the Geneva Congresses) used this phrase to express his agreement with Becker; cf. Borkheim's letters both to Marx and to Becker (IISG).

[2] Letters from Ladendorf and Goegg in Becker's *Nachlass*. Also four letters from Titus, July-August 1867, on Lausanne; one of September 1867, observing with pleasure that the League seems inclined to 'social and purely political-democratic' demands; one of January 1868, welcoming the International's preoccupation with 'the social question', and describing the democratic congress at Bamberg; and one of August 1868, regretting inability to attend the Brussels Congress as invited. These letters from Titus (on whom see further Mayer, 'Die Trennung', *loc. cit.* pp. 24–32) show that while Becker's work for the Peace Congress seemed outwardly to be winning new support for the International in Germany, it was in fact distracting him into correspondence with individuals who would be bound to fall away when the collectivist aims of the International became more apparent.

challenged. Probably it was at the Peace Congress that he first met Michael Bakunin, whose spectacular irruption into Swiss radical politics, as will be seen, was to distract him from the German scene even more disastrously a year later; but even without this, his position in Germany suffered. Marx, writing to Engels on 4 September 1867, contemptuously dismissed the League and all its works as 'the peace windbag'; and socialistic German workers, although they would not have produced so many theoretical arguments against the League as Marx, still refused to respond to Becker's enthusiasm on its behalf.

Becker's position, then, was insecure; but the alternative forms of organisation with which Bebel and Liebknecht were to supplant him were not yet in existence, and for the moment his power continued to grow. He could still count on receiving subscriptions from Sections both old and new, and on 26 September 1867, he optimistically wrote to Sorge in America: 'the Cause is making progress, of that there is no doubt'.[1] He had no reason to doubt that the leaders of the non-Lassallean labour movement in Germany were his allies, even though their positive contribution towards his work might be small; after all, as Bebel had said, their shoulders were 'already so overburdened'. In any case, there had been no sign that they might challenge his authority. Nor could he realise that his very success was undermining his position from below. Yet in Workers' Educational Clubs all over Germany, in Magdeburg and Mainz, Augsburg and Göppingen, Leipzig and Berlin, the discussions on the International's programme, started by Becker himself, were preparing the way for his first defeat (organisationally speaking) at the Nürnberg Congress of September 1868.

The year 1868 brought an increase in size and influence to every branch of the German labour movement; the main reasons for this were probably the economic recession, the existence of the new North German *Reichstag* which included some socialist members, fairly widespread knowledge of the International's

[1] Unpublished original, Schweizerisches Sozialarchiv, Zürich.

growth in Switzerland, England, France, and Belgium (described, for instance, in the pamphlet published by Eichhoff in August), and the publication late in 1867 of Marx's *Das Kapital*. The *Allgemeiner Deutscher Arbeiterverein* under Schweitzer doubled its membership in the first eight months of the year, and the sales of the *Social-Demokrat* increased from 1,200 to 3,400. Both Bebel as president of the *Verband Deutscher Arbeitervereine* and Liebknecht as a leader of the Saxon People's Party were also aware of increasing militancy among their followers.[1]

The International's Group of German-speaking Sections, too, seemed to be flourishing in the new atmosphere, to the creation of which it had in fact contributed; Becker's propaganda was rewarded with greater success than ever before in terms both of affiliations to his organisation and of subscriptions sent to Geneva.

In the first place he increased his correspondence with Sections already in existence. From Mainz, for instance, came the news that a Social-democratic Club was spreading the International's ideas, and that a formally-organised Section was also holding regular meetings (at one of which Becker's services were recognised by a resolution that he personally should receive any profits made by the *Vorbote*—a well-meant but entirely hypothetical proposal).[2] In Magdeburg the efforts of Münze and Bremer had won over a large part of the *Bildungsverein*, and Becker even received (in February 1868) a grudgingly laudatory letter from Pastor Uhlich, hitherto a determined critic of the International. The Berlin Section (led by Reimann since Vogt's departure for America in May 1867) was very active, the newly-enrolled members including the President of the *Arbeiterverein* Robert Krebs, the prominent Lassallean Fritzsche, and the gifted journalist Wilhelm Eichhoff, whose pamphlet on the International (written in close

---

[1] Mehring, *Geschichte*, Vol. III, pp. 314, 322; Bebel, *AML*, I, pp. 170–1.
[2] Stumpf to Becker 29 June 1868; *Antrag der Section Mainz ... Sitzung vom 11.I.1868* (Stumpf's handwriting), in Becker *Nachlass*.

consultation with Marx) was published in August.[1] The secretary of the Cologne Section sent (in June 1868) the largest subscription yet received from a German Section—thirty Thaler or six pounds fifteen shillings—and told Becker that Herr Schob, the president of the German Tailors' Association, was considering its affiliation to the International; from South Germany came news that the Göppingen Weavers' Association was continuing its operations; and finally, subscriptions continued to reach Geneva from the well-established Sections in Solingen and Braunschweig, as well as from individuals throughout Germany, so that Becker's receipts in the summer months of 1868 were higher than ever before.[2]

He also succeeded in establishing contact with groups and individuals in places hitherto not much influenced by his propaganda: in Kalk, near Cologne, a group of workers set up an 'international insurance scheme' (*Internationale Krankenkasse*) based on statutes supplied by Becker, which soon had a hundred members; contributions were received from leading members of the Workers' Educational Clubs of Dresden, Chemnitz and Leipzig; an effective Section was at last started in Barmen, in this case the result of correspondence going back to 1866; and Becker also exchanged ideas with Moritz Müller of Pforzheim, one of the pioneers of the still rudimentary German trade union movement.[3]

The stream of propaganda from Geneva had created a well-informed sympathy with the International in every part of

[1] *Vorbote* 1867, pp. 127, 143, & 1868, p. 32; Fritzsche to Becker 8 August 1868; Eichhoff to Becker 24 September 1868, and the Berlin police-dossier on Eichhoff (now *Landeshauptarchiv Brandenburg*, Potsdam, Rep. 30 C Tit. 94 Lit. E. Nr. 166), which describes him as being, by January 1869 'in Correspondenz und Verbindung' with Becker. Eichhoff's correspondence with Marx, however, was more important, as is shown by H. Gemkow, 'Zur Tätigkeit der Berliner Section der I. Internationale', in *Beiträge zur Geschichte der deutschen Arbeiterbewegung*, pp. 515–31.

[2] *Vorbote*, and letters to Becker from Heinrichs (Cologne) 27 September 1867, 4 February 1868, and from Bronnenmayer (Göppingen) 25 April 1868.

[3] Letters to Becker from Thiemann (Kalk) 25 December 1867, 18 February 1868; Karl Jacoby (Dresden) 30 May 1868; Carl Schelle (Chemnitz) 1 June 1868; H. Greifnich (Leipzig) 20 May 1868; Krötter, Hülsiep, Schmiedal (Barmen) 30 September 1866; Hülsiep (Barmen) 26 January 1868; H. Werth (Barmen) 22 September 1868; Müller (Pforzheim) 5 August 1868.

Germany, and in many places groups of workers had gone so far as to call themselves 'Sections' of it, despite the police surveillance which this might involve.[1] It was difficult, however, to see quite where this form of organisation could lead. Becker's authority over his flock was endangered by his inability to suggest activities which its members could collectively undertake, and which would strengthen their feeling of solidarity with the International. They could feel themselves, as Becker repeatedly said, members of an 'international revolutionary band of brothers', and they could prepare by reading and discussion for 'the coming struggle' of the revolution;[2] but in the meantime the semi-clandestine Sections could provide no focus for the day-to-day activities of militant socialists, and they inevitably tended to turn to other working-class organisations.

In most towns the centre of popular activity was the Workers' Educational Club, which served both an educational and a social purpose; many clubs remained true to the precepts of the *Verband*'s Liberal-democratic founders and avoided political discussions, but it was now more usual for the *Bildungsverein* to be a centre of socialist speculation, often inspired by members or sympathisers of the International. During 1868 trade unions were also legalised in most parts of Germany, and whether nationally or locally organised, they provided a new centre of working-class life and discussion.[3] In many parts of Germany, again, the granting of manhood suffrage and the two general elections of 1867, followed early in 1868 by the elections to the South German *Zollparlament*, led many workers to the con-

---

[1] Paragraph 8 of the Prussian *Vereinsgesetz* of 1850 (paralleled by similar laws in other states) made it illegal for any associations to be in 'organisational contact' with bodies in other countries, but its practical application varied from place to place. In Cologne, as we have seen, the Section had to be camouflaged; from Barmen, Becker's correspondent H. Werth asked (on 22 September 1868) for the *Vorbote* to be addressed to him without any mention that he was connected with the International; and in March 1869 a pamphleteer in Berlin refrained from giving detailed information on the International's German branches 'so as not to augment the material of the Berlin police' (Karl Hirsch, *Die Organisation der Deutschen Arbeiterpartei*, pp. 19, 29).

[2] *Vorbote* 1866, p. 100; Heinrichs (Cologne) to Becker 4 February 1866.

[3] H. Müller, *Geschichte der Lithographen*, Vol. I, pp. 115–31.

THE GERMAN SOCIAL DEMOCRATS

clusion that their best hope lay in electing socialists to parliament, and 'Social-democratic Election Associations' were founded with this aim.[1] Finally, of course, the majority of politically-organised workers in Germany still belonged either to Schweitzer's *Verein* or to the breakaway sect organised in opposition to him by the Countess Hatzfeldt, both of which had representatives in the *Reichstag*.

In many places, it was natural that organisations of several or all of these types should exist alongside each other: in Mainz, for instance, the members of the International's local Section had set up a 'Social-democratic Club' besides trying to win over the 'official' *Arbeiterbildungsverein*;[2] and Berlin had Sections of the International and of both Lassallean parties, a 'Social-democratic Workers' Club' started by dissident Lassalleans in 1866, and finally a large *Arbeiterverein* led by Robert Krebs, which was in close contact with Becker.[3]

Despite this competition, however, the loyalty of the International's German members to Becker was powerfully demonstrated on the occasions when he was able to give them something positive to do. For instance, it had been resolved at the International's Geneva Congress in 1866 that one of its members' tasks should be to collect statistical information about wages and the cost of living in their respective countries, and send it to the central authorities; late in 1867, when Becker reminded his German followers of this duty, he received detailed information from several parts of Germany.[4]

A more remarkable instance of his influence was the response

---

[1] Heinrichs to Becker 4 February 1868; Mayer, *Schweitzer*, pp. 211–12.
[2] Stumpf to Becker 29 June 1868.
[3] Bernstein, *Die Geschichte der Berliner Arbeiterbewegung*, Vol. I, pp. 181–3; *Landeshauptarchiv Brandenburg*, Potsdam, Rep. 30 C 95—Sect. 5 Nr. A33 contains police-reports of the social-democratic *Arbeiterverein*'s meetings; *ibid.* Nr. A37 gives details of the 'democratic *Arbeiterverein*' founded in 1868, which was connected with the International, though the police-reports wrongly confuse it with the 'social-democratic *Arbeiterverein*'. Cf. Gemkow, 'Zür Tätigkeit der Berliner Sektion der I Internationale', *loc. cit.*, p. 528.
[4] General Statutes No. 5, in *Hochverratsprozess*, p. 914. Replies to Becker from Kallen (Bayenthal) November 1867, Heinrichs (Cologne) 17 November 1867, Münze (Magdeburg) 4 February 1868.

to his appeal for help during the Geneva building strike of March and April 1868. As well as appealing in the *Vorbote*, Becker published two pamphlets explaining the situation to the workers of Germany, and although the exact total of financial help from Germany is not recorded, it exceeded anything he might have been able to expect in previous years. Sums equivalent to anything between ten shillings and six pounds arrived from groups known and unknown to Becker: the Sections in Mainz, Solingen, and Esslingen; builders' trade unions in Rostock and Schwerin; and Educational Clubs in Dresden, Leipzig, Chemnitz, München, Hanover, Hildesheim, Hamburg, and Mannheim. The Berlin Section organised a 'Grand Concert and Ball' which brought in twenty-seven pounds (122 Thaler), and the general effect of Becker's publicity was so great that workers in Germany now began to appeal to him for help when they in their turn went on strike.[1]

Reflecting on the problem of how to organise the support he had aroused, Becker concluded during 1868 (when a record number of strikes occurred in Germany, as elsewhere) that the basic organisational form of the labour movement must be the trade union—'the only way there is here', so Vogt had written to him from Berlin in April 1866, 'to get the masses moving, and remove the blinkers from their eyes'.[2] Although this view was plausible in the profoundly unsettled social and industrial climate of 1868, and was defensible in Britain or (for different reasons) in France, the priority of political problems in Germany made the trade unions always dependent on the political labour movement, and this was one reason why, as will be seen, Becker's ideas were unceremoniously rejected by the Eisenach Congress of 1869. It was impossible, even in the short run, for strike-subscriptions alone to keep the Germans interested in his organ-

[1] Babel, *La Première Internationale, ses Débuts et son Activité à Genève*, pp. 311–19; *Vorbote*; Reimann (Berlin) to Becker 20 & 30 June 1868. For appeals from Germany, cf. letters to Becker from Kugelmann (Hanover) 2 August 1868 (calling for help for 100 striking weavers) and from W. König (Barmen) 17 June 1868 (on behalf of strikers in two textile-factories). Both appeals appeared in *Vorbote* (pp. 94, 127), but the response is unrecorded.
[2] Unpublished original, IISG.

isation; and his letters from Germany in 1868 show a strong tendency for his correspondents, while remaining loyal to the ideals of the International, to meditate on forms of organisation more suited to German conditions.

In 1868 developments in the German labour movement brought an exclusion of Becker's influence nearer: the two bodies which looked like possible German centres for the International were the Lassallean party under Schweitzer and the *Verband Deutscher Arbeitervereine* under Bebel and Liebknecht, and both organisations now moved closer to the International. In each case, as will be seen, the leaders had their own tactical motives for this, but the pressure for co-operation with the International which came from the members themselves was certainly due in large part to Becker's propaganda.

In the case of the Lassalleans, growing interest in the International led to resolutions from half a dozen branches demanding affiliation, to a public declaration of solidarity at the party's Hamburg congress in August 1868, and finally, when Schweitzer seemed to turn against the International in 1869, to the stormy exodus of half the membership.[1]

This interest was partly fostered by Schweitzer himself, who published extracts from *Das Kapital* early in 1868, and carefully renewed his relations with Marx, which had been broken off in 1865;[2] but the importance of Becker's part in the new trend is clearly shown by his correspondence. In 1866, when Schweitzer had moved closer to the policy of Bismarck, Becker had been receiving letters from Lassalleans so disgusted with their party that they were prepared to break with it altogether: now that Schweitzer had moved into sharp opposition to the government, however, they wrote expressing their hopes that the party as a whole might become affiliated to the International. During the summer of 1868 (particularly in August, when the question was being discussed in the *Social-Demokrat*

[1] *Social-Demokrat* 12 August 1868; *Vorbote* 1868 p. 118; the Lassalleans' history from Hamburg to Eisenach is summarised in G. Eckert, *Aus den Anfängen der Braunschweiger Arbeiterbewegung*, pp. 23–4.
[2] *Social-Demokrat*, 22 January-24 April 1868; Marx to Engels 23 March 1868.

in connection with the resolution debated at Hamburg),
Becker received letters to this effect from Lassalleans in
Wiesbaden, Hanover, Leipzig, Hamburg and Barmen;[1] and
as Schweitzer in the *Social-Demokrat* was presenting the International as an organisation led by Marx alone, without any
reference to Geneva at all, it is clear that Becker owed his
widespread new contacts with German Lassalleans mainly to
the reputation established by his own persistent propaganda.
By this time, indeed, relations with Geneva had been spontaneously taken up by such prominent Lassalleans as Fritzsche, the
party's former vice-president (and in 1865 a strong opponent
of the International); the party-treasurer Wilhelm Bracke of
Braunschweig, who introduced the debate on Marxism at the
Hamburg Congress; and Dr Kirchner of Hildesheim, one of
the few Lassalleans who still belonged to the *Verband Deutscher
Arbeitervereine* as well, and who made a powerful speech for the
International at the *Verband*'s Nürnberg Congress in September.[2]

By 1868, then, Becker's influence on the Lassallean party was
considerable, and it contributed to the party's declaration of
solidarity with the International in August of that year: while
Schweitzer, however, was unwilling to go further than this
formal declaration of the party's support for the International
(which indeed brought the two organisations into the closest
relationship allowed by the laws of Prussia), Becker naturally
went on trying to stimulate the active interest of party-members
in the International.[3]

[1] Letters to Becker from (respectively) Bonhorst, Kugelmann, Boruttau, Bruhn,
H. Werth (all dated August or September 1868); cf. *Vorbote* July, p. 118; September, p. 139. On Schweitzer's attitude, *Social-Demokrat* 14 August.

[2] Fritzsche to Becker 8 August 1868; *Social-Demokrat* 30 August, *Vorbote*, August
(on Bracke and Braunschweig Section); on Kirchner, cf. Hirsch, *Die Organisation
der deutschen Arbeiterpartei*, p. 17, Bebel, *AML*, I, p. 188, *Archiv für Sozialgeschichte*,
Vol. II, pp. 296–7, and three letters to Becker, IISG.

[3] Becker's success in this is reflected in his letter to Conrad Rüll of Nürnberg,
dated March 1869 (Becker's copy in IISG): comparing the Lassalleans' interest in
the International with that of members of the *Verband Deutscher Arbeitervereine*,
Becker wrote, 'Our *Vorbote* has so far circulated more in the A.D.A.V. than in the
Arbeiter-Bildungs-Verein (i.e. the *Verband*), and the former has also played a bigger
part than the latter in supporting our oppressed comrades in Bâle' (i.e. the textile-
strikers).

In the *Verband Deutscher Arbeitervereine*, again, there were many different reasons why closer contact with the International was sought in 1868, including, as will be seen, the leaders' wish to profit from the popularity which it now enjoyed. Among the rank and file, however, the main cause of this very popularity was the propaganda of Becker. We have seen how in *Bildungsvereine* all over Germany, it was his writings which had started discussions on socialism and brought converts to the International; and among the letters he received in 1868 the number showing his influence on clubs affiliated to the *Verband* was greater than ever; they came, among other places, from Dresden Chemnitz, Leipzig, Hanover, Magdeburg, Berlin, Esslingen, Pforzheim, and Hamburg.

Becker, in fact, was not exaggerating when he told Sorge (on 23 August 1868) that the International's growth in Germany was due to 'my propaganda', and he certainly failed to realise that the *Verband*'s adhesion to the International, when it came in September 1868, meant not a confirmation of his authority but the beginning of its end. Bebel, indeed, wrote to him promising that the Nürnberg Congress meant the 'closest possible adhesion' (*Anschluss*) to the International, which should be carried out under Becker's own auspices; and Becker knew nothing of his assurances to the anti-socialist *Verband* leader Lange, only a few days earlier, that adhesion to the International 'could not be thought of until we have put our own house in order'—assurances which, however realistic, made nonsense of Bebel's undertaking to Becker.[1]

Becker's achievement, in spreading the International's message among the members of existing German labour organisations, was beginning in itself to weaken the basis of his Group of German-speaking Sections. He could not in the long run organise the International's relations with Germany on a scale adequate to the support which his work since 1865 had helped

---

[1] Letters of Bebel to Becker, 16 July, and to Lange, 22 June, respectively summarised and published in *AML*, I, pp. 182, 185; the significance of the letter to Becker (which Bebel summarised only in part, the complete original being in IISG) is discussed below, p. 143.

to arouse for it. The growth of the movement in Germany was therefore, in a personal sense, a tragedy for Becker; the more recruits he won for the International, the more necessary it became for the leadership to be assumed, however imperfectly, by an organisation inside Germany.

The location of this leadership, and the form it took, were in the event to be determined by the rivalry between the Lassallean party and the *Verband Deutscher Arbeitervereine*; it should not be forgotten, however, that it was Becker more than anyone else who spread the necessary knowledge of the International among the members of both organisations.

CHAPTER IV

WILHELM LIEBKNECHT AND THE INTERNATIONAL IN GERMANY, 1864 TO 1868

INTRODUCTION

Wilhelm Liebknecht, a veteran of the 1848 Revolution who spent the 1850s in London in close contact with Marx, returned to Germany in the summer of 1862. In 1868 he was partly responsible for the decision of the *Verband Deutscher Arbeitervereine*, the largest labour organisation in Germany, to adopt the programme of the International, and as the *Verband* had been founded and led by men whose aim was to keep German workers away from socialism, this has always seemed a considerable achievement. As early as 1869 Liebknecht himself assured the International's Bâle Congress that on its very foundation in 1864 he had 'immediately' started a persistent campaign 'to bring the German labour movement over to the principles of the International (*die deutsche Arbeiterbewegung auf den Boden der Internationale hinüberzuleiten*)'; and the magnitude of his achievement at Nürnberg has made most historians accept without query this suggestion of a single-minded four years' struggle.[1]

Mehring repeatedly calls Liebknecht 'the German apostle of the International', and the view is even accepted that he was 'sent to Germany by Marx as a missionary and organiser on behalf of the new movement' (i.e. the International), and that 'he was immediately successful, largely through the co-operation of Bebel'.[2] There are many reasons why such

[1] Traces of Liebknecht's claim (for which see *Hochverratsprozess*, p. 246) are evident in Mayer, *Schweitzer*, p. 149, and 'Die Lösung der deutschen Frage', *loc. cit.*, p. 261; Erich Eyck, *Der Verband deutscher Arbeitervereine*, pp. 87, 100; P. A. Steininger, *Die Ueberwindung der Lassalleschen Staatsideologie* ... (Berlin, 1955), p. 34; G. D. H. Cole, *Marxism and Anarchism* (London, 1954), p. 98; and H. Gemkow in *Beiträge zur Geschichte der deutschen Arbeiterbewegung*, Vol. I, p. 517.

[2] F. R. Salter, *Karl Marx and Modern Socialism*, p. 154; Mehring, *Die deutsche Sozialdemokratie: Ihre Geschichte und Ihre Lehre*, pp. 83, 87, 106.

estimates of Liebknecht's work in the 1860s should have persisted, but they are false.

Liebknecht did what he could to spread the ideas of Marx, as far as he understood them, but until 1868 the International played a very minor role in his activities. He did little to expound its programme and virtually nothing to enrol members for it, either in 1864–5, when he worked for Schweitzer's *Social-Demokrat*; or in the period from his break with Schweitzer to his expulsion from Prussia (February to July 1865), when he tried to organise opposition to the Lassallean leadership in Berlin; or in Leipzig from 1865 to 1868, although he lived a life of ceaseless political activity, which was interrupted only by a three-month prison-sentence in 1866–7, and which culminated in his election to the North German *Reichstag* in August 1867.

It was only in the summer of 1868, when Liebknecht and Bebel were unexpectedly able to get the International's programme accepted by the majority of the clubs represented in the *Verband Deutscher Arbeitervereine*, that their theoretical sympathy with this programme began to be expressed in action. Only now did they embark on the reorganisation which by August 1869 had transformed the *Verband* into the Eisenach Party, a body which formed, at least according to its programme, 'a branch of the International Working Men's Association'. They were helped in this by Johann Philipp Becker, although he gradually realised that the new party threatened the International's Group of German-speaking Sections which he had devotedly built up since 1865. The Eisenach Party, which ended Becker's influence in Germany, was thus created by men whose work there for the International had been considerably less than his own. To say that until the summer of 1868 Liebknecht made no systematic effort to start an organised branch of the International in Germany is not to say that it was entirely absent from his thoughts, his correspondence, or even his public speeches and writings; indeed, he quite often showed that he was aware of it. What is important is that although he sometimes referred to the

International in public, or privately assured Marx and Becker that he was doing his best to enrol members for it, he never, in practice, found himself in a situation where efforts of this kind seemed worth making—until 1868.

The reasons for this are clear if Liebknecht's references to the International during this time are examined in the context of his other preoccupations, and of the political environment in which he had to work.[1]

LIEBKNECHT IN BERLIN, 1864-5

During the winter months of 1864-5, when Lassalle's death had unexpectedly thrown together such irreconcilable figures as the ultra-Lassallean Countess Hatzfeldt, the somewhat unscrupulous opportunist Schweitzer, and the international revolutionary Marx, Liebknecht played a central role. His reasons for trying to keep the fragile alliance in being were both political, in that he sincerely hoped to use Schweitzer's paper, perhaps financed by the Countess, to spread the ideas of Marx; and material, in that he could support his family only by journalism, and was convinced that he must leave Germany if he could not earn a living in Berlin.[2] He was thus careful not to upset the partnership between Marx and Schweitzer, which he had helped to create and whose existence depended on his keeping the confidence—even though it was not total—of both partners. In this situation the opportunities for creative initiative were so small that even a more enterprising spirit than Liebknecht would have been unable to make much of them and he contented himself with a sustained attempt at mutual reassurance.

It was soon clear that Marx's aim in agreeing to work with Schweitzer had been to gain a public for the ideas of the International, and Liebknecht obediently passed on to him the

---

[1] Studies of this period of Liebknecht's career include those by Mühlbradt and Leidigkeit, already cited.

[2] Liebknecht to Engels 17 February 1865, in *Wilhelm Liebknecht: Briefwechse mit Karl Marx und Friedrich Engels*, ed. G. Eckert, p. 45.

Inaugural Address which arrived as the first contribution from London. Schweitzer, rejoicing at Marx's agreement to co-operate, was naturally delighted to print it, and Liebknecht could feel that he had already achieved something for the International. More positive efforts, however, were difficult: he was supporting his family by editorial work for Schweitzer and by writing a life of Lassalle commissioned by the Countess,[1] and when Marx summoned him to persuade 'the German Associations and Trade Unions' to affiliate to the International, he was not in a position to do much. His main contact with organised Berlin workers was through the Compositors' Association, to whom he gave frequent lectures on historical and political subjects, and he persuaded this Association, after some debate, to declare its agreement with the principles of the International.[2] It is true that this declaration was accompanied by an expression of regret that the Prussian Combination Laws prevented the Compositors from formal affiliation to the International, but this did not prevent Marx—anxious as ever to maximise the organisation's support in Germany—from giving an extravagant account of the declaration to the General Council in London.[3]

This, however, was the only personal contribution made by Liebknecht to the spreading of the International's ideas until after his break with Schweitzer: in the eyes of Marx, indeed, he was responsible for gravely neglecting the International's interests. After Marx had protested at the article in which Moses Hess seemed to cast doubts on the honesty of the International's Parisian representative, Schweitzer convinced him that the responsibility lay with Liebknecht, who, he implied, was to be regarded as responsible for everything the *Social-Demokrat* published about the International; when Marx again

---

[1] Liebknecht's own accounts in *Hochverratsprozess*, pp. 63–74, and in his Reichstag speech of October 1867 (*Stenographische Berichte*, 1867, pp. 562–3).

[2] *Chronik*, p. 236; Müller, *Geschichte der Lithographen*, p. 95, fn. 1.

[3] General Council *Minutes* (MS., IISG), I, p. 25 ('24 January 1865). On the respective *Vereinsgesetze* of Prussia and the German *Bund* cf. Karl Hirsch, *Die Organisation der Deutschen Arbeiterpartei*, pp. 26–7, and Leidigkeit, *Wilhelm Liebknecht und August Bebel*, p. 10.

took offence at remarks by Hess, Schweitzer explicitly repeated this assurance, and Liebknecht, on whom Marx turned his full fury, replied plaintively that he could see 'nothing wrong' with what Hess had said—which was merely that a 'public society' like the International would inevitably include a few unreliable elements. Liebknecht continued: 'the paper is at the disposal of the Association (i.e. the International), and will do whatever is possible. I can't help it if enemies of the Association work with the paper, but you knew about that from the beginning, just as well as I did!'[1]

The impossibility of having things all their own way was slowly made clear to Marx and Engels, but at first they were furious with Liebknecht when he pointed out (in the same letter) that 'the *Social-Demokrat* in its present form is the result of a compromise'. 'Compromise', which, they complained, meant that they should remain silent, for the sake of peace with Schweitzer, 'while the paper . . . *libels* our own aims and propaganda', had in fact been meant by Liebknecht 'in a personal sense', meaning mutual tolerance between colleagues with differing ideas.[2] (This kind of 'compromise' was one which Liebknecht, in his extremely difficult situation in Germany, was making continually, always to the incomprehending disgust of Marx and Engels.) Liebknecht had to concede a Lassallean paper's right to publish 'Lassallerei', as well as the views of Marx, but realised only slowly that this prevented him from asserting the claims of the International emphatically enough to satisfy its chiefs; it was after several days of growing disillusionment that he decided 'compromise' between Schweitzer and Marx was after all impossible, and resigned from the *Social-Demokrat* on 17 February—before either Marx or Engels formally took this step.

Liebknecht had been a member of the ADAV since 1863,

[1] Liebknecht to Marx, 3–5 February 1865, *Wilhelm Liebknecht: Briefwechsel*, p. 40.

[2] Engels to Marx 7 February, *MEB*, III, p. 273; Liebknecht to Engels 17 February, printed in *Hamburger Echo* 29 February 1926, and *Wilhelm Liebknecht: Briefwechsel*, p. 45.

although he disliked Lassalle's ideas, and particularly the party's nationalistic tone; he later justified his membership on the grounds that in the ADAV 'there was a movement there, and an organisation, even though both were still embryonic'.[1] This was no isolated case: throughout the 1860s Liebknecht repeatedly attached himself to existing organisations and tried to bring them round to his ideas, rather than himself founding anything new. It is quite characteristic that when he found further co-operation with Schweitzer impossible, he turned to another existing organisation, even though this one was even more 'embryonic' than the last.

Among Lassalleans in Berlin, as has been seen, there had been growing discontent with Lassalle's and Schweitzer's sympathies for the Prussian government, and by the spring of 1865 the local 'opposition-Section' of the party formed a compact and influential community, while the 'official' Section was reduced to five members.[2] When Liebknecht broke his links with the official party-leadership, he drew closer to this group of rebels; many of them had already told him of their distrust for Lassalle, and their leaders—August Vogt, Theodor Metzner and Siegfried Meyer—were later to contribute to the growth of the International in Germany or in America.[3]

It is clear, however, that during this period of a few months in 1865, from Liebknecht's break with Schweitzer in February to his expulsion from Prussia early in July, the International played a very small part in their thoughts and their activities; Liebknecht consoled himself for the breakdown of the *Social-*

[1] Liebknecht's article, 'Zwei Pionere', in *Neue Welt*, 1900, No. 17, pp. 131ff.
[2] Bernstein, *Geschichte der Berliner Arbeiter-Bewegung*, Vol. I, pp. 111, 132–4; Liebknecht, *Karl Marx zum Gedächtnis*, p. 112, and letter to Engels of 4 April 1865, in Liebknecht's *Briefwechsel*, pp. 53–4; J. Vahlteich, *Ferdinand Lassalle und die Anfänge der deutschen Arbeiterbewegung*, p. 83; records of the Berlin Police Headquarters on workers' clubs (now Landeshauptarchiv Brandenburg, Potsdam, C Tit. 94, Lit. A, Nr. 100), pp. 134–6.
[3] See the recent article by Heinrich Gemkow, 'Zur Tätigkeit der Berliner Sektion der I. Internationale', in *Beiträge zur Geschichte der deutschen Arbeiterbewegung*, Vol. I (1959), pp. 515–31, and for further details, Appendix IV below.

Demokrat's team of writers by the thought that it signified the breakdown of the ADAV as a whole (certainly the war of factions inside the party made this look extremely likely), and his activities in Berlin—for instance, his speeches to the Lassalleans or the Compositors—were directed towards ending the rule of Schweitzer and his colleagues or, as Liebknecht's friend Schweichel put it in a letter of 29 March 1865, 'throwing those people out of the saddle'.

This was the theme of Liebknecht's speeches to the Lassallean section and to the Compositors;[1] and if he, Vogt, and Meyer found time 'in the spring of 1865', as he later recalled, to distribute copies of Marx's *Herr Vogt*, the *Communist Manifesto*, and the *Inaugural Address* of the International, this was the most they did. Liebknecht later claimed that this Berlin group, 'in constant contact with Marx', laid 'the foundations for the organisation of a genuinely socialist revolutionary international working-class party', using the recently-founded International as 'a firm point of cristallisation';[2] but this is a characteristically tendentious exaggeration of his achievements and even of his aims.

There is only one example of practical interest for the International in Liebknecht's activities at this time: the affair of the Leipzig Compositors' strike. Early in April more than five hundred men in Leipzig went on strike over a wage-claim, and two weeks later Liebknecht and the Compositors of Berlin wrote to Marx (the International's Corresponding Secretary for Germany) to ask if the Compositors of London could help.[3] The General Council sent a deputation consisting of Marx and two English Trade Unionists, Fox and Cremer, 'to attend the Compositors Society' of London, but Fox later had to report that 'it would not be possible for that Body to grant any money for a period of three months'; Hermann Jung's comment on

---

[1] Liebknecht's speeches in Mühlbradt, *Wilhelm Liebknecht und die Gründung der deutschen Sozialdemokratie*, pp. 61–7, and in Leidigkeit, *op. cit.*, pp. 50–1, where Schweichel's letter of 29 March 1865 is quoted, p. 50, fn. 72.

[2] Article cited in note [1], p. 103 above.

[3] Bebel, *AML*, I, pp. 102, 110; *Chronik*, p. 243.

this failure was that some way of sending money should have been found, because 'the loss of this strike would have a depressing effect on the Trades of Germany generally';[1] and although these fears were unjustified, it is characteristic of the Germans' relations with the International at this stage that they should automatically be regarded as candidates for help, and not as being in a position to give it.

After 1868 things were rather different, but in 1865 Liebknecht felt that demands on the Germans for more active participation in the International's affairs would be in vain. When Marx, abandoning hope of attaching the ADAV as a whole to the International, wrote late in April to tell Liebknecht to concentrate on enrolling individual members instead (an idea which he had already mentioned late in February in a letter to Kugelmann), Liebknecht did nothing to put these instructions into practice, and for some months Marx abandoned him in disgust. (Even Engels, whose criticism of Liebknecht was less sharp than Marx's, had reminded the latter on 3 May 1865 that the International's members in Germany would soon need leadership on the spot, 'and who can do that? Eccarius would be the man, but he won't want to leave London.' Liebknecht, it seems, was completely discounted even by the indulgent Engels.) Early in July came the news that Liebknecht had been expelled from Prussia, and two months later, when he had settled in Leipzig, he wrote apprehensively to Engels: 'surely Marx won't be cross with me about the International Association? That would be unfair of him. . . . How *could* I carry on successful propaganda for the Association . . . and found branches, with all the struggles I had in Berlin?'[2]

Liebknecht's failure—on his own admission—to do anything for the International before he left Berlin is thus explained; in Leipzig again, however, he was faced with a life of 'struggles', including at first the struggle to live.

---

[1] Ms. Minutes, I, pp. 46, 48 (entries for 25 April and 9 May 1865).
[2] Liebknecht to Engels 30 August 1865, *Wilhelm Liebknecht: Briefwechsel*, p. 62.

LEIPZIG: LIEBKNECHT AND THE GERMAN
PEOPLE'S PARTY, UP TO THE CRISIS OF 1866

Liebknecht arrived penniless in Leipzig in August 1865, and had to earn a living as best he could. Fortunately, he soon met August Bebel, the President of the Workers' Educational Club, and at twenty-five already an influential figure in Saxony; Bebel arranged for him to teach English, French and History in the Club, but although his lectures soon became the most popular of all those it organised, they failed to bring him an adequate income. He was still a regular correspondent for two Liberal newspapers, one appearing in Freiburg and the other in Graz; and from these diverse sources he earned enough to support his family, though with difficulty—Bebel discovered only afterwards that Liebknecht had been forced at this time 'to take many a good book to the second-hand dealer'.[1]

Liebknecht's financial position, at least during the 1860s, was extremely precarious, and although Marx and Engels were aware of his difficulties they rarely made enough allowance for the way in which his need to prepare countless talks and news-paper-articles prevented him from serious study of their works or from carrying on careful and consistent propaganda in exactly the way they would have liked. It is certainly clearer now than it was to Marx and Engels—whose correspondence is filled with criticisms—why Liebknecht was in no position to take active steps to organise German branches of the International, depending as he did on employment as a writer and speaker, and thus being forced to avoid subjects unfamiliar to his audiences. The same tendency to cling to organisations already in existence rather than trying to found anything new, which had characterised Liebknecht in Berlin, was just as marked during his first years in Leipzig.

Here he found a flourishing organisation of Worker's Educational Clubs, of which twenty-nine in and around Leipzig

---

[1] Bebel, *AML*, I, p. 124; unpublished correspondence between Bebel and Liebknecht, IISG, Amsterdam.

had recently joined in a regional federation; and he gladly undertook to act as 'a wandering preacher' for the Educational Club movement in different parts of Saxony. 'Liebknecht came to us . . . as a godsend,' wrote Bebel of this work, 'because we lacked suitable people, whose manner of life permitted such activity.'

A month after arriving in Leipzig, Liebknecht was busily engaged in work with the Educational Clubs of Saxony, propagating as he went the anti-Prussianism which was his main political belief. When in September another vehicle for this theme presented itself, he warmly welcomed its creation. This was the German People's Party, formally created at a Congress at Darmstadt on 18 September.

The delegates at Darmstadt were prominent democratic politicians and publicists from every German state except Prussia. Their alarm at Prussia's threat to unite Germany by force had been growing for some years, and they were finally induced to create a new political party by their dismay at the Progressive Party's failure to answer Bismarck's attack on the constitution. The Darmstadt meeting agreed on no programme either politically (unanimous opposition to Prussian hegemony failing to produce agreement on how to prevent it) or socially (since the chief leader Eckhardt wanted to attract the Lassallean by demanding 'social reforms', while most delegates thought the demand for general suffrage went far enough).[1]

Despite this uncertainty Liebknecht was among the most satisfied of those present; he was enthusiastic to see a new party which embodied his own fundamental principle—hatred for Prussia—and the party's demand for general suffrage, linked with its call for full political freedom, seemed to him to make up for its other shortcomings. He became an active speaker for the People's Party as well as for the Workers' Clubs, and it was these two organisations which provided the basis for his political campaign of the succeeding years—a campaign firmly directed against Prussia, and which aimed first at trying to

---

[1] Mayer, 'Die Trennung', *loc. cit.*, pp. 10–17.

ward off the catastrophe of 1866, and later at trying to undo it.[1]

In the months before the Austro-Prussian War everything in Germany's future was uncertain: whether unity would come through agreement between the Princes, through a revolution 'from below', or not at all; whether there would be war between Austria and Prussia, and if so, who would win it; whether such a war could be prevented by a third force composed of the remaining states; and what would be the social, political, and economic structure of a united Germany, however unity came about.

To Liebknecht, who was dominated by hatred for Prussia, and who remained convinced even after Sadowa that Bismarck's armies should and could be thrown back by Austria, the army of the German Confederation, and a united rising of the German people in arms, political developments in 1865 and 1866 provided material to make everything else seem insignificant.[2]

It seems that Liebknecht did respond to Marx's instructions to send a report on Germany for the International's London Conference of September 1865 (Marx told the General Council on 19 September that 'no delegates from Germany would attend the conference, but that a report on the doings in Germany would be sent to him which he would read to the conference'), but in fact there was nothing to report.[3] Nothing, that is, on the organisation of the International, though Liebknecht was still trying loyally to provide Marx with a

[1] For Liebknecht's views on 'the German problem' cf. Mühlbradt, *Liebknecht*, pp. 82–8, and Leidigkeit, *Wilhelm Liebknecht und August Bebel*, pp. 94–109.

[2] On these developments see Bergsträsser, *Geschichte der politischen Parteien in Deutschland*; Mayer, 'Die Lösung der deutschen Frage . . .', *loc. cit.*, and Mayer, *Schweitzer*, pp. 166–7.

[3] General Council *Minutes* (MS., IISG), Vol. I, p. 62; cf. *Chronik*, p. 245. Liebknecht's report, a general survey of German socialism from 1848 to 1865, has recently been published in *The General Council of the First International 1864–1866. The London Conference 1865. Minutes*, pp. 251–60. It confirms that Liebknecht had not even succeeded in enrolling individual members for the International, though he blames this (p. 259) on general confusion in the labour movement, caused by 'the intrigues of the government'. Marx did not read the report to the Conference at all, explaining this to Liebknecht in a letter of 21 November 1865 by saying that 'too much prominence is given in it to me'. (Quoted *ibid.*, p. 434, fn. 289.)

public in Germany, in so far as this could be reconciled with his own political tactics. He told Marx in November that the editor of the *Deutsches Wochenblatt* (organ of the German People's Party) 'would be delighted if you and Engels were to write for it a few articles, but not *too* strong'; but the two exiles were unwilling to co-operate with 'a South German democrat, one of the Schwabians and Bavarians who have seceded from the *National-Verein*'.[1]

On 21 November Marx told the General Council that 'he was glad to be able to announce that our Association was at length making headway in Germany, where it had obstacles to overcome greater than those which existed in France. Steps were being taken to form branches in Berlin, Mayence and Leipsic by men for whom the speaker could vouch'. The Leipzig representative was clearly Liebknecht and those in Berlin and Mainz were respectively Vogt (or Meyer) and Stumpf.[2] Two months later, however, Marx had to tell the Council that the Leipzig Section was 'small'; Liebknecht told Johann Philipp Becker in February 1866 that he had enrolled twelve members, but the 'Section' as such seems to have undertaken no activities.[3]

A curious incident early in 1866 emphasised the difficulties which Liebknecht faced in carrying on propaganda for the International, but also the lack of realism with which he tried to solve them. After the resignation of Bernhard Becker from the presidency of the ADAV in November 1865, the contract

[1] Marx to Engels 20 November, Engels to Marx 1 December 1865; Bebel, *AML*, I, p. 128; Mayer, 'Die Trennung', p. 18.

[2] Minutes, Vol. I, pp. 83–4. Stumpf, a member of the Communist League in 1848 and now a prosperous plumber in Mainz, apparently started to correspond with Marx again at about this time (cf. *MEB*, III, p. 353, and Marx, *Briefe an Kugelmann*, p. 43). As described in Chapter III above, these Sections of the International were administratively taken over by Geneva.

[3] Minutes, Vol. I, p. 103 (23 January 1866); cf. *Chronik*, p. 249. Liebknecht's letter of 8 February, 1866 (partly printed in *Vorwärts*, Berlin, 28 March 1926) claims that the twelve members included 'den ganzen Vorstand des 500-Mitgliedern starken ...Arbeitervereins', but Bebel, the *Verein*'s president, only joined at the end of the year or even in 1867 (*AML*, Vol. I, p. 128; *Hochverratsprozess*, p. 213), and Liebknecht's claim seems greatly exaggerated.

making the *Social-Demokrat* the official party-organ had been revoked, and its editor Hofstetten now felt free to approach Liebknecht with a proposal that the paper should again become the official German organ of the International.[1] Liebknecht agreed and passed the suggestion on to Marx; he may have been encouraged by the knowledge that the *Social-Demokrat*'s contract with the ADAV had been revoked because of the paper's dealings with Julius Vahlteich of Dresden (expelled from the ADAV by Lassalle himself and now in sympathy with the International).[2] But Liebknecht must have known that the suggestion would never be accepted by Marx (who told Engels on 10 February 1866: 'I will give Wilhelm a good scolding for his feebleness. What we want is in fact the disappearance of the *Social-Demokrat* and the Lassalle-muck'); and he hardly would have put it forward if he had really regarded publicity for the International in Germany as practicable at this time.

He was, for instance, apparently not concerned in a manoeuvre in Germany undertaken by the International early in May. Alarmed by what Marx called 'the import of German and Danish tailors to Edinburgh' by employers attempting to break a strike, the General Council published on 5 May a leaflet urging German tailors not to lend themselves to this attempt and ten days later Marx was able to report that it had been printed in 'Leipsic journals'. It seems from Marx's comments to Engels, however, that this was done without any consultation or co-operation on the part of Liebknecht.[3]

The 'ass Liebknecht', as Marx called him, must indeed have regarded any talk of the International as quite irrelevant to the

[1] *Chronik*, p. 249; Mayer, *Schweitzer*, p. 144; Metzner to Marx 4 December 1865. Leidigkeit (*op. cit.* p. 94) is mistaken in thinking that Liebknecht himself took the initiative in these negotiations, and therefore exaggerates their significance as an indication that Liebknecht was anxious to work more closely with purely working-class organisations

[2] Mayer, *Schweitzer*, p. 143; Vogt (Berlin) to J. Ph. Becker 29 January 1866; Vahlteich to Metzner 6 September 1866 (IISG, Liebknecht-*Nachlass*).

[3] Minutes, Vol. I, p. 130 (15 May 1866); Marx to Engels 10 May, 17 May 1866; on the leaflet's publication in the German press, cf. *Répertoire des Sources pour l'Etude des Mouvements Sociaux* . . ., Vol. II (Paris, 1961), pp. 43–4.

situation in Germany, as the political tension increased throughout the spring, reaching by June the point of open war.
Liebknecht's determined campaign during this time was essentially concerned with the political future of Germany, and it can
be discussed here only as far as is necessary to explain the
significance of his references to the International in letters,
newspaper-articles, or speeches.[1]

In April Bismarck's challenging proposal for a reorganisation
of the German Confederation, combined with his military
alliance with Italy against Austria, made war seem imminent;
and the German People's Party and the League of German
Workers' Clubs mobilised their puny forces of propaganda to
arouse the regions of Germany threatened by 'the Prussian
solution'. In May and June Liebknecht (who had believed until
April that Prussia and Austria, rather than fight each other,
would combine to crush German democracy) spoke from dozens
of platforms in Saxony on behalf of the People's Party or the
Verband Deutscher Arbeitervereine.

On 8 May he made a violently anti-Prussian speech in a
mass-meeting in Leipzig, and a few days later followed it up by
urging the Workers' Educational Club to press for a 'people's
militia' to resist the Prussians.[2] He urgently insisted that the
forces of democracy must be better organised, and in many
meetings in Saxon industrial towns he persuaded excited audiences to join the People's Party or to found *Volksvereine* or
Arbeitervereine:[3] in Chemnitz on 2 June, he called on an audience
of 2,000 to 'form a section of the People's Party', and his message
was the same in meetings in Zwickau, Thurm and Werdau
on 9, 10 and 11 June, at the last of which 'about 3,000 men
are said to have declared themselves for adhesion to the
People's Party'.[4]

[1] Further details will be found in the accounts by Bebel, Mayer, Mühlbradt
and Leidigkeit, among others.
[2] Bebel to Liebknecht 7 May 1866 (IISG); Bebel, *AML*, I, pp. 141, 145–6;
Mayer, *Schweitzer*, pp. 166–7.
[3] Mühlbradt, *Liebknecht*, p. 86; Mayer, 'Die Trennung', p. 24; G. Benser,
Zur Herausbildung der Eisenacher Partei, pp. 38–66 *passim.*
[4] Benser, *op. cit.*, p. 56; Mühlbradt, *op. cit.*, p. 87

Liebknecht's campaign in Saxony, which was cut short by the outbreak of war on 15 June (though Bebel and others were able to continue it further West), was essentially political, but as his audiences consisted largely of industrial workers he sometimes spoke not only of resistance to Prussia but also of social problems. The social programme of the People's Party, however, to which he restricted himself, was in no way socialistic, including only a vague reference to 'improving the Condition of the Labouring Classes'; and the only speech in which he is recorded as having mentioned the International as such was at Chemnitz (2 June), when he 'recommended' his audience 'to study the social question in other countries, and to follow the efforts of the International Working Men's Association'—although even here the organisation he urged them to join was the People's Party.[1] If Liebknecht wrote telling Marx at this time that 'all the Saxon Working Men's Associations had joined the International', this was the purest fantasy.[2] In Liebknecht's mind the cause of social progress represented by the International was certainly linked with the anti-Prussian enthusiasm to which he was stirring up the workers of Saxony, but in moments of clarity he left no doubt that for the moment Prussia was the important enemy—telling the Berlin *Arbeiterverein* on 14 October 1867, for instance, that the 'social question' must be kept in the background for the time being, as it would otherwise split

---

[1] Mayer, *Schweitzer*, p. 156; S. W. Armstrong, 'The Social Democrats and the Unification of Germany', in *Journal of Modern History*, XII (1940), p. 491. Liebknecht himself told J. Ph. Becker in August 1867 (letter published in *Vorwärts*, Berlin, 28 March 1926): 'since last year I have worked successfully for the International in five public meetings with audiences of five thousand people', and this must include the meetings of June 1866. Liebknecht went on to promise Becker that he would in future 'take every opportunity of intervening decisively for the International', but he can scarcely be said to have done so.

[2] Minutes, Vol. I, p. 138, report by Marx on 12 June, 1866. Liebknecht had written on 25 May that 'the leaders of the working men's associations here have expressed a desire to become members' (*The General Council of the First International 1864–1866*, p. 417, fn. 217), and a further letter he sent on 8 June (*Chronik*, p. 251) made Marx write to Engels that 'since the noise of war began, the Saxon workers have joined the International in great numbers' (*MEB*, III, p. 405), There is no evidence, however, that anyone in Saxony joined the International as a result of Liebknecht's activities, and Leidigkeit (*Wilhelm Liebknecht und August Bebel*, p. 101) thus seems to be in error in accepting Marx's claim as true, and giving the credit to Liebknecht.

the united front opposed to Bismarck;[1] if he interpreted his popular triumphs in Saxony as victories for the International, this can best be explained by his state of general excitement and by his urgent wish to please Marx.

Liebknecht's campaign of mass-meetings was interrupted by the Prussian occupation of Saxony a few days after the outbreak of war, but he cast about him for another method of propaganda. Shortly after the preliminary peace-treaty at the end of July, and a month after the Prussian occupation began, he found it: the Liberal newspaper *Mitteldeutsche Volkszeitung* had been bankrupted by the war, and on 10 August Liebknecht told Marx that he and his friends had acquired it and would use it to spread the ideas of the International and to publish any articles Marx and Engels might be able to send him.[2] Marx was not impressed—writing to Engels on 13 August, he referred to Liebknecht's request as 'nonsense', and to the copies of the newspaper he received as 'worthless'—and so Liebknecht was left to look after the *Mitteldeutsche Volkszeitung* himself. He did indeed publish the *Inaugural Address* of the International,[3] but his main aim was to attack the Prussian occupier and to agitate for the democratic unification of Germany. (These were also the main themes of the Chemnitz Programme adopted on 19 August by the new Saxon People's Party, in which Liebknecht played a prominent part.) Within four weeks the Prussian military authorities had banned the newspaper. According to Bebel, this happened because Liebknecht attacked the Prussians so hard that 'one would have thought that he was the ruler of Saxony, and not they'; accord-

[1] Mayer, 'Die Trennung', p. 25; cf. Liebknecht to Engels 11 December 1867, 'I start from the standpoint that the fall of Prussia equals the victory of the German revolution' (Mayer, *Engels*, II, p. 161)

[2] Liebknecht to Marx (undated, probably 10 August 1866), *Wilhelm Liebknecht: Briefwechsel...*, p. 76. Liebknecht promises to publish 'the (old) Manifesto of the International ... perhaps with the omission of one or two sentences about Prussia and Poland which might become dangerous'.

[3] I am indebted to Professor E. Engelberg for the information (in a letter of 8 June 1957) that instalments of the *Inaugural Address* appeared in the *Mitteldeutsche Volkszeitung* on August 1, 9, 11, and 15, 1866.

ing to other accounts, it was because the publication of the *Inaugural Address* itself was regarded as seditious.[1]

The newspaper was suppressed in mid-August; Liebknecht optimistically told Engels early in October that it would re-appear 'when peace was concluded' (i.e. when the Prussians withdrew: peace had formally been made on 23 August), but it never did. Liebknecht assured Engels: 'The *Mitteldeutsche* will be an organ of the International Working Men's Association, and expects articles from you and from Williams (pseudonym for Marx), as well as more substantial assistance in the form of shares and abonnements.'[2] Genuine willingness to do something for the International seems in this letter to be mixed with more tactical considerations: in Liebknecht's own mind the International played a very small part, but he knew that it was extremely important to Marx and Engels. This in itself is enough to explain his promise in October—much more explicit than that of August—that the paper would be 'an organ of the International': such a promise seemed to him the surest way of getting Marx and Engels to send him articles, which they had failed to do in August. There is no evidence that the *Mitteldeutsche Volkszeitung* made a positive contribution to the spread of the International—it had scarcely more than 1,000 subscribers when Liebknecht and Bebel took it over[3]—and the next thing that happened was that Liebknecht was dramatically prevented from reviving it by his sudden arrest in Berlin.

[1] Bebel's two accounts of the paper's suppression ('Erinnerungen an Liebknecht' in *Der Wahre Jakob*, No. 368 (1900), p. 3323, and *AML*, I, p. 158) both give as the reason Liebknecht's attacks on the Prussian government. Leidigkeit, *op. cit.*, p. 103, fn. 40–1, argues on the contrary that 'Liebknecht ... had to refrain from any personal judgments in the paper on the events of 1866', and that the publication of the International's Address itself was the cause of the paper's suppression. I have been unable to consult the *Mitteldeutsche Volkszeitung* to verify this point, but Bebel would surely not have been wrong in his general impression that Liebknecht placed hostility to Prussia higher than propaganda for the International.

[2] Liebknecht ('Miller') to Engels 1 October 1866, *Wilhelm Liebknecht: Brief-wechsel* ..., p. 77.

[3] *AML*, I, p. 158. The smallness of the impression made by this publication of the *Inaugural Address* is confirmed by the fact that even Wilhelm Eichhoff was unaware of it; cf. Gemkow in *Beiträge zur Geschichte der deutschen Arbeiterbewegung*, 1959, p. 524, fn. 34.

His letter of 1 October was written from Berlin, whence he had gone in the confident belief that a recent Prussian amnesty annulled his expulsion of the previous year. On 2 October he spoke at a meeting organised by his old associates the compositors, and was immediately afterwards arrested by the police. Two weeks later a Prussian court sentenced him to three months' imprisonment for defying his expulsion-order of 1865, and he returned to Leipzig only in mid-January 1867.[1]

1867–8: ELECTION-CAMPAIGNS AND THE *Demokratisches Wochenblatt*

He returned filled with redoubled hatred for Prussia, and determined to destroy the Prussian-created North German *Bund*; the election campaign for its Constituent *Reichstag* was now taking place, and Liebknecht threw himself into electioneering. While he was still in prison the Saxon People's Party had nominated him for the 19th Saxon constituency, centred on Stollberg, Lugau and Schneeburg, but unlike his fellow-candidates Bebel and Schraps in the neighbouring 17th and 18th constituencies, he was not elected—partly because the vote took place only two weeks after his arrival.[2]

During the spring and summer of 1867 Liebknecht's attention was distracted from politics by the death of his wife, who had fallen seriously ill during his imprisonment, and who died in June. The political efforts he did make during this time were devoted above all to further electoral propaganda, which earned him a seat in the first and only legislative *Reichstag* of the North German Confederation, elected at the end of August. He soon showed how he intended to use his new platform by proclaiming to an outraged *Reichstag* (17 October 1867): 'World history will trample underfoot this North German

[1] Bernstein, *Die Geschichte der Berliner Arbeiter-Bewegung*, Vol. I, p.151, and Liebknecht's *Reichstag* speech of 21 October 1867 (*Stenographische Berichte*, 1867, pp. 562–3).

[2] Mühlbradt, *Liebknecht*, p. 98; Leidigkeit, *Wilhelm Liebknecht und August Bebel*, pp. 114, 118; Bebel, *AML*, I, p. 164; Benser, *Zur Herausbildung der Eisenacher Partei*, pp. 60–4; R. Lipinski, *Die Sozialdemokratie von Ihren Anfängen bis zur Gegenwart*, Vol. I, p. 169ff.

Confederation, which is nothing but the division, enslavement and weakening of Germany: it will trample underfoot this North German *Reichstag*, which is nothing but the fig-leaf of absolutism.'[1]

His complete inactivity on behalf of the International during all this time scarcely seems to have worried Marx and Engels, who had by now given up hope of his achieving anything tangible. They were more occupied with the completion of the first volume of *Das Kapital* than with anything else, and they seem to have lost touch with Liebknecht almost completely. On 18 February 1867, a month after Liebknecht's release from prison, Marx asked Kugelmann: 'please be so kind as to let me know what Liebknecht is up to, and where he is hiding himself (*wo er steckt*)'; and when Engels asked Marx on 12 September for Liebknecht's whereabouts, it was the first reference to him in their correspondence for ten months.[2]

The organisational growth of the International seemed at a standstill, at least in the industrially developed and politically advanced Kingdom of Saxony. Elsewhere in Germany, as we have seen, its Sections, founded and sustained by Becker from Geneva, were making slow but solid progress, but in Saxony the active workers' leaders were occupied with other things. Bebel, who had become an individual member of the International while Liebknecht was in prison, urged the chairman of the *Verband Deutscher Arbeitervereine* to follow his example in taking up contact with Geneva, but at present he saw this contact simply as a way of bringing more radical political ideas into the *Verband*, not as a step towards formal affiliation.[3] At the same time (May 1867) F. W. Fritzsche wrote to Becker from Leipzig to say that he and Liebknecht had been discussing the question of Germany's relationship to the International, but

---

[1] *Stenographische Berichte* . . .1867, p. 452; a clear account of the election-results of this period will be found in E. Wurm, ed., *Volks-Lexikon: Nachschlagbuch* . . ., Vol. IV (Nürnberg 1897), p. 412

[2] Marx, *Briefe an Kugelmann*, p. 36; *MEB*, III, p. 505. The Minutes of the General Council likewise make no reference to Liebknecht between June 1866 and August 1867.

[3] Bebel, *AML*, I, pp. 128, 166–7; *Hochverratsprozess*, p. 213.

they could reach no practical conclusions because the Combination Acts would prevent German organisations from affiliating.[1] In the circumstances, however, this scarcely amounted to more than a pretext for inaction: Liebknecht and the others could certainly have spread the message of the International if they had judged it opportune—this was demonstrated by Becker's successful activities—but they were otherwise occupied. Liebknecht, besides his personal troubles and his electoral activities, was scraping a living by petty journalism; Bebel was above all preoccupied with reorganising the *Verband Deutscher Arbeitervereine*; Fritzsche, still active in the Lassallean party, was also (and primarily) engaged in trade-union work; and Vahlteich, although he sent regular subscriptions to Geneva, was not yet materially in a position to do anything more active.[2] Certainly Becker was exaggerating the efforts of Liebknecht when he wrote to Sorge in September 1867: 'He (Liebknecht), Bebel, and J. Vahlteich in Germany are working diligently (*fleissig*) for our Association.' Becker was right in thinking that his correspondent in America would be impressed by this parade of three of the outstanding names in the German labour movement; but in reality their minds were on quite different things from the International.[3]

After Liebknecht's election to the North German *Reichstag*, late in August 1867, his correspondence with Marx and Engels again became more frequent, but it was not until July 1868

[1] Fritzsche to Becker, May 1867 (IISG, *Partei-Archiv*). A few months later Liebknecht sent a telegram of greetings to the International's Lausanne Congress 'in his name and on behalf of the *Volks-Vereine* of Zwickau, Meerane, Werdau, Crimmitschau, and Leipzig' (*Vorbote*, Oct. 1867, p. 153), but there is no evidence that members of these *Vereine* actually joined the International. Similar telegrams had been sent by the '*Volks-* and *Arbeitervereine* of Crimmitschau, Zwickau, Berlin, Leipzig and Dresden' to the Geneva Congress of the League of Peace and Freedom (*ibid.*, p. 150).

[2] Vahlteich to Liebknecht 19 March 1865, and to Metzner 6 September 1866 (both IISG, Liebknecht-*Nachlass*) on Fritzsche, cf. Eckert, *Aus den Anfängen*, p. 7.

[3] Becker to Sorge 26 September 1867, unpublished original in Sozialarchiv, Zürich. By March 1868 Becker was much less optimistic about Liebknecht, whose new *Demokratisches Wochenblatt* was competing with the *Vorbote* in Saxony; still, said Becker, 'Liebknecht is putting up a good fight, and thus serving our cause indirectly' (*Briefe und Auszüge aus Briefen . . . an F. A. Sorge*, p. 5).

that he mentioned the International, and by this time their suspicion about whether he was capable of any serious action seemed quite reasonable. Liebknecht was possessed during this time with hatred of Prussia and of 'the work of 1866': his one goal, as Gustav Mayer put it, was the 'reversal of Bismarck's revolution from above by a revolution from below', and his political activity and attitudes were governed by the search for allies in this task. Enemies of Prussia, whoever they might be, were his political friends, and if this obliged him to disregard the 'social' struggle against capitalism, he freely admitted, for instance in two Berlin speeches of October 1867, that social reforms were worthless until political agitation had first put the state on a more democratic (i.e. non-Prussian) basis, and that 'the social question must be left aside for the moment, so as not to disturb the co-operation of the workers and the Liberal bourgeoisie'.[1]

Liebknecht's purely destructive attitude to the North German Confederation was shown in his refusal to consider its parliament as a possible place for constructive work, and his insistence that its only right use for socialists was as a platform for propaganda 'to the masses outside'. He made provocative speeches which were regularly drowned in angry protests; he refused to support even such a progressive measure as Schweitzer's factory-safety bill, on the grounds that legislation of any kind would strengthen the Confederation as a political entity; it was at this stage, as we have seen, that he revived and popularised the slogan that the *Reichstag* was 'nothing but the fig-leaf of absolutism'.[2]

In the search for allies in the struggle against Prussia and the Confederation, Liebknecht consciously abandoned for a time the purely working-class audiences which he had addressed in

[1] Speeches quoted in Mayer, 'Die Trennung', p. 25 fn., *Schweitzer*, p. 207; correspondence in *Chronik*, pp. 262–3, Mayer, *Engels*, II, pp. 160–1, 542, and *MEB*, IV, p. 93.
[2] Liebknecht's anti-parliamentarian views were developed in a Berlin speech of 31 May 1869, published as a pamphlet entitled *Die politische Stellung der Sozialdemokratie, insbesondere mit Bezug auf den Reichstag*; in old age he changed his views, as can be seen from his preface to the *Hochverratsprozess* (1894), pp. 26–7.

industrial Saxony during his campaign of 1866. He was not even present at the fourth Congress of the *Verband Deutscher Arbeitervereine* (in Gera, 6 & 7 October 1867), at which Bebel became President, the organisation of the League was strengthened, and a series of social problems, including notably mining accidents, formed the subject of debates.[1]

On the other hand, his connections with non-socialist enemies of Prussia grew stronger. When the democratic forces of South Germany met again (at Bamberg on 22 December) to discuss the organisation of the now moribund German People's Party, Liebknecht was an active participant; although he criticised the more extreme anti-Bismarkians for their utopian dreams of a federalistic future for 'Greater Germany', he was delighted to see new signs of life in the anti-Prussian forces defeated in 1866. It is absolutely clear that his aim at this stage was much less the building of a labour party extending throughout Germany than the creation of an alliance that would tear down what Bismarck had built in 1866, as a first step to any progress either political or social.

At a further People's Party Conference in Bamberg, in February 1868, Liebknecht and Bebel urged the party to take an active part in the elections to the German tariff-parliament (*Zoll-Parlament*), which would provide a further platform for democratic ideas; and after a number of prominent democrats had been elected, they organised a public meeting in Berlin in May, which Liebknecht used for more 'diatribes against the victors of Königgratz', leaving 'the social question...hardly touched'.[2] It is scarcely surprising that Marx and Engels gave up their attempts to persuade him to do something for the International, and never referred to him in their correspondence except with contempt.

Their contempt was concentrated in particular on the *Demokratisches Wochenblatt*, which Liebknecht edited in Leipzig from January 1868 onwards. It was in vain that they accused

[1] Bebel, *AML*, I, pp. 166–9.
[2] Bebel, *AML*, I, pp. 178–9; Mayer, 'Die Trennung', pp. 32–4.

him of losing all sense of proportion in his attacks on Bismarck and his complementary praise for all the Chancellor's enemies, notably Austria; the *Demokratisches Wochenblatt* lived up to its title 'organ of the German People's Party', and although it found its main support in Saxony, where the Party's members were mostly working-class and relatively advanced on the way to socialism, the feelings common to the party as a whole (which the editor himself was only too inclined to stress) were enmity to Prussia and sympathy for Austria. In the first six months of its existence the *Demokratisches Wochenblatt*, for the sake of the united front against Bismarck, infuriated Marx and Engels by doing no direct propaganda for socialism, failing to publicise *Das Kapital* in a satisfactory way, and making no attempt to enrol members for the International. When, in mid-July 1868, Liebknecht wrote to say that the *Verband*'s Nürnberg Congress was about to vote to affiliate to the International, Engels was expressing the justified scepticism of them both when he told Marx that he would 'wait for performance before giving an opinion'.[1]

CONCLUSION: LIEBKNECHT'S DIFFICULTIES BETWEEN 1864 AND 1868

Before discussing the circumstances which had produced this rash promise from Liebknecht (after nearly a year's complete silence on the subject of the International), it is worth summarising the reasons why his activity on its behalf had been so small for almost four years—during which Marx and Engels had been forced to regard him (as Engels reminded Marx on 7 August 1865) as being, despite his faults, 'the only reliable contact we have in Germany'.

There were five main reasons: first, the Combination Acts

---

[1] Engels to Marx 29 July 1868, *MEB*, II, p. 93; for further examples of criticism, cf. *ibid.*, III, pp. 545, 548, 551, 553, IV, pp. 1–95 *passim*, and Marx to Kugelmann 24 June 1868 (*Briefe an Kugelmann*, p. 65): 'Liebknecht is becoming more and more simple-minded in this South German stupidity; he is not enough of a dialectician to criticise two sides at once.' Bebel himself disagreed with Liebknecht's immoderate Austrophilia, as he explains in *AML*, II, p. 61.

which made open affiliation to the International illegal; secondly, Liebknecht's material dependence on non-socialists and non-socialist organisations; thirdly, his personal conviction that propaganda against Prussia was more important than propaganda for the International; fourthly, the fact that the audiences with whom he had to deal usually shared these feelings themselves; and finally, his lack of gifts as an organiser.

First, Liebknecht's own excuse for his inactivity on the International's behalf—that the Combination Acts (*Vereinsgesetze*) forbade any formal founding of Sections in Germany—was certainly valid up to a point. In Prussia, Saxony, and a number of smaller states, laws (dating usually from the early 1850s) forbade political associations to enter into any organised relationship either with each other or with bodies in foreign countries. In spite of uncertainty about how firmly these laws might be enforced—the police tended to be really strict only in times of crisis, as in 1866 or 1870—it was essential for Liebknecht and Bebel to respect them in any organisation they founded.[1]

Throughout most of Germany Sections of the International could not have been established openly; but if Liebknecht had been really concerned to win members for it he could either have founded semi-clandestine Sections in the German States where this was legally possible (in Baden, for instance, the Lörrach Section was officially registered with the police, and in Saxony-Weimar there was no *Vereinsgesetz* at all),[2] or finally—and most promising of all—concentrated on the perfectly legal procedure of enrolling individual members. In 1869, when the Eisenach Party was anxious to present itself as the German representative of the International, its committee declared (in the *Demokratisches Wochenblatt* of 28 August 1869) that 'no law

---

[1] Karl Hirsch, *Die Organisation der Deutschen Arbeiterpartei*, pp. 26–7, discusses the *Vereinsgesetze*; Bebel in *Hochverratsprozess*, p. 144, describes how they were interpreted by the police; Eichhoff's letter of 18 July 1868 to Marx (quoted by Gemkow in *Beiträge* ..., Vol. I, p. 523, suggests a way to circumvent them by enrolling individual members only.

[2] The Lörrach Section is described in Chapter V below. On Saxony-Weimar, cf. Bebel, *AML*, II, pp. 83–4.

in the world can forbid people to belong to several political Associations at the same time', and recommended strongly that 'every member of the Social-demccratic Workers' Party should also become an individual member of the International Working Men's Association'.[1] This form of membership was quite legal in Germany; Marx—as we have seen—had urged Liebknecht for years to enrol individual members, and the fact that he did virtually nothing about it suggests that considerations of legality were by no means alone in holding him back from action.

There was, secondly, the vital factor of his material dependence, during all these years, on other people and on organisations already in existence. Until 1868 he was rarely in a position to speak his mind openly, because he was a subordinate contributor to newspapers owned by others. The *Social-Demokrat* was the organ of the ADAV, the *Grazer Tagespost* and *Oberrheinische Curier* were mouthpieces of South German democracy, the *Deutsches Wochenblatt* of 1865–6 and even the *Demokratisches Wochenblatt* of 1868 were 'organs of the German People's Party', the *Frankfurter Zeitung* was firmly anti-socialist, and the one newspaper personally controlled by Liebknecht, the short-lived *Mitteldeutsche Volkszeitung* of August 1866, would have been condemned by its precarious finances to an early death even if the authorities had not banned it.[2]

Just as Liebknecht could not risk losing his income by addressing the readers of these journals too openly on unfamiliar subjects (e.g. Marxist socialism or the International), so he was forced to make concessions to the views of the individuals and organisations on which he depended. These included in turn the Lassallean leadership, the Countess Hatzfeldt, the Lassallean opposition, the Saxon Workers' Clubs,

[1] *Hochverratsprozess*, pp. 249, 253–4; Nicolaevsky, *loc. cit.*, p. 255; Bracke, *Der Braunschweiger Ausschuss . . .*, pp. 156–7.
[2] The date at which Liebknecht began to write for the *Frankfurter Zeitung* is uncertain. The *Geschichte der Frankfurter Zeitung* (Volksausgabe, Frankfurt a.M., 1911), does not mention him, and the surviving letter to him from the editor Sonnemann, dated 3 December 1869 (IISG), suggests only that by this date he was a regular and well-trusted contributor.

the German People's Party, and his constituents of the People's Party in Saxony; co-operation with all these was materially essential to Liebknecht's existence, and this helps to explain why he was forced into compromises horrifying to the doctrinal purity of his distant censors Marx and Engels, and why in particular he neglected the International.

Thirdly, Liebknecht's limitations of character and intellect meant that he was not always aware of the potential theoretical importance of socialism, and the consequent significance of the International; his blind refusal to accept the *fait accompli* of 1866, and his confident faith that Bismarck's work should and could be undone, make it an exaggeration to say that 'he never lost sight of the political aims he had set himself along the lines of the *Communist Manifesto* and the *Inaugural Address* of the International'.[1]

Quite apart from his perpetual need to support his family by hack journalism, he could, in Gustav Mayer's phrase, 'never stick it out long with books',[2] and had nothing like the far-sighted sense of political strategy, for instance, of Schweitzer. Marx and Engels were justified in criticising him for allowing his detestation of Prussia to carry him to a point where he became an ally of all Prussia's reactionary enemies: Austria, South German particularists and federalists, and the royal families dispossessed by Bismarck. They repeatedly urged him not to neglect 'social agitation' in the attempt to destroy the political 'work of 1866', and to use 'dialectical application' in attacking not only the reactionary Bismarck but also his reactionary enemies because (as Marx put it in a letter of 27 November 1867 to Engels) 'they aren't worth anything either'.

It was all in vain: Liebknecht insisted in reply that the essential task was to prevent Prussia from consolidating the still unfinished 'work of 1866'; the Confederation was weaker than they realised, he said, but if it was allowed to consolidate

[1] Mühlbradt, *Liebknecht*, p. 74; cf. Leidigkeit, *Wilhelm Liebknecht und August Bebel*, p. 117.
[2] Mayer, *Engels*, II, p. 128.

itself, the German revolution would have to wait until the German people had evolved enough to make it spontaneously, and that would take 'several generations'. 'I start,' he continued, 'from the standpoint that the fall of Prussia equals the victory of the German revolution'[1]—and allies had to be found and prized for their usefulness in this task, not in the spreading of socialism. As Marx rightly said, discussing 'our Wilhelm' in a letter of 17 December 1867 to Engels, 'hatred for Prussia is the only passion which give him verve and singleness of purpose'.

The appearance of socialist conviction was lent to this hatred of Prussia (although it usually meant agreement with anti-socialists outside Prussia) because Liebknecht's enemies included the National Liberals, the party of the Prussian (or, in Saxony, pro-Prussian) middle class; Liebknecht's socialism, however, was on the whole a by-product of his faith in democracy, and consequently he left the International in the background.[2]

Fourthly, even if Liebknecht had been economically independent, and intellectually capable of carrying on wholehearted propaganda for Marxism and the International, it is unlikely that he would have been listened to before 1868. Marx and Engels, like the other émigrés of 1848, had long been forgotten by the mass of the German people, and until the publication of Das Kapital late in 1867, well-publicised by Engels, most German socialists refused to believe that Lassalle's ideas were anything but original; thus, for instance, Liebknecht, when he reprinted an article by Engels in the Demokratisches Wochenblatt, felt obliged to cut out the denunciation of Lassalle's plagiarism to avoid offending his numerous disciples.[3] The

[1] Liebknecht to Engels 11 December 1867, quoted ibid. p. 161
[2] In a letter of 10 July 1869 to Kugelmann, Engels denounced 'the South German-republican-spiessbürgerlich stupidities which Liebknecht systematically pumps into the workers', to which Kugelmann replied 'the socialist element has got into him [Liebknecht] through the chance of personal acquaintanceships'; Marx & Engels, Ausgewählte Briefe, p. 254; Mayer, Engels, II, p. 542.
[3] Mayer, Engels, II, pp. 156–9.

revival of German socialism embodied in Lassalle's party had been calculated to fill a precise gap in the German political scene before 1866, demanding—as no other party did—universal suffrage and social reform; working-class forces of a positively socialist character, distinct from the ADAV, could only be gathered together on a large scale by about 1868, when German radicals were becoming at the same time reconciled to the Confederation's existence, and dissatisfied with its social and economic arrangements. Until then, the main objectives of progressive thought in Germany were political democracy, the destruction of militarism, and above all the weakening or isolation of Prussia.[1] Liebknecht concentrated on these points not only because to him they were the most important, but because they came first for his audiences as well; a purely socialist campaign would not have been understood unless it had taken the nationalistic lines of Lassalleanism, and in that case Saxon or South German audiences would have rejected it. Liebknecht's readiness to adapt himself to this environment is reflected in a letter he wrote on 8 August 1867 to Johann Philipp Becker:

If we do not do much here directly for the International Working Men's Association, the fault is with the circumstances; we are forced into the political arena. With propaganda on purely social lines, like that desired by the official Social Democrats [i.e. the ADAV] in Berlin, we would play into the hands of the common enemy of all honest German democrats, socialists, and patriots, namely Prussian caesarism. That must not happen at any price.[2]

Again, as Liebknecht explained to Engels on 20 January 1868,

here I am not dealing with a lot of trained communists, but only with recruits for communism, who have certain prejudices that must be considered. . . . Criticise, as much as you like . . . but don't only criticise. I have won a position here. To hold it and strengthen it is my next task: to *use* it in *our* party's interests, is your business.[3]

[1] Mayer, 'Die Trennung', pp. 30–1.
[2] Printed in *Vorwärts* (Berlin), 28 March 1926; on the isolation and unpopularity of the ADAV in Saxony at this time, cf. Benser, *Zur Herausbildung der Eisenacher Partei*, pp. 52–3.
[3] Mayer, *Engels*, II, p. 161.

Liebknecht was at this stage, indeed, so dependent on politicians who would have been horrified to hear him connect his 'party's interests' with 'communism' that 'strengthening his position' often took some very curious forms: as late as June 1868 his relations with the non-socialist People's Party were still so close that its leader Sonnemann could describe him as 'extremely well suited' to undertake a propaganda tour on its behalf;[1] and in mid-August, three weeks before the Nürnberg Congress actually adopted the programme of the International, Liebknecht set such store by the unity of all democratic and anti-Prussian forces that he insisted on the 'harmlessness' of the programme, which would imply no 'artificial conflict' between the People's Party and the workers represented at Nürnberg.[2]

By this time, indeed, circumstances made the adoption of the International's programme suitable and even necessary (suitable, that is, in view of the rapid expansion of the German working class, which provided a basis for a more strictly socialist party, and necessary to Liebknecht personally, if he was to compete with Schweitzer), but Liebknecht was alarmed at its implications; this was the effect on him of several years in which open propaganda for the International had been inappropriate.

A fifth and final reason why Liebknecht did nothing to organise support for the International in Germany was that he was not by nature a capable organiser. He clung to the movements led by Lassalle, Eckardt, Sonnemann, or Bebel not only because it was materially necessary and politically opportune, but because he had no patience with the details of organisation; and he preferred to limit his demonstrations of sympathy with the International to a hasty printing of its programme or a warm recommendation in a speech, rather than troubling himself with the complicated business of organising Sections for it under the difficult German conditions. Characteristically, it was Bebel who took all the active steps concerned with both the

---

[1] Sonnemann to Jacoby 1 June 1868, in 'Die Trennung', p. 35.
[2] *Ibid.*, pp. 37–8; Leidigkeit, *op. cit.*, pp. 124–5.

Nürnberg and the Eisenach Congresses: it was he who conducted the correspondence, prepared the documents, examined the delegates' credentials, and guided his proposals through the long debates, while Liebknecht appeared essentially as the brilliant and effective mass-orator.[1]

It should be clear what were the reasons which prevented Liebknecht from doing anything effective for the International before 1868; in the light of this, it is scarcely possible to give any further credence to the widely-accepted legend that the International's 'work of recruiting and liaison in Germany fell above all to the younger friend of Marx, Wilhelm Liebknecht'.[2]

[1] Joll, *The Second International* (London 1955), p. 9; Engelberg, *loc. cit.*, p. 647.
[2] Karl Renner in *Der Wiener Hochverratsprozess* . . . (Vienna, 1911), p. 102.

CHAPTER V

THE TURNING-POINT: THE GERMAN LABOUR CONGRESSES OF 1868 TO 1869

INTRODUCTION

At the meeting of the International's General Council on 21 July 1868, 'Citizen Marx' was able to announce the possible affiliation of the Lassallean party in Germany; he had learned, he said, 'that the General Working Men's Union was going to do in a round-about way what the Prussian Law prohibited to be done directly'. Moreover, 'there was another working men's union in the Southern and Western States of Germany who had some affiliations in Switzerland and they are (*sic*) also going to join'. Marx had had preliminary news about the plans of this second 'union' (i.e. the *Verband Deutscher Arbeitervereine*) from Liebknecht, and a week later, after receiving a letter of confirmation from its President August Bebel, he gave the General Council further details; the Council then agreed to send a representative to the 'Conference at Nuremberg, where the question of the affiliation of the whole of the Societies, numbering 100, is to be decided'.[1]

What was the significance of this unprecedented information, reported under the Council minute-book's routine heading 'Correspondence from Germany'? What had caused Liebknecht and Bebel, after years of hesitation over the International, to make such surprising promises to affiliate the *Verband* to it? The answer is indicated by Marx's reference on 21 July to the 'General Working Men's Union' (i.e. Schweitzer's ADAV), and by Liebknecht's revelation in a letter of 17 July that he had concluded 'a sort of alliance' with his enemy Schweitzer.[2] Bebel and Liebknecht, in fact, would probably not have over-

---

[1] Minutes 21 & 28 July; Bebel to General Council 23 July, *AML*, I, p. 187.

[2] Liebknecht to Marx 17 July (*Chronik*, p. 270); *MEB*, IV, pp. 93, 95; Mayer, *Schweitzer*, pp. 208–11, *Engels*, II, p. 164.

come their deep reluctance to organise anything for the International as early as this summer of 1868, if they had not seen in Schweitzer a dangerous rival for the esteem of Marx and of German socialists in general, and if it had not seemed urgent for them to affirm publicly their adherence to the International to prevent him from further improving his position by making his own declaration first.

As recently as 1865 it would have been unthinkable that Schweitzer should try to compete with Liebknecht for the favour of Marx, once the two of them had broken with his *Social-Demokrat*. It would have been equally unthinkable that Liebknecht and Schweitzer, the sworn enemy and the apparent friend of Bismarckian Prussia, should regard themselves as competitors for the same German public (Schweitzer, after all, had concentrated on recruiting industrial workers, mainly in Prussia, who were willing to accept Bismarck's 'work of 1866' and socialism as preached by Lassalle, whereas Liebknecht, leaving socialism in the background, had appealed to South German and Saxon democrats of all social classes to join him in the struggle *against* Bismarck). It would have been quite inconceivable, finally, that either of them should expect to enhance his prestige in Germany by publicly declaring his sympathy with the International. Even in Liebknecht's anti-Prussian campaign of 1866 and his electioneering in 1867, virtually nothing had been said of the International; why then, by July 1868, did both Schweitzer and Liebknecht strive so eagerly for Marx's personal recognition, and the public recognition of the German working class, as the International's representative in Germany?

After 1866 the position of the ADAV, still the only socialist party in Germany, was less simple than during Lassalle's lifetime, or when Schweitzer had founded the *Social-Demokrat*; instead of being able to choose sides between Bismarck's government and the Progressive Party, locked in seemingly irreconcilable strife, the Lassallean leaders, as we have seen, were faced, now that the opposition had surrendered to Bismarck, by a solid-looking front of ruling class and 'National Liberals', united against all socialist demands.

In this new situation Schweitzer (who was in complete control of the party after May 1867) could no longer expect governmental concessions in return for support against the Liberals, and took a decisive step leftwards (and into outspoken independence of the government) by adopting the demands for political liberty and international conciliation which the new 'National Liberalism' seemed to be abandoning. Schweitzer's criticism of the government, indeed, was at this point so sharp that it became clear even to his most mistrustful critics that he was now much less in sympathy with Bismarck than with the oppositionist minority of the old Progressive Party, the Prussian democrats led by Jacoby, and even the politically-minded (and therefore anti-Bismarckian) elements in the *Verband Deutscher Arbeitervereine*.

The ADAV's independence, however, was to be as jealously guarded from these new allies as from the government (at least on the surface) before 1866: after July 1868, when Jacoby proposed that the apparent unity of purpose between all these groups should be expressed in a closer organisational link, Schweitzer reacted by denouncing 'permanent co-operation between socialists and non-socialists' as impossible, and by rebuking the influential Lassalleans whom Jacoby's proposal had attracted.[1]

By the summer of 1868, then, the ADAV (which, at least in economic matters, had always been purer in its socialism than the miscellaneous groups under Liebknecht and Bebel), had become visibly more radical and emphatically more independent; Schweitzer had also shown his determination to maintain his autocratic control over the party. For reasons presently to be made clear, moreover, he now felt that this control would be reinforced if he could show his followers, and the German public in general, that he was in contact with Marx and the International.

[1] Mayer, *Schweitzer*, pp. 219–20.

At the same time as the ADAV was making clear its independence of the government by taking up an uncompromisingly left-wing standpoint, the workers organised in the *Verband Deutscher Arbeitervereine* were showing that they too intended to act independently (in their case, independently of their Liberal-democratic patrons) by starting to discuss problems that were explicitly political in a spirit that was implicitly socialist. Bebel, rather than Liebknecht, had been responsible for the *Verband*'s increasing radicalism and its structural reorganisation, and it was Bebel who now took the lead in urging that only the adoption of a formal programme could end 'the political ambiguity in the Verband'. Liebknecht was at this point still anxious lest the adoption of too precise a political programme on explicitly working-class lines would disrupt the *Verband*'s alliance with the anti-Bismarckian bourgeoisie, but he was inevitably aware of Schweitzer's prestige as a firm exponent of socialism, and deeply resented his growing influence.[1]

The mutual antipathy between Liebknecht and Schweitzer, and the irreconcilability of their political views, were notorious, especially after their bitter exchange of insults in the *Reichstag* in October 1867; their rivalry continued, and Liebknecht, in order to keep on level terms with his adversary, now agreed to Bebel's argument that the forces on their side needed a more effective organisation and better-defined public aims. Bebel's search for a political programme to consolidate the *Verband*, and Liebknecht's need to strengthen his position against Schweitzer, made both of them reflect (as Schweitzer on his side was already reflecting) on the use that might be made of a closer association with the International.[2]

How had the International, ridiculed in 1865 and ignored even by Liebknecht in 1867, become by 1868 a source of prestige

[1] *AML*, I, pp. 167–9, 180; *MEB*, IV, pp. 69, 95.
[2] *Reichstag* debate of 17 October 1867, *Stenographische Berichte* . . . 1867, pp. 451–71; Mayer, *Schweitzer*, pp. 207–11; Bebel, *AML*, I, pp. 150–82 *passim*.

THE GERMAN SOCIAL DEMOCRATS

which both he and Schweitzer determinedly set out to monopolise? Three contributory causes each played a part: the publication of *Das Kapital* in September 1867; the way in which impressive news of the International's growth abroad coincided with increasing working-class radicalism inside Germany; and the steady campaign of propaganda carried on from Geneva by Johann Philipp Becker.

The publication of *Das Kapital* early in September 1867 was soon recognised as an extremely important event. Socialist conviction was becoming firmer in every branch of the German labour movement, and the prestige of natural science inspired both socialists and their opponents to seek 'scientific' support for their views. The *laissez-faire* economics of Schulze-Delitzsch, despite the attacks of Lassalle, were widely quoted as unanswerable, and socialists gave a warm welcome to Marx's 'scientific' argumentation, which offered, as one left-wing speaker put it 'a criterion, a yardstick which stands unshifting above the unleashed passions' to prove their side of the case.[1] This recognition of the book's importance was naturally encouraged by Marx's friends, particularly Engels, who undertook a campaign of propaganda for it in the German press. Reviews of the book (many of them written by Engels himself) appeared in middle-class newspapers as well as in the socialist publications controlled by Johann Philipp Becker, Schweitzer and Liebknecht, and gradually Marx's work began to achieve more prominence still, through critical replies by well-known anti-socialist economists.[2]

To say that *Das Kapital*'s importance was widely recognized among socialists, however, is not to say that the book was thoroughly understood, or even much read; the largely symbolical nature of its effectiveness at this stage is clear enough when we learn that Bebel, for instance, read it only two years later and that Liebknecht, months after its appearance, had, or so

[1] Schweichel at Nürnberg, *Hochverratsprozess*, p. 762. On the popularity of Schulze, cf. Jantke, *Der Vierte Stand*, p. 192
[2] *Marx-Engels Archiv*, I, pp. 427–62; Mayer, *Engels*, II, pp. 156–9; *MEB*, IV, pp. 28 *et seq.*, 140; Borkheim to Marx 8 October 1868 (IISG).

at least Marx thought, 'not yet read fifteen pages' of it.[1] Socialist newspapers in Germany agreed in recognising the book's importance, but almost all of them limited themselves, when publishing extracts, to the relatively uncomplicated Introduction, and even on this (with the exception of Schweitzer's *Social-Demokrat*) they attempted no detailed commentaries.[2] The significance of the book to the German public was typified in the speech, already quoted, in which Robert Schweichel commended the International's programme to the Nürnberg Congress in September 1868. He started by arguing that although the working class might be able to refute capitalistic arguments by exposing the class-determined prejudice of those who used them, the same method could also be turned against the workers:

Is not their judgment, too, clouded by self-interest and the passions of the heated struggles? Certainly, gentlemen; but there is a criterion, a yardstick which stands unshifting above the unleashed passions, and this . . . is science. Measured by this . . . the demands of the International . . . are no faults of judgment. Historical experience as well as political economy (*Volkswirthschaft*), which Karl Marx has lifted high above the economic science of the capital-party, they both stand on our side.[3]

It is noteworthy that the historical and statistical evidence with which Schweichel went on to support his assertions was taken not from *Das Kapital* but from the International's *Inaugural Address*, written by Marx in 1864 and much easier to read; but the irrefutable economic proof of the socialist movement's 'certainty of victory' (as Liebknecht again put it after Schweichel had sat down) was supposed to have been provided by *Das Kapital*. A fragmentary but widespread knowledge of the

---

[1] Marx to Engels 25 January 1868; on Bebel, cf. *AML*, I, p. 128.
[2] List of newspapers in *Chronik*, p. 261; *MEB*, IV, p. 39.
[3] Report in *Hochverratsprozess*, pp. 762-4 (Schweichel), 778-82 (Liebknecht). Cf. Becker's description of *Das Kapital* as 'this Bible of socialism, this testament of the new Gospel' (*Vorbote*, August 1868, p. 127). It was the German delegates to the International's Brussels Congress who proposed—successfully—a resolution praising 'Karl Marx's great work *Das Kapital*' (Freymond, ed., *La Première Internationale*, Vol. I, pp. 427-30).

book's message, and a universal conviction of its importance, rendered the German labour movement in 1868 liable to be impressed by the ideas and the name of the International. This process was hastened by the general political and economic evolution of Germany, and the prestige won for the International by its achievements in other European countries. The International had now made itself better-known to the European public through its two successful Congresses in Geneva and Lausanne, and was in a good position to publicise its activities, at a time when the social development of industrial Europe itself was such as to make them seem more significant.

An economic recession in 1866, accompanied by bad harvests in two successive years, produced social tensions leading to violent conflicts in one country after another. The three outstanding incidents were a major lock-out in the Parisian bronze industry in February 1867, the Geneva building-strike of March and April 1868, and the savage repression by the Belgian government of a demonstration by impoverished miners near Charleroi slightly later. In each case, although the International had not been responsible for the conflict, its General Council and local organisations took effective steps to make known the sufferings of the workers involved and to collect aid for them. These events, as well as a series of less spectacular occasions on which the International acted to collect strike-funds or to prevent effective strike-breaking, led to a great increase in public awareness of its existence and purpose; and as large sections of the ever-increasing German working class were suffering from the economic hardship affecting all Europe, there was an economic motive—as well as the purely political motive of rising disappointment with the North German Confederation —for the Germans' increasing respect for the International.[1]

Finally, the leaders of the German labour movement knew in 1868 that the International's significance had been incessantly

[1] Mayer, *Schweitzer*, p. 221; Leidigkeit, *Wilhelm Liebknecht und August Bebel*, pp. 132–3 (economic crisis); Dolléans, *Histoire du Mouvement ouvrier*, Vol. I, pp. 301–3 (Paris); Babel, 'La Première Internationale ... à Genève', pp. 310–15 (Geneva); Eichhoff, *Die Internationale Arbeiter-Association ...*, pp. 92–3 (Charleroi).

urged on the German public, and its prestige augmented, by the propaganda of Johann Philipp Becker. It has been shown in detail how his efforts since 1865 had resulted in widespread knowledge of the International's purpose; his influence had been strong not only in the Southern and Western parts of Germany untouched by Lassalleanism, but also among the most active members of the ADAV itself. By 1868, it is true, German socialists were beginning to ask themselves whether the organisational structure of Becker's Group of German-speaking Sections was suitable to German conditions, but the importance of his ideas was widely recognised, whether by Sections of the International founded from Geneva, groups of ADAV or Educational Club members, or individual subscribers to the *Vorbote*.[1]

RIVALRY BETWEEN SCHWEITZER AND LIEBKNECHT: THE ADAV'S HAMBURG CONGRESS

In these circumstances efforts to make use of the International came increasingly to preoccupy the rival leaders Schweitzer and Liebknecht. In the struggle which now ensued each of them had certain advantages: Schweitzer was right, as the letters of Marx and Engels show, in thinking he had earned their approval (however reluctant) by his capable and laudatory reception of *Das Kapital*, his unquestionably socialist reputation in economic and industrial matters, and his general energy; and Liebknecht, although realising that he was in disfavour with Marx (and even with Engels, who admitted to Marx on 2 May 1868 that Schweitzer 'put Liebknecht in the shade'), had the advantages of working in parts of Germany where

[1] A further aspect of Becker's work (which lies outside the scope of this study) was propaganda for the International in Austria, where his influence is evidenced by material in *Der Wiener Hochverratsprozess*, pp. 300–11, 495–542, 651, etc., in Brügel, *Geschichte der Oesterreichischen Sozialdemokratie*, Vols. I and II *passim*, in H. Steiner, *Zur Geschichte der österreichischen Arbeiterbewegung 1867–1888*, and in numerous letters in IISG. The favourable impression of the International's Austrian strength given to Liebknecht on his visit to Vienna (Leidigkeit, *op. cit.*, pp. 124–5) probably contributed to his decision to suggest the International's programme to the *Verband Deutscher Arbeitervereine*.

Becker's internationalist propaganda had been particularly effective, and of being pushed along, sometimes against his own will, by the clear-sighted and efficient organiser Bebel. By 1869 Liebknecht and Bebel, by turning Becker's achievements to their own advantage, could win Marx's recognition, and that of the world of socialism, as the International's leaders in Germany; but it is clear that in the early stages of the process their actions (especially Liebknecht's) were mainly inspired by fear that Schweitzer might act before them and capture the International's prestige for himself.

This fear was justified, since Schweitzer was beginning in the spring of 1868 to use his improved relations with Marx in a typically masterly way. Hearing that Marx had overruled his publisher's objections to publication of extracts from *Das Kapital* in the *Social-Demokrat*, Schweitzer found an excuse to re-open the correspondence broken off in 1865. Late in April he politely asked for Marx's advice on how the socialists in the *Reichstag* should vote in the forthcoming debate on iron tariffs. In spite of Engels' profound distrust of Schweitzer's motives, Marx sent him a reply. He was careful to limit this to the precise subject of the enquiry, and comforted Engels with the argument that Schweitzer had to be answered, being (as member of the *Reichstag* for Elberfeld) 'a representative of workers in one of the most industrialised areas'. Schweitzer, after using Marx's letter in an article on the subject, sent a reply which assured Marx that the party's 'debt' to him would be publicly acknowledged at its Congress in August, and ended flatteringly: 'I know how much I have to learn from you.'[1]

Schweitzer succeeded by this contact with Marx in securing some defence against the repeated criticism of him in Liebknecht's new *Demokratisches Wochenblatt*, and Liebknecht, now apparently realising that he would be able to carry on this criticism only at the price of taking up openly socialistic propaganda which would ruin his relations with the People's Party,

---

[1] *Social-Demokrat*, 22 January–13 May 1868; *Chronik*, p. 267; Schweitzer to Marx 29 April, 13 May, *SAR*, pp. 255–6; *MEB*, IV pp. 60–1.

THE TURNING POINT: LABOUR CONGRESSES

'found himself obliged to conclude a sort of cartel with Schweitzer.'[1]

On Liebknecht's initiative the two rivals met in Berlin late in May or early in June, and although their main purpose was to negotiate terms on which their mutual attacks could be stopped and the German labour movement united, their conversation naturally turned to the International; this body, thanks to its increased prestige in progressive circles, was the obvious touchstone by which the respective professions of the two men could be tested.[2]

Liebknecht and Schweitzer, it was clear, could give a public guarantee of their good faith by agreeing to work together 'in the spirit' of the International. But what exact form could this guarantee take? And in what form did they in fact agree to declare their allegiance to the International? A year later, when Liebknecht appeared at the International's Basle Congress as representative of the newly-founded Eisenach Party, he asserted that he and Schweitzer had agreed to affiliate respectively the *Verband Deutscher Arbeitervereine* and the ADAV to the International as constituent organisations; and that whereas the *Verband* at Nürnberg had fulfilled this promise by 'accepting the programme of the International', the ADAV had not: 'Schweitzer gave me his word of honour—and broke it.' Liebknecht, however, was exaggerating when he claimed that Schweitzer had promised to 'affiliate his *Verein* to the International'; this claim is intrinsically implausible because of the notorious illegality of such corporate affiliations under the

[1] Marx to Engels 29 July 1868, *MEB*, IV, p. 95. Criticism of Schweitzer in *Demokratisches Wochenblatt* 8 February, 15 February, 7 March 1868; Mayer, *Schweitzer*, pp. 208–11; *Engels*, II, p. 164.

[2] Liebknecht later said that he had been encouraged to meet Schweitzer 'by friends, in the interest of unity' (*Hochverratsprozess*, p. 247); one of the friends was probably Karl Hirsch (still a member of the ADAV, though also a contributor to Liebknecht's newspaper), who told the Berlin *Arbeiterverein* on 8 June that Liebknecht's meeting with Schweitzer had led to 'an understanding' (Mayer, *Schweitzer* p. 217). This confirms Liebknecht's own statement that the meeting took place 'in spring' (*Hochverratsprozess*, p. 869); Engels' remark of 24 September that it took place 'noch nicht 4 Monate' previously (*MEB*, IV, p. 119) also dates it in late May or early June. Leidigkeit (p. 135) thus seems mistaken in placing it 'in the first days of July', though it was not until July that Liebknecht told Marx of the meeting.

Prussian Combination Laws, and is in any case contradicted by Liebknecht's private account to Marx of his negotiations with Schweitzer. He said simply that Schweitzer had promised to 'recognise' Marx and the International, and this is obviously as far as the undertakings went.[1]

The ADAV congress in Hamburg did in fact give extensive 'recognition' both to Marx's work and to the importance of the International; Schweitzer had found no difficulty in promising this to Liebknecht, because he knew that the socialist doctrines of Marx and the International would be more welcome to his own followers than to the anti-socialist members of the People's Party who were associated with Liebknecht, and because his own relations with Marx were at this time much closer than Liebknecht's. (Schweitzer wrote at least four times to Marx between April and mid-July, whereas Liebknecht's letters apparently ceased completely between January and mid-July.)

Late in June Schweitzer wrote telling Marx that 'in consideration of his quite exceptional services' to the cause of labour, he was being invited as a guest of honour to the Hamburg Congress. After Marx's letter of reply had urged the ADAV to declare its affiliation to the International and to send a delegate to the Brussels Congress in September, Schweitzer wrote again (8 July) that the 'breaches of the law' involved in formal affiliation could not be risked, but that 'we will thoroughly do away with the suspicion that we do not value the international significance of the movement', and that he would 'try to make it possible' to come in person to Brussels.[2]

In the event, this was not possible: by September, Schweitzer was busily occupied in founding Trade Unions (something which Lassalle had ignored, but which his successor found necessary in response to the labour movement's new needs in 1868, given the rapid increase in the number of industrial

[1] *MEB*, IV, p. 93; *Chronik*, p. 270; *Hochverratsprozess*, pp. 247, 869; Mayer, *Engels*, II, p. 165.
[2] *SAR*, pp. 273–4; *Chronik*, p. 269; further details of the Basle resolution's role in the dispute between the two German parties are given by Eckert, 'Zur Geschichte der Braunschweiger Sektion', *loc. cit.*, pp. 147–50.

workers, and now an unprecedented wave of strikes); and the ADAV's relations with the police were by this time so strained that its official representation at Brussels would certainly have led to catastrophe. (Its headquarters were in any case closed down by the Leipzig police in September, though they soon reopened in Berlin.)[1] On the other hand, public 'recognition' of the importance of Marx and the International could hardly have gone further than it did at the Hamburg Congress. From the flatteringly-worded invitation to Marx (which he declined, with the excuse of preparatory work for Brussels) up to the final resolution on the ADAV's 'duty...to go forward with the workers' parties of other countries', the congress showed a collective recognition of Marx's importance unparalleled in Germany at the time, and an international spirit unique in the ADAV's history. The great question of Trade Unions and strikes, which was raised by Wilhelm Bracke, a member of the International, challenged the traditional Lassallean refusal to have anything to do with activities that were not purely political. The congress resolution on this subject, inspired by Schweitzer, declared that strikes might after all 'promote the class-consciousness of the workers', train them for political action, and even abolish 'certain oppressive social evils, such as excessively long working-hours, child labour, and the like', but when Schweitzer suggested actually founding Trade Unions the Lassallean tradition was strong enough to force him (with the cigar-workers' leader F. W. Fritzsche) to do this independently of the party.

Despite such reminders of Lassalleanism, however, the International was constantly praised in the Hamburg debates, and the congress unanimously passed Schweitzer's motion that 'Karl Marx, through his work...*Capital*, has rendered an indispensable service to the working class'.[2]

[1] Mayer, *Schweitzer*, p. 239; Bebel, *AML*, II, p. 57; Schroeder, *Geschichte der Sozial-demokratischen Parteiorganisation*, pp. 9 *et seq.*

[2] *Social-Demokrat*, 14, 19, 30 August, 3 September; Mayer, *Schweitzer*, pp. 226–33; *Chronik*, p. 271; Engelberg, *loc. cit.*, pp. 654–6. Schweitzer's letter expressing solidarity with the International, addressed to the Brussels Congress, is summarised in Freymond, ed., *La Première Internationale*, Vol. I, p. 246.

It seemed that the ADAV had come very close to the International, and the Lassalleans who became prominent at the time of the Hamburg Congress—Kirchner, Fritzsche, Bracke, Karl Hirsch and Karl Klein—all had some understanding of Marxism and, as we have seen, more or less close contacts with Johann Philipp Becker. In fact, however, Schweitzer's *rapprochement* with the International remained superficial; he wrote to Marx in mid-September that he would 'always spread your opinions as much as possible', but his immediate concern was with the ADAV's temporary dissolution by the Leipzig police, and with his new Trade Union organisation. He did nothing to demonstrate his new-founded sympathy with the International in any concrete way, and the dictatorial constitution of his Trade Unions soon revived the extreme disapproval of Marx.[1]

From October onwards Schweitzer lost the advantage he had seemed to possess over Liebknecht, and the ADAV's striking *rapprochement* with the International became less significant in itself than for its wider repercussions. Inside the ADAV the results of Schweitzer's tactics were felt only in 1869, when the group of socialists encouraged by his line at Hamburg resented their later disappointment keenly enough to break away. On Liebknecht, however, the effects of Schweitzer's manoeuvres were immediate and drastic: he was forced to make decisions and to take steps which were at this stage most unwelcome to him—though of course this did not prevent him, when their consequences proved fortunate, from claiming that he had planned them all the time.

LIEBKNECHT'S RESPONSE: THE NÜRNBERG CONGRESS
OF THE *Verband Deutscher Arbeitervereine*
Liebknecht's reluctance to take up Schweitzer's challenge is shown by his move in negotiating for an 'armistice' with him in May or June which would, he hoped, make steps to alter the

[1] Schweitzer to Marx 15 September; Marx to Schweitzer 13 October, *SAR*, pp. 277, 279–81.

status quo unnecessary. His own claim, that he now promised Schweitzer that he and Bebel would affiliate the *Verband Deutscher Arbeitervereine* to the International, has been shown to be implausible, to say the least: for one thing, any such affiliation would have been illegal; for another, Bebel was still uncertain as late as July whether even the committee of the *Verband* would accept the International's programme;[1] and thirdly, Liebknecht was still unhappy about the possible effect on his allies in the People's Party of an open demonstration for the International. Liebknecht, in fact, cannot have told Schweitzer in the spring of 1868 that the *Verband* would give the International anything more than the symbolical 'recognition' which was also to come from the ADAV, and there he would have been content to let the matter rest.

Far from acting, in Franz Mehring's phrase, as 'the German apostle of the International', impatient to secure the *Verband*'s affiliation, Liebknecht now ignored the International for two months, becoming active again only when he learned from Bebel that the *Verband* would certainly adopt a precise programme of some kind at its Nürnberg Congress in September. For Bebel, the main issue was the strengthening of the *Verband*, and its transformation from a loosely-organised educational federation into an actively political body, united on the basis of some kind of radical programme; the programme's actual contents were relatively immaterial.[2] The question arises: what was it that made Bebel choose to put forward the programme of the International (rather than that of the Saxon People's Party, which he had considered after Leopold Sonnemann—certainly no socialist—had refused his original request

[1] *AML*, I, p. 182.
[2] *Ibid.*, pp. 180, 182, where Bebel discusses the rumour that he was intending to but forward the (Chemnitz) programme of the Saxon People's Party. Liebknecht contributed to this rumour by reprinting this programme next to his notice calling on clubs to elect their delegates to Nürnberg (*Demokratisches Wochenblatt* No. 27, 4 July 1868). The surprise when Bebel put forward the programme of the International (*Deutsche Arbeiterhalle* No. 13, 12 July) should be attributed to his own previous uncertainty rather than to any determination to force this programme on the *Verband* by deceit (as it is by Eyck, *Der Verband Deutscher Arbeitervereine*, p. 86).

to draft a programme)? The answer seems to be: Liebknecht's alarm when he realised that Schweitzer, through his correspondence with Marx, threatened to give the ADAV a monopoly of the International's prestige in Germany, and his realisation that the *Verband* must forestall this by acting first.[1] Thanks to the energy of Schweitzer on one side and of Bebel on the other, Liebknecht at last found himself taking active steps on behalf of the International—though his role during the proceedings which led up to the Nürnberg Congress was still subordinate to Bebel's.

From an organisational point of view, what Bebel and Liebknecht did at Nürnberg was to 'capture' the organisation built up since 1865 by Johann Philipp Becker, and to start the destruction of his influence in Germany. Their dependence on his work is shown by the extent to which they relied on him for information and help in the early stages of the process (though they afterwards tried to deny or hide the extent of this reliance). The first proposal to adopt the programme of the International had come from the *Arbeiterbildungsverein* of Dresden, whose president Vahlteich was one of Becker's correspondents, and when Bebel decided in July to support the Dresden proposal in the *Verband*'s committee, it was to Becker that he turned for help.[2]

Bebel wrote to Geneva in mid-July explaining that 'the Dresden *Verein* has proposed that we attach ourselves to the programme and organisation of the International Working Men's Association', and asking for documentary material, as the committee wanted to let the affiliated clubs 'debate the thing thoroughly': he asked Becker to send him two hundred copies of the General Statutes, and the first few numbers of the

[1] Bebel to Becker 16 July 1868 (IISG) makes clear Liebknecht's enthusiasm for the programme of the International—the earliest evidence of such enthusiasm.
[2] The *Verband*'s committee decided for the programme of the International on 7 July (*Deutsche Arbeiterhalle*, 12 July), and the drafting of a version suitable for Germany was entrusted to Robert Schweichel, a friend and journalistic colleague of Liebknecht's (Bebel, *AML*, I, p. 180). On Vahlteich's connection with Becker, see Chapter III above, and on his more recent connection with Marx (via Eichhoff), see Gemkow, *loc. cit.*, p. 524.

1866 *Vorbote* containing Becker's opening 'programme-article' *Was Wir Wollen und Sollen*, as 'I want to get it reprinted in the *Demokratisches Wochenblatt* and in the *Arbeiterhalle* [the organ of the *Verband*]'. Bebel did indeed warn Becker that the *Verband*'s affiliation to the International could only take a collective form, as they could not 'oblige each separate club to join as a Section and to pay the full subscription', and as Liebknecht had assured them that 'simple affiliation, with acceptance of the programme and of any form of organisation ... suitable to German conditions' would be enough; but by his repeated use of the word 'affiliation' and by his pressing invitation to Becker to come to Nürnberg in person, he implied that in return for Becker's help and information the *Verband* would regard itself as enrolled in the International under the aegis of his committee in Geneva.[1]

The fifth congress of the *Verband Deutscher Arbeitervereine*, which assembled at Nürnberg on 5 September, was notable both for the record number of delegates attending (there were 115 of them, representing about 13,000 members) and for a general atmosphere of excitement. Both were due—as several speakers pointed out in the first evening's debate—to the presence of 'the programme-question' as the first item on the agenda. Several delegates—some of them obviously sympathisers of the National Liberal Party, others perhaps genuinely non-political —tried hard to postpone or prevent discussion of the 'programme-question', and Sonnemann argued that to avoid the *Verband*'s complete disintegration, the question should go to a committee containing representatives of all viewpoints. The congress, however (which had elected Bebel as chairman by 69 votes out of 94 cast), rejected Sonnemann's proposal with shouts of 'No compromises!', and insisted on deciding the

---

[1] Bebel to Becker 16 July 1868 (IISG). The version given by Bebel (*AML*, I, pp. 182–3) has omissions and distortions which hide the extent both of his debt and of his promises to Becker; the request for Becker's help is omitted, and Bebel's original assurance that the *Verband* was agreed 'about affiliation to the International' ('*wegen Anschlusses an d.I.Ar.Ass.*': Bebel's abbreviations) is weakened in the published version to read 'with regard to our relationship to the Internationale' ('*in Bezug auf das Verhältnis zur Internationale*').

'programme-question' even if it split the organisation in two.[1]
The result, after a day's vigorous debate, was that the clubs
represented, by a majority of 61 against 32 (whose delegates
thereupon walked out of the congress), accepted as the *Verband*'s
programme four paragraphs from the Preamble to the International's Statutes, written by Marx in 1864. The *Verband*'s
new programme accordingly committed it to the proposition
that 'the emancipation of the working class must be the task
of the working class itself', to condemnation of 'the worker's
economic dependence on the monopolist of the means of
production', to the belief that 'political freedom is the essential
precondition for the economic emancipation of the working
class', and to calling for 'a fraternal bond of unity between the
working classes of different countries'.

On the basis of these paragraphs the *Verband* declared 'its
adherence to the aims of the International Working Men's
Association', and thus adopted 'a definite political programme'
which could be broadly summed up as 'social-democratic'; its
supporters described it as 'detailed and clear', and its opponents
as 'useless' or 'too far-reaching', but all were agreed that it
represented a new departure for the *Verband Deutscher Arbeitervereine*—'a political programme'.[2]

The preceding debate had been confused, however, and this
seems to have happened partly because Bebel and his fellow
committee-members failed to agree until shortly before the
congress on the wording of the programme, or indeed on what
'the programme of the International' actually was. The four
paragraphs written by Marx in 1864, which were finally
adopted, had indeed been published on 25 August in the
Deutsche Arbeiterhalle and on 29 August in the *Demokratisches
Wochenblatt* as the committee's proposal on the 'programme-
question'; but for a month already Bebel and his colleagues had
been propagating Johann Philipp Becker's article of 1866,
Was Wir Wollen und Sollen, and describing it to their readers as

---

[1] Nürnberg report in *Hochverratsprozess*, pp. 758–60.
[2] *Ibid.*, pp. 775, 776, 789; the new programme, *ibid.*, pp. 782–3.

'the programme of the International Working Men's Association'.[1] Bebel's letter to Becker of 16 July, already quoted, makes clear the two reasons why this was done: first, Bebel regarded Becker as the International's official representative for Germany, and depended on him automatically as a source of information and documentation; and secondly, Bebel was convinced, at least when he wrote his letter of 16 July, that Becker's article was in fact 'the programme of the International'.[2] Some of the delegates at Nürnberg were thus arguing on the basis of Becker's 'programme', and others on that of the passage from Marx finally proposed by the committee. (The International's *Inaugural Address*, on the other hand—also written by Marx in 1864—was clearly unknown to most of them, and despite its inclusion in Eichhoff's book on the International, published on 1 August, its influence appeared only in the platform-speeches of Schweichel and Liebknecht, and in a contribution from Hermann Greulich of Zürich.)[3]

An attempt was made during the debate to explain that Becker's article was not in fact the 'programme of the International', but this was of little importance to the delegates.[4] The main point of 'the programme-question' was whether the *Verband* should or should not adopt any political programme at

[1] The Committee's proposal (Marx's text) in *Deutsche Arbeiterhalle* 25 August, and *Demokratisches Wochenblatt* 29 August; Becker's article in the former journal 27 July and 12 August, and in the latter 1, 8, 15 August (originally in *Vorbote*, January 1866, pp. 1–8).
[2] Bebel's erroneous impression that Becker's article was 'the programme of the International' is confirmed by his letter of 23 August 1868 to the General Council (*AML*, I, p. 187, reprinted—with the omission of the relevant passage—by Leidigkeit, *loc. cit.*, p. 140). Marx was thus mistaken in accusing Liebknecht of forcing on the congress 'the confused wishy-washy of Becker' in order to remain on good terms with the People's Party (*MEB*, IV, p. 111).
[3] Eichhoff's book, containing the *Inaugural Address* and other material by Marx, appeared in time to be advertised in the *Demokratisches Wochenblatt* on 1 August, and commended by Bebel in the *Arbeiterhalle* on 25 August. The *Address* had already appeared in German in the *Social-Demokrat* at the end of 1864 (as described in Chapter II), in the first numbers of the *Vorbote*, alongside Becker's own programme (January-March 1866), and (as described in Chapter IV) in Liebknecht's *Mitteldeutsche Volkszeitung* a few months later. Interesting details of Eichhoff's publication are given by Gemkow, *loc. cit.*, pp. 524–5.
[4] *Hochverratsprozess*, pp. 767, 769.

all; and 'the programme of the International' came into the discussion not because the International as an organisation was of any great interest (except to a few leaders like Liebknecht, Bebel, Schweichel and Vahlteich) but because it was vaguely regarded as a natural source of socialist, or more precisely, working-class political principles—'the outpost of labour, the pioneer of the great social labour movement of our time', as even Venedey, an opponent, described it.

None of the speakers was able to question the gravity of 'the social problem', as Schweichel had depicted it in an opening speech based partly on the International's *Inaugural Address*; the debate concentrated on the question (raised in the *Arbeiterhalle* and *Demokratisches Wochenblatt* before the congress even met) of whether the *Verband* should strive to solve problems of social injustice by adopting a political programme. As Liebknecht summed it up: 'the main point in dispute . . . is the indivisibility of the political movement and the social movement'. His own argument was that 'only the state can solve the social question . . . but the state today is in the hands of the propertied classes: it is class-rule, politically organised. . . . Because the social question and the political question are indivisible, the interests of the working class demand that they separate themselves politically from those who are their enemies socially.'

Much of Liebknecht's speech consisted of such (for him) unusually sharp formulations of purely proletarian and socialist demands; in concluding, however, he reverted to his more usual call for a united movement of all democrats, whether socialist or not: '...democratic and socialistic are for me altogether identical expressions, and as the workers form the great part of the democratic army...the democratic People's Party must simply unite itself with the democratic workers' party'.[1]

The purpose of the Nürnberg Congress was thus, for Liebknecht, to strengthen the forces of 'greater-German' democracy, and at the same time to give more weight in its programme to 'the social question', which, as he said, 'poses itself wherever

[1] *Ibid.*, pp. 780–2.

the German question is discussed'. The name of the International Working Men's Association had been invoked, and its principles recognised, in order to give Liebknecht an answer to the accusations of his rival Schweitzer that he was interested exclusively in political questions, to the neglect of socialism. There were several reasons, however, why Liebknecht and Bebel, although they needed to use the International's name, could not turn the *Verband Deutscher Arbeitervereine* into an effective part of its organisation.

First, as a speaker at Nürnberg pointed out, close links with the International might mean 'legal difficulties and collisions with the authorities' in Germany;[1] secondly, the *Verband*'s leaders had to use all their limited financial and administrative resources for developing their own organisation; and thirdly, if they identified themselves too closely with the International, the non-socialist leaders of the People's Party, such as Sonnemann, would abandon them.[2]

As things were, the People's Party, following the hint given by Liebknecht at Nürnberg, proceeded in its turn (at its Stuttgart Congress later in September) to declare its own 'adherence' to the programme newly adopted by the *Verband*. This decision was made possible by the leftward evolution of the

[1] Hochberger's speech, *ibid.*, p. 776.

[2] How little the *Verband* thought of joining actively in the work of the International is shown not only by Bebel's private assurance to Lange that 'joining the International could not be thought of until we have put our own house in order' (letter of 22 June, *AML*, I, p. 185), but also by the progressive dilution of the programme's wording on organisation, before the Congress finally adopted it. Vahlteich's original motion on behalf of the Dresden *Verein* had been that the Congress should 'adhere to the programme and organisation of the International . . .', and recommend the clubs represented to re-constitute themselves as Sections of the above-mentioned body' (*Arbeiterhalle*, 12 July; *Vorbote*, July, p. 105). As published by Bebel before the Congress the draft resolution read simply that the *Verband* should 'make the programme of the International . . . its own, and in accordance with it' declare its belief in certain enumerated political and social principles (*Arbeiterhalle*, 25 August). Finally, in the version presented by Bebel to the actual Congress, even the reference to the International programme becoming the *Verband*'s 'own' was dropped, and it simply declared 'its agreement in the following points with the programme of the International Working Men's Association', before going on to quote the relevant sections of Marx's preamble—though not of the International's organisational statutes (*Hochverratsprozess*, p. 782).

People's Party under the influence of Jacoby, by its own international connections, and by the general realisation that the party was now so weak that it virtually depended on the *Verband Deutscher Arbeitervereine* for survival.[1] The decision ensured that co-operation between the two organisations would not be broken by the nominal acceptance of an explicitly proletarian programme in Nürnberg, and also that the *Verband*, despite its new programme, did not evolve yet into an unmistakably socialist party—an evolution which at this stage was desired as little by Bebel and Liebknecht as by the People's Party leaders such as Sonnemann.[2] Bebel and Liebknecht had made use of the International's name for the purposes for which they needed it, and they did not intend to let the Nürnberg decision imply the abandonment of the People's Party for a course of undiluted socialism.

Bebel claimed that he and Liebknecht, as a result of the Nürnberg Congress, found themselves at the head of 'a socialist party, which stood on the basis of the International'; but the *Verband*'s inadequacy as a branch of the International is indicated by the contempt of Marx and Engels, its failure to win a convincingly socialist reputation is suggested by the persisting vitality and popularity of the ADAV under Schweitzer, and both confirmed by the continued effectiveness and importance in the German labour movement of Becker's organisation based on Geneva.[3]

Although the *Verband*'s position was so equivocal, Liebknecht

[1] Mayer, 'Die Trennung', pp. 33–42.

[2] Sonnemann's attempts to keep the two organisations together are described in a letter from Schoeppler (Mainz) to Becker, 18 October 1868 (IISG).

[3] Bebel, AML I, p. 193; the ADAV's strength is shown by its membership increase from 8,192 in August 1868 to 12,135 in March 1869 (Müller, *Geschichte der Lithographen*, p. 279). The contrast between Marx's public and private views of the Nürnberg Congress is, as usual, striking: in telling the General Council of it on 22 September he optimistically added that 'a committee of 16 had been appointed to carry out the resolution and to act as the Executive Committee of the International Association in Germany' (Minutes, II, p. 153), but to Engels he had expressed the very different view that 'Liebknecht in Nürnberg has been guilty of an action quite useless (and even contrary to the statutes) in forcing Becker's confused wishy-washy on them as "the programme of the International"' (*MEB*, IV, p. 111).

now urged Marx to issue a proclamation in the name of the General Council, confirming his own position as representative of the International in Germany and condemning Schweitzer as a traitor. Marx refused, partly because of Liebknecht's ambiguous relationship with the People's Party, and partly because he and Bebel, despite the Nürnberg resolution, were doing nothing active for the International's cause in Germany; they had used Becker's help in preparing their congress (the latter's correspondents—Vahlteich, Kirchner, Hirsch and Bremer—had also played a leading part), and although Marx was scarcely pleased to find Becker's 1866 article being described as the 'programme of the International', he was annoyed when the Germans failed to do anything in return.[1]

The General Council did indeed provide Liebknecht, on 22 September 1868, with a 'mandate' appointing him as 'its correspondent and representative',[2] but this gave him no authority to denounce Schweitzer in the International's name, and he was too busy to make any other use of it. His indifference to the International, indeed, was confirmed during the winter of 1868–9, when a group of coal-miners from Lugau (in his own *Reichstag* constituency) wrote to Marx applying to join the International, 'of which they had read in various newspapers and in a book by W. Eichhoff'. Marx gave them the necessary information, enrolled them as members, and persuaded the General Council to endorse a long report (written by Engels) on the injustices of the compulsory insurance-schemes in the Saxon mines, which was then published in several British and German newspapers. To Engels, however, he wrote angrily (in March 1869) that 'Wilhelm and Co. haven't taken a single step, since the Nürnberg Congress, as far as the International is concerned, so that the poor devils in Lugau felt they had to

---

[1] *Chronik*, p. 273; Mayer, *Engels*, II, p. 165; the German's reliance on Becker is further shown by an appeal for his help from the circulation-manager of the *Demokratisches Wochenblatt*, 15 October 1868 (IISG).

[2] Text of the 'mandate' in *Wilhelm Liebknecht: Briefwechsel mit Karl Marx und Friedrich Engels*, pp. 90–1.

write directly to London'.[1] Marx and Engels did not always show enough understanding of Liebknecht's difficulties, but their accusation that he gave little attention to the International was quite justified.

Liebknecht's public assurances that members of the International in Germany should not be called on to pay any 'particular contributions', and that 'simple affiliation, with acceptance of the programme' would be enough, also led to tension with Geneva. Liebknecht may have believed, as he complained to Marx, that Becker's 'financial administration and accounting for money' were not impeccable, but Becker felt for his part that the precarious finances of his organisation were threatened by Liebknecht's renewed announcements that membership of the International cost nothing, and that 'anyone could join without paying'.[2]

The Nürnberg Congress, with its claim to set up a new organisation representing the International in Germany, was bound sooner or later to create rivalry between Liebknecht and Becker, the President of all the German-speaking Sections; and in such questions as this one of finance, the conflict began to appear. It was not yet serious, however, because in 1868–9, as the Lugau affair showed, Bebel and Liebknecht did not intend to assert their right to represent the International to the point where it conflicted with Becker's own jurisdiction. Their threat

[1] Report by Marx to General Council 24 November 1868 (Minutes, II, p. 160–1) and letter of Engels 29 March 1869 (*MEB*, IV, p. 210). Engels' report (in Marx-Engels-Lenin-Stalin, *Zur Deutschen Geschichte*, Vol. II, pp. 860–6) was debated by the General Council on 23 February 1869 (Minutes, II, p. 180). Numbers of new members are unknown: a letter of 6 January 1869 from Lugau to the General Council (Jung-*Nachlass*, IISG) lists twenty-seven applicants 'to join the International . . . as direct members'. There were more than this, but Becker's reports of enrolments running into thousands (*Vorbote*, February 1869, p. 26) are of course greatly exaggerated. The episode is discussed in the book by Engelberg, Rössler, and Wächtler: *Zur Geschichte der sächsischen Bergarbeiterbewegung* (Berlin, 1954), which has unfortunately been unobtainable.

[2] Liebknecht's statements were reported by Bebel to Becker 16 July 1868 (IISG), by Marx to Engels 5 December 1868, and in the General Council on 15 December 1868 (Minutes, II, p. 164). His complaint about Becker (who indeed published no systematic accounts after June 1868) is mentioned by Marx to Engels 28 January 1869 (*MEB*, IV, p. 181).

to this jurisdiction, though it was to be decisive when it came, was still veiled.

BECKER'S PROBLEMS IN 1868–9:
GERMANY, SWITZERLAND—AND BAKUNIN

In 1868–9, indeed, the Group of German-speaking Sections enjoyed such an expansion in Germany that the Nürnberg Congress seemed to have had no effect on its previous rate of growth. Four delegates from German Sections played an active part in the International's Brussels Congress of September 1868, and if the Nürnberg Congress had not been meeting at the ame time, Becker's efforts would have ensured the presence of others.[1]

After the Congresses of the summer of 1868, the International's Sections and individual members all over Germany continued to look to Geneva for leadership. The sums of money which Becker received this winter in subscriptions and donations from Germany were slightly smaller than during the summer, but the quantity of his correspondence continued to increase.[2] Some of his letters came from individual members and supporters of the International—Kugelmann in Hanover, Martini in Kaukehmen, Meincke in Hamburg—but most were from flourishing Sections founded by Becker in 1866 or 1867, from Sections which had already led a nominal existence but which now became more active, or in some cases from Sections founded for the first time after Nürnberg.

From Magdeburg, for instance, Bremer wrote frequently throughout the spring of 1869, reporting that the local 'Workers' Social Reform League', with a programme based on that of the International, had about 2,000 members, that its meetings attracted as many as 3,000 or 5,000 people, and that it was

---

[1] Freymond, *La Première Internationale*, Vol. I, pp. 239–447 *passim*; Bremer (Magdeburg) to Becker 5 January 1869.

[2] Financial details in *Vorbote* and Appendix II below; the surviving letters from Germany in Becker's *Nachlass* (IISG) total 6 from 1864, 29 from 1865, 60 from 1866, 73 from 1867, 100 each from 1868 and 1869, 60 from 1870, 41 from 1871, and 10 from 1872.

considering putting up its own candidates at the next *Reichstag* elections. Bremer was determined to remain neutral at this stage in the struggle between Schweitzer's party and the followers of Bebel and Liebknecht; to him they all seemed 'good social-democrats', and it was not until July 1869 (when Becker had probably made clear his own preference, on balance, for Liebknecht) that Bremer wrote to say that he and his friends were also working against Schweitzer, and to ask Becker to come to the Eisenach Congress.[1]

Another active Section was that of Mainz, which held meetings sometimes in its own name and sometimes under the more cautious title of 'Social Democratic Club'. It was represented at the Brussels Congress by the carpenter Schoeppler, and it must have been he who advised the local Carpenters' Union to apply for membership of the International early in 1869. The International's members in Mainz were prompt in paying their subscriptions to Geneva and in responding to Becker's appeals on behalf of Swiss strikers, and Paul Stumpf, the most active of them (he had been a member of the Communist League in 1848), kept Becker informed of the continuing struggle between Schweitzer and Liebknecht, urging him to take sides more openly in favour of the latter.[2]

In Cologne and Braunschweig, although the majority of Becker's correspondents were still active in the Lassallean party, they paid contributions to the International, and took an obvious pride in belonging to it: Heinrichs of Cologne wrote in October 1868, when the ADAV was temporarily banned by the police, that this would oblige its members 'one and all to come over to the International', and when the ban was after all lifted he wrote (1 April 1869) that 'the idea' of the Inter-

[1] Bremer to Becker 5 January, 2 February, 13 May, 22 July 1869; *Vorbote*, May 1869. Cf. Dlubek, Rolf & Herrmann, Ursula, 'Die Magdeburger Sektion der I. Internationale' in *Beiträge zur Geschichte der deutschen Arbeiterbewegung*, Vol. IV, (1962), Sonderheft, pp. 189–218.
[2] Schoeppler to Becker 8 October 1868; 'Die Gewerkschaft der Schreiner in Mainz an den Vorstand der I.A.A. in Genf' 6 January 1869; Schott to Becker 2 August 1868; Goebel to Becker 3 February 1869; Stumpf to Becker 6 January 1869, etc.

national was still making progress through the local members' work in the ADAV and the Trade Unions; in Braunschweig, early in May, a mass-meeting was persuaded by Bracke and Lüdecke to vote a fiery motion of sympathy with Belgian strikers killed and wounded by the military authorities, which closed with the words: 'Workers of the world, unite! Long live the social-democratic Republic!', and showed that Bracke, though still treasurer of the ADAV, thought in more radical terms than his leader Schweitzer.[1]

In Solingen again, Becker's correspondent Klein was still active in the ADAV (in fact, with Fritzsche, he became a Vice-President of Schweitzer's new trade-union organisation), but he remained in contact with Becker, he joined with other members of the International to defend it against a propaganda campaign run by the Countess Hatzfeldt, and he continued to increase the local sales of the *Vorbote*.[2]

In Barmen and Leipzig, two places where Becker's success, despite considerable correspondence, had so far been limited, lively Sections were now in existence, started in each case by groups of workers who felt that the deadlock between Schweitzer and his opponents could only be broken by common efforts in the name of the International—a striking echo from below of the professions made by the rival leaders from above: from Barmen, for instance, after a preliminary request for the programme and statues of the International, Becker heard from Gustav Werth (11 April 1869) that about twenty local socialists, who disagreed with Schweitzer, wanted to join the International 'as there would be no point here in founding a club on Bebel's model'; in Leipzig, Becker was in touch with the bookbinder Ernst Werner, who made it clear (12 April) that he considered Liebknecht's attack on Schweitzer at the recent Elberfeld

---

[1] Text in *Vorbote*, May 1869, p. 74; a copy (perhaps sent by Bracke to the General Council?) in Jung's *Nachlass* (IISG). The social democrats of Braunschweig and Wolfenbüttel had already sent a telegram of greetings to the Brussels Congress in September 1868: Freymond, *op. cit.*, Vol. I, p. 438.

[2] From 1869 until his death in 1871 Becker's main correspondent in Solingen was Fritz Moll, many of whose letters are in IISG.

congress a mistake, and that the 'group of the most intelligent workers' who now joined the International in Leipzig did so to break the deadlock between the rival leaders. (Werner, incidentally, was also in correspondence with Marx, but this was mainly on the limited question of co-operation between British and German Trade Unions, whereas with Becker he discussed general political problems. Shortly before the Eisenach Congress of August 1869 he foresaw that it might mean the end of the ADAV, but he still thought the new party-organisation to be created in Germany should be firmly under the control of the International, as represented by Becker; it was only at the Congress itself, as will be seen, that he changed his mind.)[1]

Completely new Sections were started at this time, nominally at least, in Siegburg near Bonn (where Becker's correspondent was the first working-class Marxist philosopher, the tanner Joseph Dietzgen), and in Lörrach in Baden, where groups of textile workers were roused to action in the winter of 1868–9, apparently by the strikes in nearby Basle.[2]

From Berlin came steady contributions (both from the Section and from the Carpenters' Union) for the strike-funds and the general treasury of the International, and a request for

[1] Werner to Becker 28 July 1869, and many other letters from Leipzig and Barmen; *Chronik*, pp. 279, 281.

[2] Siegburg, cf. *Vorbote*, November 1868, January 1869; Dietzgen to Becker 6 November 1868, 10 January; F. Ellinger (Uckerath) to Becker 28 April 1870; Dietzgen's autobiography in Marx, *Briefe an Kugelmann*, pp. 48–51. The foundation of the Lörrach Section (October 1868) was announced in *Vorbote*, November 1868, p. 176. For further details the writer is indebted to Professor Dr Ernst Engelberg for the kind loan of his notes on material in the Baden public archives relating to the Lörrach Section (Badisches Generallandesarchiv, Zugang 1924, Nr. 56, entitled *Die Internationale Arbeiter-Association betreffend*). Apart from many details of the weavers' strike in Basle, the documents record the Lörrach Section's foundation, its early holding of well-attended meetings in nearby villages, and the growing disquiet of local textile-employers at its expansion. (The names of 113 members are given—these lists were circulated among the employers—and some meetings are said to have been attended by up to 150 men.) The Section was dissolved by the authorities as early as December 1868, and although it reconstituted itself in June 1869 to debate an address to the Grand Duke demanding 'free right of association and public meeting, as well as the repeal of the Combination Laws', it was never again very active, and the occasional strikes which broke out in the summer of 1871 seem to have been unsuccessful.

Becker's views—and for Marx's—on the accusations made by Bebel against Schweitzer.[1] There also came a noteworthy confirmation of Becker's authority: the President of the Berlin *Arbeiterbildungsverein*, Robert Krebs, had spoken against the programme proposed by Bebel at Nürnberg, but he enraged Wilhelm Eichhoff and other Berlin socialists by insisting that he still regarded himself as a loyal member of the International; Eichhoff's protest to Marx provoked the answer that Krebs had been enrolled by Becker's authority and it was therefore Becker who had to publish—as he did—an announcement that Krebs had failed to comply with 'the obligations laid upon him by the statutes', and was therefore expelled from the International.[2]

Among the workers of Nürnberg itself, Becker's continued activity produced a strange epilogue to the congress which the *Verband* had recently held there, an epilogue which in 1870 was to influence the relations between the International and the whole Eisenach Party. The majority of the Nürnberg *Arbeiterbildungsverein*'s members, for a start, were dissatisfied with the ambiguous attitude to the International which the *Verband* had now adopted. Early in November 1868 Becker received a letter from one of them, Conrad Rüll, who assured him that their *Verein* would 'unanimously' declare itself a Section of the International if only the Bavarian Combination Laws allowed it; instead two dozen of them joined as individual members, *Vorbote* articles and the Brussels congress-resolutions were discussed and propagated, and groups of sympathisers were soon started in the Bavarian towns around Nürnberg—Fürth, Augsburg, Bamberg, and Hof. These consisted of socialists who mistrusted the pro-Prussian sympathies of Schweitzer, but were repelled by the 'social indecisiveness' and the 'confusing

---

[1] Letters to Becker from G. Liebkert, 21 February 1869; Reimann 21 October 1868, 1 April 1869, 5 August 1869.

[2] Eichhoff to Becker 24 October; *Vorbote*, October 1868, p. 160. Gemkow's article, *loc. cit.*, pp. 527–30, adds interesting details on the repercussions of the Nürnberg resolution in Berlin, but errs in attributing Krebs' expulsion to the General Council rather than to Becker.

federalism' of Liebknecht's *Demokratisches Wochenblatt*, which seemed, as Steinbacher of Augsburg put it, quite out of place in 'a subsidiary organ of the International'.[1]

Early in March 1869 Rüll wrote again from Nürnberg, asking Becker's advice on how to deal with an imminent visit by Lassallean speakers who were trying to secure the allegiance of Bavarian socialists to the ADAV. Becker's detailed reply— which is of great interest as virtually his only surviving letter to a local leader in Germany—argued that 'in both camps (i.e. in Schweitzer's and his rivals') there is something rotten, though again each...is in some respects ahead of the other'. Schweitzer, continued Becker, abused the appeal of nationalism, and 'betrayed political freedom', but against this the Lassalleans had 'more socialist fire' than their rivals, and were at least clear about the importance of 'the conflict between proletariat and bourgeoisie, i.e. class-consciousness'; Liebknecht and Bebel, on the other hand, were satisfactorily energetic in the political field, but were 'caught up in too much particularism', and through their collaboration with '*spiessbürgerlichen Elementen*', were 'prisoners of the illusion that the socialist proletariat and the democratic bourgeoisie could have a common aim and could bring anything into the world but a monster'. Becker explained that to destroy Schweitzer's harmful influence, German socialists would have to take the initiative effectively against him, 'which unfortunately Liebknecht and Bebel have so far failed to do'; the eventual reunification of the two factions, he said, would become progressively more feasible as more of their members found common ground by joining the International as individual members and subscribing to the *Vorbote*. He therefore advised the Bavarian socialists to remain independent both of Schweitzer and of Liebknecht, relying for the time being on the pure socialist message of the International,

---

[1] Rüll to Becker 5 November, 4 December 1868, 3 March 1869. Letters to Becker from Löwenstein (Fürth) 28 March, 29 April 1869; Steinbacher (Augsburg) 31 January 1869; Vollrath (Hof) 10 July 1870; circular of July 1869 from Bamberg, cited below, p. 157.

'which keeps itself free from such failings' as those which he ascribed to both the German parties.[1] In July, when the struggle in Germany was reaching its climax with the gathering of all Schweitzer's critics at the Eisenach Congress, the International's members in Nürnberg acted on Becker's advice: holding themselves aloof from the nationally-significant developments which had resulted, as will be seen, from a new split in the ADAV, the self-appointed 'Secretaries of the Social Democratic Party in Bavaria', Rüll and Karl Hirsch, sent out a circular calling a congress in Nürnberg for the establishment of a separate 'social-democratic party embracing all Bavaria', whose members were to 'recognise the principles of the International'.[2]

The effects of this step were not apparent for some time, as the labour movement in Bavaria had always been somewhat independent of national organisations, and the Eisenach Congress overshadowed the meeting called in Nürnberg, as well as the various trade-union conferences—separate ones for engineering workers, carpenters, etc.—which the Bavarians called at the same time. The new nucleus created by the Bavarian 'Internationalists', however, was already beginning to attract local Lassalleans, and when several influential ADAV members were drawn into it at the end of 1869—including Neff, the editor of the Lassalleans' Munich newspaper *Der Proletarier*—the results included first, a breach between Schweitzer and his Bavarian followers, and later—in 1870—a serious modification of the Eisenach Party's attitude towards the International.[3]

It should not be forgotten that the existence of this Bavarian group was due partly to the influence of Becker, whose authority

[1] Rüll to Becker 6 March 1869; Becker to Rüll 10 March 1869 (Copy in *Nachlass*, Nr. 3457, *Theilweise Abschrift eines am 10. März 1869 an die Sektion Nürnberg gerichteten Briefes*). The portion of Becker's letter in which he criticises Schweitzer is printed in the article by Dlubek & Herrmann, *loc. cit.*, p. 210 fn.
[2] Copies of circular (MS., 3 pp.) in Becker & Jung, *Nachlässe*, IISG (latter addressed to General Council); extract in *Vorbote*, July 1869, pp. 109–10.
[3] J. Faaz (Nürnberg) to Becker 27 June, 1869, Rüll to Becker 6 November 1869; *Vorbote*, 1869, pp. 93–5, 109; Eckert, *Aus den Anfängen der Braunschweiger Arbeiterbewegung*, p. 29; Gärtner, *Die Nürnberger Arbeiterbewegung 1868–1908*, pp. 25, 36–8.

in Germany was clearly unimpaired by the Nürnberg Congress: in some ways, the new situation actually seems to have increased it. His failure to realise the implicit threat to his position in Germany is shown by his actions in turning with renewed devotion to the labour movement in Switzerland, and in associating himself closely with Michael Bakunin.

Taking the latter first, Bakunin's explosive impact on the International cannot be discussed here at length; it is important, however, in that its effects included the distraction of Becker's attention from Germany during the crucial period between the Nürnberg and Eisenach Congresses, and his consequent failure to realise in time that his position there was being undermined.[1]

Becker and Bakunin probably met as early as September 1867, at the Geneva Peace Congress, and they may have been in contact again in March 1868; their close collaboration, however, dates only from the summer, when Bakunin (perhaps foreseeing the difficulty of persuading the League of Peace and Freedom to include socialism in its aims as well) seems already to have envisaged the anarchist grouping which in October 1868 took shape (so to speak) as the 'Alliance Internationale de la Démocratie Socialiste'.[2] One reason why Becker was attracted by Bakunin's activities was that the holding of the International's annual congress in Brussels instead of in Switzerland gave him more leisure than he had enjoyed during the two previous summers; in any case, he was enraptured by the idea that 'Russian idealism' would rejuvenate the International in Switzerland, and even, so Bakunin later claimed, 'déclara a maintes reprises que seule le groupe de l'Alliance représentait la véritable Internationale à Genève'.[3] He and his friends joined the 'provisional Central Council' of the Alliance, and in November 1868, in response to Bakunin's plea to 'aid us with

---

[1] On Bakunin see the biography by E. H. Carr, and Riazanov's articles 'Sozialdemokratische Flagge und Anarchistische Ware', in *Neue Zeit,* Vol. 32/1 (1913–14).
[2] *Grünbergs Archiv,* Vol. V (1915), pp. 182–99.
[3] J. Guillaume, *L'Internationale,* Vol. I, pp. 109–10. Becker's cosmopolitan background and his experience in genuinely international bodies clearly made him approve both of the spirit and of the organisation of the Alliance.

all your influence', Becker asked the General Council in London to admit the Alliance to corporate membership of the International.[1]

Becker's request to the General Council naturally did a good deal in itself to weaken his claim to responsibility for the International's German branch; his attention was further distracted from Germany when he began to write for *l'Egalité*, the Bakuninist organ of the International's 'Fédération Romande'. His work on its editorial board seems to have taken much of his time during the year 1869, and it was only in February 1870 that he resigned. He now concluded that Bakunin was 'more of an egoist than a communist', and broke off all relations with him, remarking sadly that he had 'done a lot of harm' to the International's branches in Switzerland; he still gave no sign of realising, however, that co-operation with Bakunin had handicapped him in dealing with the threat to his own authority in Germany.[2]

Becker's growing involvement in the Swiss labour movement in general is reflected at this time in the pages of the *Vorbote*, where news from Germany increasingly takes second place to news from Switzerland, and where, despite the paper's growing sales in Germany, German news tends to be presented in carefully simple terms, as if Becker's main public was in Switzerland.[3] In the winter of 1868-9 Becker was also deeply involved in organising relief for workers affected by a long strike of dyers and weavers in Basle, as well as by renewed conflicts in the Geneva building-industry. His reports on these events to the General Council, although they earned the scorn of Marx for their failure to contain 'a single precise fact', reflected a deep

[1] *Ibid.*, p. 76; *Grünbergs Archiv*, Vol. V, pp. 190-1; *Chronik*, p. 275; General Council Minute-book (MS., IISG), II, p. 164; Engels to Marx 18 December 1868.
[2] Marx to Engels 28 January 1869; unpublished letters from Borkheim to Marx and to Becker (IISG); J. Ragaz, *Geschichte der Arbeiterbewegung in der Westschweiz*, pp. 113-14 (on *L'Egalité*); Minutes, III, p. 50, Borkheim to Becker 21 June, 20 December 1869, Marx to Engels 12 February 1870, Becker to Sorge (*Briefe und Auszüge aus Briefen*, p. 12) 3 & 5 May 1870 (on Becker's work for *L'Egalité*, his resignation and his criticism of Bakunin).
[3] E.g. *Vorbote*, July 1868, pp. 104-5; May 1868, pp. 78-80.

concern for Swiss problems which, like his connection with Bakunin, inevitably distracted Becker's attention from Germany.[1]

SCHWEITZER AND HIS RIVALS
AFTER THE CONGRESSES OF 1868

One reason why Becker was able to continue enrolling members undisturbed, and to receive recognition as the International's representative in Germany, was that the struggle between Schweitzer and his rivals (which now figured so prominently in Becker's correspondence from Germany) was assuming a form which made both sides reluctant to challenge him. The spring and summer of 1868 had seen a struggle in which both the ADAV and the *Verband Deutscher Arbeitervereine*, for reasons of prestige, had sought recognition as the German branch of the International; the public declarations of the Hamburg and Nürnberg Congresses marked the end of this stage of their rivalry, but the position was still far from being clarified. In the public eye, nothing was settled: both Schweitzer and Liebknecht claimed that their respective congress-resolutions had won them the favour of the International, yet the International itself irritatingly refused to come down openly in favour of either. Marx had allowed Schweitzer to make public use of his correspondence, and the General Council (in response to an urgent request by Bebel) had been represented by Eccarius at part of the Nürnberg Congress; but once the excitement of the various congresses had died down, the leaders of both factions in Germany discovered that the International was not to be moved to open support by anything so platonic as a simple 'declaration of agreement'.

In 1868–9 the conflict between Schweitzer and his detractors (who now launched a series of systematic attacks on him) was one in which public reference to the International was less frequent than in the summer, but in which both sides were nevertheless acutely aware of the advantages of claiming its

[1] *Vorbote*, 1869, *passim*; Becker to General Council 21 December 1868 (copy in *Nachlass*); Marx to Engels 13 January 1869.

support if possible. They were anxious to use its name, but were unwilling to pay the price it demanded, that is to say really energetic support. Throughout this winter and the spring of 1869, the important questions for the International were those asked by Engels soon after Nürnberg: 'What is Wilhelm's organisation to date, what is the result of the Nürnberg resolution? Have associations really joined, paid subscriptions and so on?'[1]

As the answer, throughout the year, was that neither 'Wilhelm's organisation' nor Schweitzer's *had* 'really joined', the official support of the International could be given to neither. There were, indeed, occasions when one side or the other seemed for a time to have found a way of using the International's name without paying for it, but these attempts were usually cut short by the strict public neutrality of Marx, the General Council, and Becker's 'Central Committee'. As will be seen, it was only in July 1869 that Liebknecht manoeuvred them into casting this neutrality aside.

Their symbolic victory at Nürnberg encouraged Liebknecht and Bebel to attempt the destruction of Schweitzer's power and the ending of the policies for which he stood. Conflict was inevitable between the Lassallean labour leader and these radical spokesmen of South German democracy: Schweitzer welcomed Bismarck's forcible creation of the North German *Bund* and used its *Reichstag* as a platform for demanding social reforms from the government; his rivals, who in 1866 had fought the hopeless battle to forestall Bismarck's 'revolution from above', were now fighting the yet more hopeless battle to undo it, and this involved them (particularly Liebknecht) in purely negative opposition to the *Bund*, its *Reichstag* and all its doings, and in alliance with all the enemies of Prussia from the most radical to the most reactionary.

Liebknecht and Bebel were convinced that to build a nationally organised socialist party which would, in contemporary terminology, 'combine political with social agitation', they had

[1] Engels to Marx 30 September 1868, *MEB*, IV, p. 177.

first to destroy Schweitzer's ADAV. Their political background
and environment made it inevitable that they should regard
victory over Schweitzer as far more urgent than clarifying
their relationship with their non-socialist allies; indeed the
whole-heartedness of their attack on Schweitzer may be
explained partly by their realisation of how ambiguous their
position was, as spokesmen of a variegated coalition united
only by hostility to Prussia. Liebknecht and Bebel were certainly
socialists, in the sense that they desired, finally, the destruction
of capitalism, but in the meantime the destruction of Prussia
seemed—particularly to Liebknecht with his memories of 1848—
more important. They anathematised Schweitzer partly because he accepted the 'work of 1866', and partly because he
continually—and convincingly—taunted them for choosing
anti-Prussian allies rather than anti-capitalist ones. It would
have been extremely tactless for Liebknecht to remind the
People's Party that both they and the *Verband*, by their agreement with the International's programme, were committed
to such radical propositions as that 'the emancipation of the
working classes must be the task of the working classes themselves'; it was better to concentrate on those aspects of the
International's message which made it a weapon against
Schweitzer, and this meant in practice turning it into the
symbol of a very vague socialism indeed.

Liebknecht's great expectations of this weapon, however,
were clear from the start. While he announced to the German
public that the agreement of both the ADAV and the *Verband*
with the International had created 'a road along which all the
workers of Germany can march in solid ranks of brotherly unity'
he was showing privately the terms on which he desired this
unity by pressing Marx to issue, in the name of the International,
a 'proclamation' to the German workers, welcoming the
Verband Deutscher Arbeitervereine as the official German branch and
denouncing Schweitzer as a traitor: a similar request was
made by Liebknecht's associate Wilhelm Eichhoff.[1]

[1] *Demokratisches Wochenblatt*, 12 September 1868; Mayer, *Engels*, II, p. 165;
MEB, IV, pp. 119–20, 125.

Schweitzer for his part no longer had any such hopes of positive public support from the International, but after the Hamburg Congress he had some claim to Marx's sympathy, and he was not slow in moving to protect himself against Liebknecht's manoeuvres; his letter to Marx asserted more outspokenly than ever his respect for 'the head of the European labour movement', suggested that Marx might restrain the hostility of his 'followers', and taking, up an accusation of his own indifference to the International, pointed out quite rightly that in the matter of 'adhesions' he had been 'the driving force, not the driven'.[1]

As both the *Verband* and the ADAV had publicly declared their agreement with the International, Marx and Engels decided despite their mistrust of Schweitzer that 'complete neutrality between him and Wilhelmchen—at least in public pronouncements' was the only possible course, 'until firstly, the emptiness of Schweitzer's game comes more to light' (which they regarded as imminent) 'and secondly, Liebknecht and Co. have really organised something' (which, they had reason to know, might take a long time).[2]

Because Schweitzer succeeded in retaining and even increasing his popularity (Becker was right in telling Conrad Rüll, on 10 March 1869, that 'the campaign opened by Liebknecht and Bebel' would not shake Schweitzer's popularity: the ADAV's membership had risen from 8,000 to 12,000 in the seven months since August 1868), and above all because 'Liebknecht and Co.' were far from the thought of 'really organising' anything for the International, the struggle in Germany had to be fought out without its official intervention.[3] Though lacking its official support, however, Bebel and Liebknecht did all they could to suggest that they had its sympathy. When they founded Trade Unions in opposition to those of

---

[1] Schweitzer to Marx 15 September 1868, *SAR*, p. 277.
[2] Marx to Engels 29 September, Engels to Marx 30 September, *MEB*, IV, pp. 124–5.
[3] Becker to Rüll 10 March 1869 (copy in IISG); ADAV membership figures in Müller, *Geschichte der Lithographen*, p. 279.

Schweitzer, they called them 'International Trade Unions' in order to monopolise an attractive symbol—though the Unions themselves for a long time achieved scarcely more than a nominal existence.[1] When Schweitzer published an article which defended the centralised organisation of the Lassallean party and called the structure of the *Verband* a 'confused wishy-washy', Liebknecht indignantly denounced this as an attack on the International, calculating that if Schweitzer were thought guilty of this, he would lose support.[2] In October 1868, when the local branch of the ADAV in Altona announced its decision to affiliate to the International, and to persuade other branches in Schleswig-Holstein to do the same, Liebknecht greeted the news as a token of his growing influence in the rival camp—although there was little in his own performance to justify this assumption that he represented the International.[3]

During the winter months of 1868–9, when Schweitzer was in prison, Liebknecht and Bebel used his absence to undermine his authority among the more thoughtful and active members of his party; their main thesis, evolved and elaborated in scores of speeches and articles, was that 'Schweitzer, either for money or by choice, had systematically tried since the end of the year 1864 to hold up the organisation of the labour party, and played the game of Bismarck ...'. In February 1869 Liebknecht challenged Schweitzer to let him and Bebel 'prove' these accusations in a public debate at the forthcoming ADAV Congress in Barmen-Elberfeld—and again, to convince the German public of his sincerity, he offered to submit the dispute to the best-respected court of European socialism, the General Council of the International.[4] Schweitzer refused to submit to this kind of arbitration: his correspondence with Marx had been broken off two months earlier, and now he rightly feared

[1] *Demokratisches Wochenblatt*, 27 October, 7 November, 1868; Bebel, *AML*, I, p. 202.

[2] *Social-Demokrat*, 16 September, *Demokratisches Wochenblatt*, 26 September 1868.

[3] *Vorbote*, September 1868, p. 141; *Demokratisches Wochenblatt*, 10 October; Bruhn (Altona) to Becker 25 August, 21 November 1868.

[4] Bebel, *AML*, I, pp. 212–13; *Demokratisches Wochenblatt*, 20 February 1869.

a judgment against him, since Marx, while praising his 'energy and intelligence', had strongly condemned the statutes of his new trade union organisation, and the Lassallean doctrines which they reflected. Despite this, however, and despite Marx's failure to respond to a hint that in view of the Hamburg resolution, 'which the whole world regarded as an affiliation to the International', he (Marx) should induce Liebknecht and Bebel to stop their 'hateful attacks', Schweitzer still wished to appear as a recognised representative of the International: he was well aware, as was Liebknecht, of the advantages which this might bring.[1] Before Liebknecht's challenge was published, even, Schweitzer announced that the *only* resolution to be debated at the Elberfeld Congress, to be proposed by himself, would declare that the ADAV 'attached itself to the programme and the aims' of the International, failing to affiliate fully only because this was illegal; and that until formal affiliation became possible, the ADAV would strive 'to remain in real agreement and real co-operation' with the International.[2]

Bebel and Liebknecht, as they prepared to present their case against Schweitzer at the Elberfeld Congress, realised that a declaration of this kind could do much to preserve his authority, both among his wavering followers in the ADAV, and among socialists outside it, and they tried to reduce its possible effects. The evening before their appearance at the Congress, Bebel wrote to Marx from Elberfeld, where he and Liebknecht were 'sitting with a small group of our comrades, preparing plans of campaign for tomorrow's battle'. His main purpose in writing was to warn Marx that the Congress seemed likely to pass the resolution on the International, but (as Schweitzer's motive was 'to strike us a deadly blow and to batter down the large opposition elements or to bring them over to his side') to re-

[1] Schweitzer to Marx 15 September, 8 October, 2 December; Marx to Schweitzer 13 October; Mehring in *SAR*, pp. 278–85.

[2] *Social-Demokrat,* 3 February 1869; Mayer, *Schweitzer,* pp. 281–3; Bebel's view (*AML*, II, pp. 63–4) that Schweitzer mentioned the International largely to answer the critics in his own party is confirmed by a letter from the Lassallean Bonhorst to Becker (10 February 1869; IISG) suggesting a secret meeting in Basle 'from which we expect great things for our congress'.

quest Marx to leave the resolution 'unnoticed for the moment, or at least to answer it very cautiously'. Marx's reaction was one of fury at being asked to repulse Schweitzer's profession of attachment to the International in order to help Liebknecht and Bebel, when they themselves had 'not taken a single step' for the International. (He must also have reacted to the fact that Liebknecht, in disgrace over his failure to account for missing copies of one of Marx's books, had delegated the task of writing to London to Bebel, whom Marx had not yet met.) His reluctance to intervene openly in the German struggle, however, made him do as Bebel asked. He does not seem to have informed the General Council of the Elberfeld resolution (though the Congress had passed it unanimously), and he certainly did not write to Schweitzer to acknowledge it. Becker also gave the resolution a cold reception, merely reprinting it without comment in the *Vorbote*.[1]

At the Congress itself, the accusations of Bebel and Liebknecht produced strong but mixed reactions. The Lassallean audience was enraged when Liebknecht described Bismarck's 'work of 1866' as anti-patriotic aggression, and when Bebel accused their president Schweitzer of being a government agent, but something of the speakers' arguments was believed. When Schweitzer insisted on a vote of confidence, one-third of the 42 delegates, representing nearly half of the ADAV's 11,000 members, abstained from voting; more significant than the numbers was the fact that the abstainers included those influential members, led by the party-treasurer Bracke, who had been brought into prominence by Schweitzer's *rapprochement* with the International in 1868. They were now uncertain where he was leading them, and although (as Bebel had predicted) Schweitzer's resolution in favour of the International kept them from open desertion, their continued mistrust inspired them to pass a resolution limiting his presidential powers; with this decision, and a clear threat of more tension in the future, the Congress ended.[2]

[1] Bebel to Marx 27 March (Bebel, *AML*, II, pp. 63–4); Marx to Engels 29 March (*MEB*, IV, p. 210); *Vorbote*, May 1869, pp. 77–8.
[2] Mayer, *Schweitzer*, pp. 285–91; Bebel, *AML*, II, pp. 64–5.

As Engels commented to Marx on 8 April: 'Wilhelm has again had the good fortune of stupidity. The vote of 6,500 against 4,500 (i.e. abstentions) was a great defeat for Schweitzer, though not an outright victory for Wilhelm.' This result, and Marx's renewed refusal to issue a 'proclamation' against Schweitzer, were reflected on 14 April in a new 'armistice' between Schweitzer and Liebknecht. They made an informal agreement not to attack each other in public; but their profound differences made it impossible for this to last long. Public polemics soon restarted, first on the question whether socialism or democracy was more important for the working class (when Schweitzer predictedly put socialism first, and Liebknecht just as predictably preferred democracy); then on what was the proper socialist attitude to the *Reichstag*—when Liebknecht attacked Schweitzer's participation in social and economic debates with a public onslaught culminating in the slogan, later famous: 'whoever parliamentarises with the enemy comes to terms with him'.[1]

The pressure of renewed criticism by Liebknecht and Bebel, and the risk of the ADAV's disintegration, made Schweitzer lose his nerve. He concluded that his authority could only be restored by his party's reunion with the sectarian 'Lassallean ADAV' run separately by the Countess Hatzfeldt since 1867: it is possible, though there is no evidence, that he had been planning this for some time. On 18 June, he and Mende (the president of the Countess's party) made the startling announcement that their parties would be reunited on the basis of Lassalle's original statutes of 1863 (thus reviving the presidential powers weakened by the Elberfeld Congress); and in an attempt to stifle criticism they gave the local branches no time to debate their *coup d'état*.[2]

Schweitzer had realised that in the struggle for the outright favour of the International he was handicapped, despite his

---

[1] Bebel, *AML*, II, p. 67; Mayer, *Schweitzer*, pp. 299, 303-8; Mühlbradt, *Liebknecht*, pp. 137-41.

[2] Mayer, *Schweitzer*, pp. 310-12, 318; Leidigkeit, *op. cit.*, pp. 177-8.

theoretical advantages over Liebknecht, but he may have
hoped that Marx and also Becker would at least retain their
public attitude of neutrality, despite his action; in any case,
his reunion with the hyper-dogmatic and fossilised 'Lassallean
ADAV' finally ended his chances of Marx's support, and it also
provoked the immediate exodus from his party of the open-
minded and influential leaders who had hoped he would stick
to an 'internationalist' line.

Within four days of Schweitzer's *coup d'état*, in Magdeburg,
Bracke and his friends met Bebel and Liebknecht, with whose
encouragement they issued a proclamation to the Lassalleans
still under Schweitzer's leadership, calling on them to attend a
'general Congress of all the Social Democratic workers of
Germany ... where the basis can be laid for a really democratic
organisation of the party, attached to the international movement'.[1]

THE FOUNDING OF THE

SOCIAL DEMOCRATIC WORKERS' PARTY AT EISENACH

The reference to 'the international movement' was by now
almost obligatory, given the International's permanent role as
a touchstone for the true socialist faith of those who invoked it;
and the preparations for the great Congress of Eisenach (which
was to unite dissident Lassalleans and the *Verband Deutscher
Arbeitervereine* in a new party strong enough to overshadow any
remaining adherents of Schweitzer) were dominated by the
same problem which had faced Bebel and Liebknecht before
Nürnberg a year earlier. Again the problem was how the
organisers could get the maximum of public support and private

[1] Bebel, *AML*, II, pp.71–4. A simultaneous proclamation by Bebel and Liebknecht
praised the International even more specifically: *Demokratisches Wochenblatt* 1869,
No. 26, quoted in *Hochverratsprozess*, pp. 119–20. In 1872 Liebknecht admitted
(*ibid.* p. 120) that their motive for this was that 'vis-à-vis Schweitzer we found it
necessary, for tactical reasons alone, to declare ourselves for the International in
this way, as he had been constantly praising it to his followers as the highest, so
to speak the model organisation for the proletariat, and it was vital for us to make
clear our standpoint to the ADAV members, to whom Schweitzer had been
persistently denouncing us as "bourgeois democrats"'.

help from the International's authorities, without being forced in return to make efforts on its behalf which would either bring trouble with the German police or handicap the organisation of the German party itself. As in the weeks before Nürnberg, Bebel and Liebknecht found Johann Philipp Becker much more willing to help than Marx. Marx had been trying for some months to get Liebknecht to enrol members for the International in Germany, so that an official German delegation could attend the Basle Congress in September;[1] but Liebknecht's other tasks, as always, had condemned these efforts to failure. When a letter from Liebknecht now announced that 'three-quarters of the ADAV' were on the point of deserting Schweitzer, and attempted to lure Marx into attending the Eisenach Congress by requests for International membership-cards and promises that the new party's paper would be 'an organ of the International', he very firmly refused. He would come to Germany, he replied, 'when they had really joined the International and given themselves a decent party-organisation', since 'the Nürnberg meeting showed how little one can trust simple promises, tendencies, etc.'; he continued by saying firmly that the new organisation must break with the People's Party, and that a new version of the *Communist Manifesto*, which Liebknecht had demanded, could wait (like his own visit to Germany), until the results and value of the Congress became clear.[2]

While Liebknecht was seeking in vain to move the General Council from its uncompromising neutrality, Bebel tried a new approach to the source from which he had been so effectively helped at Nürnberg, the International's Group of German-speaking Sections in Geneva. At the end of June he appealed to

---

[1] Marx to Engels 8 April, 3 July, 17 July 1869, *MEB*, IV, pp. 216, 239, 246.
[2] Liebknecht to Marx 29 June 1869, Marx to Liebknecht 3 July 1869, *Chronik*, p. 281; Mayer, *Engels*, II, p. 167; *MEB*, IV, pp. 239–40, 243. Engels to Kugelmann 10 July 1869, also denounces Liebknecht's alliance with the People's Party, and says that 'of course' he and Marx 'have much less in common with the People's Party, as a bourgeois party, than with Schweitzer's Lassalleans, who are at least a working-class sect' (*Ausgewählte Briefe*, pp. 254–5).

Becker thus: 'I ask the Central Committee of the German Section of the International to declare its agreement with the work of unification in Germany. I think we shall bring off the *coup de grâce* this time.'[1] In other words, Schweitzer was to be overthrown, with the help of the International's name.

Bebel's request for the Group's official support posed a grave problem to its President, Johann Philipp Becker. If Liebknecht and Bebel transformed the *Verband Deutscher Arbeitervereine* into an explicitly socialist party with an effective organisation, it would offer a much more powerful German centre for the International than his Group of German-speaking Sections, and his authority—which he could already feel weakened by the indifference of the General Council—would be seriously threatened. The Nürnberg Congress had potentially damaged his position, and a further consolidation in Germany, which would be bound as usual to exploit the name of the International, might this time take on the reality as well. On the other hand, the organisation of a great socialist party opposed to Schweitzer was inevitable whatever Becker did, and in any case so many of his own associates in Germany were active in preparing the Congress that he was bound to wish them success.[2] He therefore published a short statement welcoming the proposed unification of the German parties, and offering his Central Committee's help in organising the planned Congress;[3] and having thus ensured that he would continue to be consulted, he worked out a scheme which might allow him to keep some of his influence in Germany.

Becker was impressed by the democratic and anti-Prussian convictions of Liebknecht and Bebel, but thought that their inadequate work for socialism needed to be supplemented

---

[1] Bebel to Becker, written in margin of a printed circular declaring *Verband* Committee's agreement—28 June 1869—with declaration of Bremer, etc.: unpublished original in IISG, *Partei-Archiv*.

[2] Becker had long been in correspondence with the leading Lassallean rebels—Bracke, Bremer, and Fritzsche—as well as with their new associates Bebel and Liebknecht. A pro-Becker resolution by his new correspondents in Leipzig, also, is cited on pp. 173–4 and 176 below.

[3] *Vorbote*, July 1869, pp. 102–3, and an earlier statement *ibid.*, May, p. 77.

from another source; and this he saw in the Trade Union movement, whose growth in response to German economic conditions had in 1868 and 1869 been extremely rapid, as we have seen. If the organisation of the International Trade Unions of Germany could be made a reality, and made into the central part of the new party's structure, the way would be found to keep Liebknecht and Bebel firmly on the path of socialism, and to keep a share of the movement's control in his own hands; for these two reasons Becker replied, when Bebel wrote again to invite him to Eisenach, by publishing a long memorandum, whose basic argument was that 'only the Trade Unions offer a proper form for workers' associations and for the society of the future altogether'.[1] This document, which Becker proposed to lay before the Congress, contained the very clear suggestion that the whole organisation of the new party should be based on Trade Unions, and the less obvious implication that their international structure would put supreme authority in the hands of the German-speaking Committee in Geneva.

This was not in the least what Bebel and Liebknecht had in mind when they published 'Relations with the International Working Men's Association' as one of the main points on the Congress-agenda; they wanted, as usual, to use the prestige of the International's name without giving up their freedom to organise the party according to purely German needs. The only source from which they could get an official authorisation to reject Becker's proposals was the General Council in London, and Bebel thus had to seek the help of Marx.

By the end of July, two weeks before the Congress was due to begin, Marx was furiously angry with Liebknecht for giving way to the temptation to publish a completely false announcement that he (Liebknecht) had the General Council's official support against Schweitzer. Marx had already refused Lieb-

---

[1] *Ibid.*, July, pp. 103–7, in reply to Bebel's letter to Becker of 15 July 1869 (IISG), which enclosed money for pamphlets on the Basle strike, promised that Bebel would attend the International's next Congress, and assured Becker that his presence in Eisenach 'would give us all great pleasure'—which was indeed the case, for more than one reason.

knecht's request to draft a programme for the new party, and in letter after letter to Engels he was denouncing Liebknecht's recourse to 'official lies ... about non-existent resolutions of the General Council'.[1] Whatever he felt about Liebknecht's methods, however, he agreed with him and with Bebel on the impracticability of allowing Becker's control in Germany to be continued and shortly before the Congress he sent them the General Council's authorisation to repulse it.[2]

The social-democratic Congress which assembled at Eisenach on 7 August was the largest yet held in Germany; there were 263 delegates, claiming to represent a total of 14,000 workers. In addition 110 ADAV members loyal to Schweitzer arrived in Eisenach, with instructions to disrupt the proceedings of the Congress; they successfully did this by barracking and singing during the first session, but were then excluded while the Congress turned to its work. Its task was to continue the process began at Nürnberg a year earlier: the building of a progressive political party opposed to the ADAV, and standing for democracy as well as socialism. The Social Democratic Workers' Party founded at Eisenach fulfilled these demands; it consisted of the old *Verband Deutscher Arbeitervereine* (which was now disbanded) and of about a thousand of the most active ex-members

---

[1] E.g. Marx to Engels 24 July 1869: *MEB*, IV, pp. 249–51; *Chronik*, p. 282; *Demokratisches Wochenblatt*, 17 July 1869.

[2] At Eisenach Bebel effectively countered Becker's proposals by announcing that he 'had a letter from the General Council in his pocket' (report quoted in *Hochverratsprozess*, pp. 129, 136), and in his memoirs (II, p. 82) he gives the impression that Marx had taken the initiative in writing to him; significantly, however, just as Bebel tried to gain Becker's goodwill by sending him an unexpected remittance (cf. Note 1, p. 177), he won the favour of Marx at the moment when his support *against* Becker was needed, by the unprecedented gift of 25 Thaler for strikers in Belgium (Bebel to Marx 14 July 1869: unpublished original, IISG). The impression made on Marx is clear from *MEB*, IV, pp. 255–6. On 30 July, when Bebel acknowledged Marx's advice and encouragement to overthrow Becker's authority, he promised that 'the amount of the subscriptions' from new German members of the International would soon be discussed, and repeated that he himself would 'certainly' attend the Basle Congress, but these promises aimed mainly at making sure of Marx's support; as will be seen, virtually no subscriptions were paid to the International from Germany, and Bebel soon abandoned any intention of going to Basle (cf. his speech at Eisenach, quoted in *Hochverratsprozess*, p. 136). It is scarcely surprising that Bebel omitted this part of his letter from the version published in his memoirs (*AML*, II, p. 82; original in IISG).

of the Lassallean party. Power in the new party was shared between a committee consisting largely of former Lassalleans living in or near Braunschweig (the most prominent being Bracke, Bonhorst and Spier) and the former *Verband* leaders Bebel and Liebknecht, who edited the party-paper *Demokratisches Wochenblatt* (now renamed *Volksstaat*) in Leipzig.

The wording of the party's programme reflected the diversity of its members' backgrounds. It included many phrases inspired by the programme of the International, including a denunciation of 'the economic dependence of the worker on the capitalist', and a demand for factory-legislation and 'the introduction of the normal working-day'; in other passages the influence of the former ADAV members led to the inclusion of Lassallean demands for 'the free people's state', 'the full product of labour' for every worker, and 'state credits for producers' cooperatives'; and finally, the strong 'pure-democratic' tradition still counted for so much with Bebel and Liebknecht that the programme insisted on 'political freedom' and the essential need for 'a democratic state'. The influence of the People's Party was so strong, even on Bebel, that he was persuaded by Sonnemann to propose that the new party should call itself simply 'Democratic Socialist Party', and not 'Workers' Party' at all, because so many of its members were not workers: this proposal was only defeated at the Eisenach Congress by the former Lassalleans present.[1]

The mixture of Marxist, Lassallean and 'pure-democratic' ideas in the Eisenach programme, however, created no difficulties for a time; Liebknecht and Bebel could count on the unity of the ex-*Verband* and ex-ADAV members of their party (as well as on the continued sympathy of the People's Party) in the struggle against Schweitzer which was the immediate task.

To strengthen the party's unity, great stress was laid on the fact that its members had come together on what the Leipzig members' proclamation had called 'the only possible basis for agreement ... that of the International Working Men's Associa-

---

[1] Mayer, *Schweitzer*, p. 338; Leidigkeit, *loc. cit.*, pp. 185, 192–3.

tion'. The new party's loyalty to the International was emphasised throughout the Congress, and shouted in a vigorous 'Long live the international labour movement!' just before the delegates separated; and it was only at the mention of organised relations with the International that the limitations of this loyalty became apparent. Johann Philipp Becker arrived at Eisenach determined to press his proposals on the party's relationship to the International, not knowing that Marx had already authorised Bebel to reject them because they would give too much power to Geneva.

Bebel first attempted to dissuade Becker from presenting his proposals, but the old man insisted, so Bebel had to wait until the Congress turned to debate the relevant point—'relations with the International Working Men's Association'—then persuaded it that all discussion of Becker's document should be 'postponed'. With very little difficulty Bebel then got the Congress to adopt his own resolution on the International, which stated simply:

Considering that the emancipation of the working class is neither a local nor a national, but a social task, which embraces all countries where modern society exists, the Social-Democratic Workers' Party considers itself, as far as the Combination Laws allow it, as a branch of the International Working Men's Association, to whose efforts it attaches itself.

This resolution, like the one passed at Nürnberg, was designed to associate the German party with the International without committing it to anything more positive. Answering the question of what the party's relationship to the International would in fact be, Bebel insisted: 'whatever happens, the social-democratic party in Germany must first construct itself, because besides the international organisation, national organisations are indispensable; and the former without the latter would be a mere shadow'.[1] For Bebel, as for Schweitzer, the building-up of a national organisation came first; but the leaders of the Eisenach Party wished, partly for the purposes of their struggle

[1] Bebel at Eisenach, *Protokoll*, p. 73; the new programme in Bebel, *AML*, II, pp. 85–8.

against the ADAV, to have at least a nominal contact with the International. The furthest they would go in response to Becker's and Marx's requests for more active participation was to appoint a small commission 'for closer examination and satisfactory settlement' of the question, and to recommend all members of the party to become at the same time members of the International—a recommendation whose practical consequences were very limited indeed.[1]

The Eisenach Congress, from the point of view of creating a strongly-organised party consisting of the most open-minded ex-Lassalleans and the former members of the *Verband Deutscher Arbeitervereine*, was a great success.[2] The practical significance of the new party's role as a 'branch of the International', on the other hand, was not altogether certain.

THE END OF BECKER'S GROUP
OF GERMAN-SPEAKING SECTIONS

For Becker, the first and most effective pioneer of the International in Germany, the Eisenach Congress had a special significance: it was a blow from which his Group of German-speaking Sections never recovered. Many of the delegates at Eisenach, he was not surprised to discover, were men with whom he had corresponded, local leaders of his network of Sections in Germany;[3] some of them had even come with the firm intention of ensuring that Becker's authority would be preserved, but when they arrived, they succumbed to the excitement of the occasion, the conviction that the first object was to build up a centralised German party against Schweitzer, and the determination of Bebel and his fellow-organisers to prevent the

[1] On Schweitzer's attitude, cf. Chapter II above and Mayer, *Schweitzer*, pp. 326–7, 340, 350; on the special commission (Rittinghausen, Greulich, Liebknecht, Becker) cf. *Vorbote*, August 1869, p. 116, and Nicolaevsky in *Die Gesellschaft*, 1933, p. 255.
[2] Report in *Hochverratsprozess*, pp. 791–4; Bebel, *op. cit.*, II, pp. 89–90; Mayer, *Schweitzer*, pp. 339–40; Eyck, *Der Verband Deutscher Arbeitervereine*, pp. 94 *et seq.* (where the Liberal historian gives the *Verband* up for lost after its adoption—even nominal—of a socialist programme).
[3] *Vorbote*, August 1869, pp. 115–16.

party's adherence to the International from becoming more than nominal.

There were five delegates, for instance, from Leipzig, where a Section started by Becker had been flourishing for over a year; its leaders (who appear to have had little direct contact with Liebknecht and Bebel, though they too were in Leipzig) had gone so far as to publish in the *Demokratisches Wochenblatt* their conviction that 'the new organisation' to be created at Eisenach should 'attach itself fully and completely to the International', and the five delegates had set off for the congress with instructions to propose that the new party's programme should be 'that of the International' instead of Bebel's, and that its 'central authority' should be the Geneva Committee.[1] When the congress began, however, they took no steps to fulfil this mandate.

A month later one of them, Wilhelm Taute, wrote to Becker to explain that he, alone of the five, had tried to speak up for 'the international programme', but had been 'rudely forced into silence' and had received 'no support whatever' from his comrades, even from Ernst Werner. (The same Werner had assured Becker before the congress of his determination to see that the German movement 'took its adhesion to the International seriously', and 'straight-forwardly took up its place' under the International's existing authorities.)[2]

Werner's *volte-face* (although this was obviously unknown to Taute) was perhaps inspired by Marx. Certainly Werner had been in correspondence with London for some months, and it is probable that Marx now tried to ensure the removal of Becker's authority not only from above by condemning it in his letter to Bebel, but also from below, when an occasion presented itself, by encouraging German workers like Werner to vote against it.[3] Marx regarded Becker as unreliable because of his connec-

[1] *Demokratisches Wochenblatt*, 10 July 1869, quoted by Benser, *Zur Herausbildung der Eisenacher Partei*, pp. 109–10; Werner to Becker, 1 August 1869, and Leipzig resolution (Werner's MS), IISG.

[2] Taute (Leipzig) to Becker 20 September 1869; Werner to Becker, 1 August.

[3] *Chronik*, pp. 279, 281, 283; General Council Minutes 3 August 1869; Marx to Engels 17 July, 27 July 1869.

tion with Bakunin, dangerous because of such actions as his impulsive declaration of the International's support for Liebknecht, and also generally incompetent; he was furthermore convinced that the International must henceforth be based on nationally-organised parties in each country, and no longer on such entities as the language-group led by Becker. The delegates at Eisenach, partly owing to Marx's own pressure, agreed with him, and Becker's role in Germany was ended.

The final decline of the Group of German-speaking Sections was in fact slow. Becker was welcomed and even revered as an advisor of the Eisenach Party, whose creation he enthusiastically described as a 'world-historical event', and he was entrusted with the drafting of its 'Manifesto to the Rural Working Population'. In this he expounded socialist policy for agriculture —a subject which soon assumed a burning importance for the International's associates in Germany, when the Basle Congress of September 1869 voted for the nationalisation of the land.[1]

After the failure of the Basle Congress (at which Liebknecht represented the new German party) to produce any more concrete arrangements for the party's relations with the International than those decided at Eisenach, there were still many Sections of the International in Germany who continued to pay their subscriptions to Geneva as before. Gradually, however, the number of letters and subscriptions arriving from Germany dropped, as more and more Sections turned themselves into local branches of the new German party; for instance, Becker's Leipzig correspondent Werner was asking Marx within a few days of the congress how the International's Leipzig Section should affiliate to the Eisenach Party, and Bronnenmayer, of Göppingen, also transferred his allegiance from Becker to Liebknecht.[2]

In January 1870 the Secretary of the party's Central Committee in Braunschweig (who was Ludwig von Bonhorst, a

[1] Mayer, *Schweitzer*, p. 343; *Vorbote*, August 1869, p. 116, December 1869, pp. 177–84; *Hochverratsprozess*, pp. 473, 876–83.
[2] *Chronik*, p. 283; Bronnenmayer to Liebknecht 3 January 1870 (IISG, Liebknecht-*Nachlass*).

former Lassallean and a long-standing correspondent of Becker's) wrote to Geneva with the following questions:

(1) How do things stand with regard to your adhesion to the social-democratic party? [a striking reversal of roles]
(2) [going even further] Will not the General Committee for the German language be simply wound up in favour of the party, so that we take up direct relations with the General Council? Or what else do you propose?[1]

Becker refused to allow his connection with Germany to be ended in this abrupt way, and insisted that the Central Committee's past contributions to the German movement entitled it at least to 'a federal relationship on equal terms' with the Eisenach Party, and that both organisations should stand 'in direct communication with the General Council'.[2] Becker considered that he still had a right to advise the Eisenach Party, and was shocked when a long memorandum (proposing a new advisory commission), which he sent to the party's Stuttgart Congress in June 1870, was not followed up because the creation of a further organ controlling the party 'would obstruct the unity of our propaganda'. Becker was thanked for his 'continued moral co-operation', but it was made clear to him that his intervention in the day-to-day running of the party would not be welcome.[3]

By this time the *Vorbote* was printing far more news from Switzerland than from Germany, and Becker's Central Committee was generally regarded as being concerned only with the Swiss Sections of the International. For instance, when the war of 1870 made it imperative for the General Council to receive resolutions from national representatives, proposing the postponement of the Congress planned for September, Marx

[1] Bonhorst (for the party *Ausschuss*) to Becker 26 January 1870 (original in IISG, partly published in *Hochverratsprozess*, pp. 343-4).
[2] Becker to Bonhorst 4 February 1870 (Becker's copy in IISG; original seized by police in September 1870, and a short extract published in *Hochverratsprozess*, p. 344).
[3] Bonhorst to Becker 21 June 1870 (IISG); *Vorbote*, June 1870, pp. 94-6; Liebknecht's evidence in *Hochverratsprozess*, pp. 346-8; further details in Eckert, 'Zur Geschichte der Braunschweiger Sektion', *loc. cit.* p. 157.

wrote to the Braunschweig committee asking for 'a formal motion from Germany' to this effect, but from Becker, to whom he sent a copy of the same letter, he requested 'a formal official motion from the German-Swiss Group and from the Geneva Romance Group'. Becker's reply 'in the name of the Central Committee of the Group of German-speaking Sections' had a certain insistent dignity, and his letter re-affirmed his belief that the International should be organised in 'groups of Sections', but neither the title nor the idea any longer corresponded to the reality.[1]

The decline of Becker's authority in Germany can be measured by his relations with the annual German congresses from 1868 onwards: the Nürnberg Congress of 1868 could hardly have succeeded without his help; in 1869 the organisers of the Eisenach Congress had sought his assistance and his presence as a matter of urgency; in 1870 the Stuttgart Congress, though it neglected to debate his proposals, at least sent him an apology; but in 1871 he made no attempt even to communicate with the Dresden Congress, confining himself to reprinting its agenda and its main resolutions in the *Vorbote*.[2]

The war of 1870 helped to speed the decline of Becker's influence. The various German Sections which had continued to pay subscriptions now stopped doing so; and when the German party, persecuted for its attitude to the war and to the Paris Commune, set out to reconstruct its organisation in 1871, it was too much concerned with its own problems to welcome even the 'moral co-operation' of Becker. The financial difficulties of party-members prevented most of them from buying the *Vorbote*, and at the end of 1871, handicapped further by the growth of a strong Swiss labour movement with its own organ *Die Tagwacht*, it stopped publication.

[1] Marx to Braunschweig Committee 2 August 1870, printed in Marx and Engels, *Briefe an A. Bebel, W. Liebknecht* (Adoratski, ed.), p. 489. Marx to Becker 2 August 1870, original in IISG, printed in Russian translation in Marx-Engels, *Sochineniya*, Vol. XXVI, p. 64. Becker to General Council 7 August 1870, original in IISG, Jung-*Nachlass*.

[2] *Vorbote*, June 1871, pp. 94–5; September 1871, pp. 236–7.

The list of Becker's achievements given in the last number of the *Vorbote* is impressive enough in itself, in view of the difficulties he had faced: 58 Sections had been founded (nearly half of them in Germany, the rest mainly in Switzerland), ten societies had joined in affiliated membership, and 385 individual members had been paying subscriptions.[1] These figures, however, represented only a beginning: many of these Sections and individual members had worked with the energy of their leader, hundreds of his 4,281 letters had had their effect, and his work had made possible the growth of the International under the nominal patronage of Liebknecht, the Lassallean party's *rapprochement* with the International at the Hamburg Congress, the reorganisation of the *Verband Deutscher Arbeitervereine* at Nürnberg, and the creation of the *Sozialdemokratische Arbeiterpartei* at Eisenach.

A significant stage in the growth of international socialism in Germany was ended; but although since 1869 the message and name of the International had been adopted and applied there in ways which were not entirely welcome to Becker, it was his work which helped to ensure that they were adopted at all.

---

[1] *Vorbote*, December 1871, pp. 177–83 (*Unsere Letzte Nummer*), partly summarised by F. Berghoff-Ising: *Die Socialistische Arbeiterbewegung in der Schweiz*, pp. 32–3.

CHAPTER VI

THE EISENACH PARTY AND THE INTERNATIONAL, 1869 TO 1872

INTRODUCTION: ORGANISED RELATIONS BETWEEN
THE PARTY AND THE INTERNATIONAL, 1869–72

In August 1869 the Eisenach party became, in name at least, 'a branch of the International Working Men's Association', in time to witness the three most dramatic years of the International's existence: at the Basle Congress of 1869 its programme became outspokenly socialistic; in 1870 its opposition to the Franco-Prussian War caused it to be regarded as a major conspiracy against the accepted ideals of patriotism; and in 1871 its support for the Paris Commune made the governments of Europe take collective measures for its extirpation. At the same time it went through the struggle between Marx and Bakunin which split its organisation into two, and which caused its explosive disintegration at the Hague Congress of 1872. Here Bakunin was expelled, his doctrines were formally condemned, and a reliably 'Marxist' General Council was empowered to direct the International's remains from a safe refuge in New York.

In this agitated period the German party's political attitude towards the International underwent a series of interesting variations; its organised relations with the International, on the other hand, remained embryonic and, in the judgment of the latter's leaders, wholly unsatisfactory. For this there were two main reasons.

The first was already indicated in the party's formal declaration of its membership '. . . as far as the German Combination Laws allowed it'. With the growth of socialism, and the increasing political and social tensions of the later 1860s, these Combination Laws were beginning to be more strictly applied.

181

In 1867 or 1868 Johann Philipp Becker had been able to found Sections of the International in many German towns without fear of systematic persecution of their members, and an eminent servant of the Prussian State, Lothar Bucher, had subscribed to the *Vorbote* with thoughts not of immediate police-measures but simply of 'informing himself about the revolutionary goings-on in Switzerland'.[1] By 1870, however, European governments were much more suspicious of working-class organisations: in many German states, socialist meetings attracted increased attention from the police, and after a series of trials in France and Austria had attempted to destroy the International's branches there, the German Social Democrats in their turn had to undergo systematic persecution. In 1869 and 1870 their leaders were often subjected to short periods of arrest,[2] and when they raised their voices during the war of 1870 to oppose the annexation of Alsace-Lorraine, they were despatched in chains to the East Prussian fortress of Lötzen for 'agitation endangering the military security of the State'. The war led to the Paris Commune, which gave rise to a wave of governmental repression taking the form in France of transportations and massacres, in Germany of long prison sentences for 'High Treason', and throughout Europe of vigilant measures to ward off 'the red peril'.

In these circumstances (even these of 1869–70, and still more those of 1871–2) the Eisenach Party had one obvious reason for not allowing its organised contacts with the International to go beyond prudent limits, and for rejecting the far-reaching demands made by Marx as its Secretary for Germany; but it also had a reason of its own. The party's central authorities, the Executive (*Ausschuss*) in Braunschweig and Wilhelm Liebknecht (editor of the party paper) in Leipzig, saw their main task in the creation of a well-organised anti-Lassallean party in Germany; there were some questions of policy which

---

[1] Moritz Busch, *Tagebuchblätter*, Vol. III, p. 105.
[2] A list of those arrested is given by W. Bracke, *Der Braunschweiger Ausschuss . . . vor dem Gericht*, p. 153.

divided them (broadly speaking, Liebknecht clung to his alliance with the People's Party, while the Executive demanded an explicitly socialist party-line on every point), but about the International they all agreed. Its name had been a valuable rallying-cry at Nürnberg and Eisenach, but nothing ought to be done to enrol German socialists as members of the International until the party in Germany itself was firmly established.

Representing the Eisenach Party at the International's Basle Congress in September 1869, Liebknecht assured the delegates that all the party's members were obliged to join the International as well, but this was an exaggeration—all that had really happened was that Marx had sent several hundred International membership-cards for free distribution to the Germans, so that they might 'legitimately' be represented at the Congress, and they paid no subscriptions either now or later. The German party-leaders did indeed recommend their followers to become individual members of the International, but with so little insistence that the number who did so remained very small.[1]

The Party Executive, although its members met Marx in Hanover in October, 1869, entered into effective correspondence with the General Council only in the New Year, and even then made no serious move to carry out Marx's wishes about organisation. Bracke wrote in March 1870 assuring him that they could 'easily dispose of' 3,000 membership-cards, and would 'send in the money as it reaches us', but although the cards were sent, no money ever reached London in exchange.[2]

The International accepted the invitation of the German party to hold its 1870 congress in Germany, but the report of the Germans' own congress, held at Stuttgart in June, shows

---

[1] Liebknecht at Basle, *Hochverratsprozess*, p. 249; free distribution of cards *ibid.*, p. 342, and *MEB*, IV, p. 246; German party-leaders' recommendations in Bebel's speech at Eisenach (*Protokoll*, p. 73), and in *Demokratisches Wochenblatt*, 28 August 1869 (*Hochverratsprozess*, pp. 136, 253–4). Marx complained in a letter to Berlin of September 1871 (*Die Gesellschaft*, 1933, p. 260) that no money had been received from Germany 'since 1869'.

[2] Eckert, *Aus den Anfängen der Braunschweiger Arbeiterbewegung*, pp. 7–9.

that they scarcely gave any consideration to the party's relations with the London General Council.

The war of 1870-1 brought arrests and persecution of German socialists which nearly destroyed the party, making all communication with London difficult and a tightening of organisational contacts unthinkable. Even the party's reconstruction in 1871, although it was accompanied by assurances of loyalty to the International, was so exclusively concerned with the German party-organisation itself that Marx refused to take these protestations seriously.

The International had held no Congress in 1870 or in 1871: but after a small delegate-conference had met in London in September 1871, Marx began to take systematic steps to counteract the indifference of the German leaders. He complained early in September to a leading member of the Eisenach Party in Berlin that 'Germany was not represented at the Congress, and has sent neither delegates nor subscriptions since 1869'; when Liebknecht wrote to complain at this direct approach to a local branch of the party, Marx curtly replied that 'as we are very dissatisfied here with the way the affairs of the International' (in Germany) 'have been handled until now, it is my duty, in the name of the General Council, to take up direct communication with the main places in Germany, which I have already begun to do'.

Marx's view, as he told his Berlin correspondent, was that 'the laws may destroy a regular organisation' (i.e. of relations between the party and the International) 'but they cannot prevent the . . . Social Democratic Workers' Party from doing in practice what is done in all other countries, enrolling individual members, paying subscriptions, sending reports. . . .' Liebknecht, on the contrary, felt (as he told Engels) that 'one should not expect too many individual memberships in Germany, and *entre nous* I don't regard it as necessary'.[1]

[1] Marx to Kwasniewsky (Berlin) 25 September 1871, in *Die Gesellschaft*, 1933, pp. 260-1; Marx to Liebknecht 17 November 1871, in Adoratski, p. 40; Liebknecht to Engels 8 December 1871, *ibid.*, p. 46, and other letters to Engels in Mayer, *Schweitzer*, pp. 439-40: cf. Eckert in *Wilhelm Liebknecht: Briefwechsel mit Karl Marx und Friedrich Engels*, pp. 109-12.

Under steady pressure from London the German party-leaders were indeed made to see the desirability of strong German representation at the International's next Congress, to protect the General Council against the Bakuninists; but they would never try hard to enrol paying members.[1] A subsidiary reason why they were unwilling to organise support for the International was that they still feared a revived threat to their authority from Johann Philipp Becker in Geneva—surprisingly, as his influence in Germany had received a death-blow at the Eisenach Congress. The fears of the Eisenach Party were revealed early in 1872: a young German engineer named Cuno (who had met Bebel in Chemnitz in 1871) had been expelled successively from Saxony and from Vienna as an 'agent' of the International, and settled in September 1871 in Milan. During the winter he organised there a Section of the International (which, unlike the other Italian Sections, sided with the General Council against Bakunin) and thus came into lively correspondence both with Engels, now the General Council's Secretary for Italy, and with Becker in Geneva. By corresponding with Becker, Cuno aroused German suspicions that a move was being made to revive the Group of German-speaking Sections, and he paid the price for this when he arrived in Bavaria in April 1872. Although he had neither money nor possessions (his political activities having led to his being deprived of his job, thrown into prison and deported penniless from Italy) he was suspected of being 'an agent of Becker's, sent with the task of leading the German International back into the lap of Geneva', and was cruelly ostracised by the Eisenach Party's members in several German towns, including Leipzig itself. Engels later repaired the situation by tactful letters both to Liebknecht and to Cuno, who remained a useful member of the International and played a leading part at the Hague Congress before emigrating to America. His experiences in Germany, however, had revealed

---

[1] Liebknecht to Engels June 1872 (Mayer, *Schweitzer*, p. 440); Engels to Liebknecht 18 January and 15 February 1872 (Adoratski, pp. 52, 56).

the extremely jealous attachment of the German party-leaders to their national organisation, and had indicated an additional reason why they refused to keep up any organised relations with the International.[1]

The General Council could count on declaration of solidarity from Germany, like the one passed by a mass-meeting of Saxon socialists in January 1872 but this was all; the German delegates who helped Marx to victory over Bakunin at the Hague Congress, though all nominally mandated by German Sections, in fact represented only a tiny number of paid-up members.

The Congress, and Marx's Pyrrhic victory, meant the end of the International's effective life in Europe; and to the end the Germans, as far as organised relations went, adopted (in Marx's words) the 'purely platonic' attitude to it which they had taken since 1869 and indeed earlier. As Engels explained to Cuno in a letter of May 1872, 'the German labour movement's attitude to the International never really became clear. It remained a purely platonic relationship, there was no real membership of individuals either, and the founding of Sections was forbidden by law...Liebknecht etc.... in fact wanted to subordinate the International to their specific German aims and to make use of it for these aims ....'[2]

THE PARTY'S CHANGING POLITICAL ATTITUDES
TO THE INTERNATIONAL, 1869–72

The Eisenach's Party's organised contacts with the International thus form an unbroken story of failure, thanks to the Germans' constant fear of the law, and their need to concentrate

---

[1] Nicolaevsky, 'Aus der Geschichte der I. Internationale', in *Die Gesellschaft*, 1925, pp. 445–75; letters of Cuno to Becker, IISG; Engels to Cuno, 7–8 May 1872 in *Marx-Engels-Lenin-Stalin: Zur deutschen Geschichte*, Vol. II, p. 1275; Engels to Liebknecht 7 May 1872, Adoratski, p. 64; *Chronik*.

[2] Engels to Cuno, *loc. cit.*; on the Saxon declaration of January, cf. Adoratski, p. 52, Engels to Cuno 24 January 1872 (Marx & Engels, *Ausgewählte Briefe*, 1953, p. 332), and Bebel, *AML*, II, p. 205. The list of dubious German 'Sections' represented at the Hague includes Crimmitschau, Breslau, Düsseldorf, Celle and Chemnitz: Freymond, ed., *La Première Internationale*, Vol. II, pp. 329–30.

on their own organisation; the party's political attitude to the International, again, although it changed significantly between 1869 and 1872, did so mainly in response to tactical needs inside Germany. This is confirmed by a study of the three successive attitudes adopted by the party during this period.

In the first phase, from the Eisenach Party's foundation to the outbreak of the Franco-Prussian War (August 1869 to July 1870), the German leaders acted as they had done during the Eisenach Congress and earlier: they tried to reap the benefits of contact with the International—the recognition of Marx, his public support against the Lassalleans, and even financial help—without, in exchange, giving up their freedom to work with non-socialist parties in Germany, fully acknowledging the International's programme, or even paying membership dues.

In the second and much more troubled phase, from the outbreak of war to the suppression of the Paris Commune (July 1870 to May 1872), German socialists could do little except comment helplessly on the rapid course of events, and the uncompromising internationalists (notably Bebel and Liebknecht) at times completely isolated themselves by flatly disagreeing not only with prevailing German opinion but also with the majority of their own party; they could not, of course, undertake open propaganda for the International in these circumstances, but their public pronouncements failed to take account of it as its leaders, particularly Marx, would have liked.

In the third phase, from the suppression of the Commune up to the Hague Congress (May 1871 to September 1872) the German party was busy rebuilding its organisation, again on a national basis, and the International was split into two rival camps arming for the final struggle; by this time the German leaders had realised that close contact with the International would bring them neither political prestige nor financial support, and although they responded to Marx's appeal to save the General Council by sending delegates to the Hague Congress, they did this without enthusiasm and without feeling that the International any longer had any very great significance.

From 1869 to 1872, although the German leaders were by no means indifferent or disloyal to the International, they always—and quite understandably—subordinated this loyalty to considerations affecting their own party.

THE FIRST ATTITUDE: FROM THE EISENACH CONGRESS TO THE FRANCO-PRUSSIAN WAR (AUGUST 1869–JULY 1870)

In 1869–70 the Eisenach party's leaders made use of the International as a source of prestige in their struggle with the Lassalleans; they expected it to provide financial help; and they took these attitudes at a time when they were refusing to acknowledge parts of its programme as long as it suited them better not to do so.

The International as a source of prestige and financial support, 1869–70
In the months after the Eisenach Congress the new party's leaders concentrated on developing it into a strong nation-wide organisation, capable of competing for members and influence with Schweitzer's ADAV, and even of replacing it altogether. Power in the new party was divided between Braunschweig, where a five-man Executive under Bracke directed its organisation and policy, and Leipzig, where Liebknecht and Bebel edited the party's newspaper, and drew a certain additional prestige from their position as its representatives in the *Reichstag*.[1] Now as during the Eisenach Congress, they all accepted the view of the International which had prevailed in Germany since 1868: that it was an influential and powerful body which could help them in many ways, without the need for much contribution on their part in exchange. It was not surprising that the members of the Braunschweig

---

[1] W. Schroeder, *Geschichte der Sozialdemokratischen Parteiorganisation in Deutschland*, pp. 14–19; on the actual working of the new party's constitution, cf. the reports of the Leipzig and Braunschweig trials, and the letters published by Eckert in *Aus den Anfängen der Braunschweiger Arbeiterbewegung*.

Executive (who had all until recently belonged to the ADAV, and knew relatively little about the International, except what they knew from Becker's propaganda and from the lavish praise published by Schweitzer in 1868) should accept this view; but even those who might have been better informed, notably Liebknecht, saw the International as a source of all kinds of political and material benefits, which could be earned by a mere declaration of allegiance.

Ideally, Liebknecht and his colleagues would have liked to publish a certificate from the chiefs of the International that the Eisenach party was the only German representative of honest socialism, and that Schweitzer and his followers were sectarians and traitors. Marx and Engels, however, despite their hostility to the ADAV, refused to allow their names to be used in a public and formal condemnation of this kind, particularly by an Eisenach Party which still held to its ambiguous alliance with the anti-socialist People's Party; and although Liebknecht must have been tempted to use their name and that of the International without asking permission, he doubtless remembered the furious reactions in London when he had dared to do this on the eve of the Eisenach Congress, and the temptation was resisted. This, however, did not prevent the party, in its struggle against the Lassalleans, from exploiting its nominal adherence to the International in other ways.

The party's Secretary Bonhorst, sent a formal demand to the International Basle Congress that in Germany its membership cards should be issued 'to members of the Social Democratic Workers' Party, and to them only'; and the party's delegates to the Congress, Liebknecht and Spier, made the most of the monopoly of German representation given them by this move, as well as by the Lassalleans' reluctance to appear at the Congress at all. Liebknecht in particular gave a highly coloured 'report on Germany' which attacked Schweitzer as a discredited traitor and Bismarckian agent, and the unquestioning reception of this by a distinguished international audience was prominently reported in the Eisenach's Party's paper, the

Demokratisches Wochenblatt. The paper also emphasised the Basle Congress's recommendation that all 'sections and affiliated societies should abolish the office of President'. The editorial comment on this—'we particularly hope the Germans will appreciate this point and act on it'—was aimed directly at the ADAV's presidential constitution, which the Eisenach Party had carefully refrained from copying.[1]

Another way, already mentioned, in which it tried to turn its connection with the International account, as in 1868–9, was in giving the name 'international' to the Trade Unions under its auspices, and in publicising the superior benefits claimed for these over 'nationally-organised' unions; the 'International Trade Unions' failed for a long time to win any substantial support, and Bebel later admitted the largely propagandist purpose of their title by explaining that it 'was meant to give expression to the outlook (*Tendenz*)'—not the reality.[2]

In these ways the Eisenach Party's leaders manoeuvred against the ADAV during the first months of their nominal connection with the International; as will be seen, they were to adopt other methods later.

The party overestimated not only the prestige and influence of the International, but also its financial resources: Eichhoff's pamphlet of 1868, for instance, had given prominence to details of financial aid organised by the International for strikers in France, Belgium and elsewhere, and even Becker's propaganda campaign had tended to stress this potential advantage of membership—though he did often appeal to the Germans themselves to send money for strike funds in Switzerland. All this, however, was no justification for the frequent requests now made by the Eisenach party for financial assistance from the General Council. When the party's leaders, even before the Eisenach Congress, had already asked for money, Marx expressed his wonder at 'the idea these Germans have of our financial

---

[1] *Demokratisches Wochenblatt*, 11 September 1869.

[2] Bebel, *AML*, I, p. 202; occasional reports of Trade Union activities in the first few numbers of the *Volksstaat* (which replaced the *Demokratisches Wochenblatt* on 1 October 1869).

means', when in fact 'the General Council is five weeks in arrears with its rent, and is in debt to its secretary'. The Germans, said Marx, had 'never sent a penny', and Engels in reply went further: 'In my opinion, it would be very ill-advised for the International Working Men's Association to send a single farthing to the Germans, until they have paid regular contributions for some time themselves.'[1]

This insistence that the International was in no position to help, followed by its disappointing response in the following months to two further appeals from German strikers, showed some of the more realistic German leaders, including Bebel, that their expectations had been too great. 'It might have been better', wrote Bebel to the Braunschweig Executive in December 1869 'if you hadn't given the people in Waldenburg' (striking coal-miners) 'the prospect of so much support from the International Working Men's Association. The organisation of the International is not at all in a position yet to be able to give any effective material help.'[2]

Bebel's warning went unheeded, however, and throughout the early months of 1870 the General Council continued to receive requests for financial help from Germany. In February and early March the Braunschweig Executive was appealing to the International for a subsidy to help pay the costs of 'the newspaper and officials' salaries' and to help propaganda campaigns.

Even after Marx had pointed out that help of this kind should not be expected, the party-secretary Bonhorst still ruefully referred to the party's need 'to let our faithful Finance Minister's laments wail even to you', and Marx's only consolation to him was that 'the finances of the General Council are at nil, or rather in perpetually increasing deficit'. A further appeal by Bracke to Engels to remember that 'our party, founded under

[1] Marx to Engels 22 July, Engels to Marx 24 July, 1869, *MEB*, IV, pp. 251, 254. Further evidence on the Germans' financial expectations, *ibid.*, pp. 246–7; Minutes, II, pp. 226–7; Eckert, *Aus den Anfängen*, p. 22.

[2] *Hochwerratsprozess*, pp. 509–10; Minutes, III, pp. 6, 23, 37; Mayer, *Schweitzer*, pp. 367–8.

the most difficult conditions, needs the strongest support of all its friends', met with no response except good advice on methods of accountancy, and the German leaders now seem to have realised that they had been deluding themselves in expecting much help from the International.[1]

Their misapprehension, however, had lasted from the foundation of their party almost to the moment when the outbreak of the Franco-Prussian War threatened to destroy both it and the International.

1869–70: land-nationalisation as seen by the International and by the party

The German leaders' expectation during this period, that the International would give them moral, political and financial support, was the more remarkable in that they refused for several months to accept an important point of its programme.

In September 1869 the Basle Congress of the International voted by a large majority in favour of the abolition of private property in land. Liebknecht and the school-teacher Spier, who represented the Eisenach Party at the Congress, realised at once that the resolution, while it was in harmony with the socialist points in the Eisenach Programme, put the party in a very difficult situation. Despite these points of the Eisenach Programme, most members of the bourgeois People's Party were still prepared to work with the Eisenachers as they had done in the years before 1869; they had enough in common with the followers of Liebknecht and Bebel for both parties to value their alliance against Prussianism and Lassalleanism, and to emphasise their common political ideals rather than the social problems which potentially divided them. If the Eisenach Party's leaders, who had continually stressed their loyalty to the International, now had to admit that its programme included specific demands for land-nationalisation, the anti-socialist leaders of the People's Party would take fright, and the alliance would be

[1] Correspondence of February, March & April 1870 in Eckert, *Aus den Anfängen*, pp. 5–6, 8–10.

ended. Realising this at the Basle Congress, and realising also that talk of land-nationalisation would alienate the German peasantry from the party, Liebknecht was in no doubt what to do; although he was wholeheartedly 'in agreement with the resolution in principle', the political situation in Germany forced him to consider its tactical implications, and particularly its effect on electoral co-operation with the Peoples' Party. He therefore did all he could to prevent the Congress from putting the resolution to the vote at all, and when he finally failed in this he only voted for it ('giving way to his communist conscience' as Gustav Mayer put it) with grave forebodings about the consequences. So restrained, indeed, did Liebknecht and his German colleagues appear that an American delegate, A. C. Cameron, recorded that they 'seemed to our entire satisfaction to steer clear of ultra views, and allowed their reason, rather than their passion, to control their judgment'.[1]

Liebknecht's concern was justified. The International was now firmly associated with the policy of land-nationalisation, which alarmed its critics more than anything in its programme had done before, and Liebknecht's own position was particularly difficult. From September 1869 until February of the following year he and Bebel, who were in agreement with the resolution but preferred not to admit it, manoeuvred in an attempt to escape from their dilemma, before deciding that further equivocation would harm them more than open admission of their agreement; at this their relations with the International improved at once, but it is remarkable how long they had subordinated its declared policy to their own tactical necessities, and the whole episode is worth examining in some detail.

As soon as the Basle resolution become known in Germany, the alarm was sounded by the People's Party newspaper in Mannheim, whose editor had always mistrusted the party's connection with Liebknecht; within a few days the 'communistic' implications of the resolution were the subject of

[1] Commons and Andrews, *A Documentary History of American Industrial Society*, Vol. IX, p. 248.

perturbed articles in the *Stuttgarter Beobachter* and even in the *Demokratische Korrespondenz*, whose first report on the Basle Congress two weeks earlier had noted 'with joy and respect . . . how faithfully and bravely Liebknecht had defended our common programme at the Congress of the International': from this side, Liebknecht and Bebel were subjected to increasing pressure to disavow the Basle resolution, and they were threatened with the secession of the whole People's Party if they refused.[1]

They were obliged, however, to take account of criticism from other quarters as well. Schweitzer had always insisted that Liebknecht's followers, and the workers whom Bebel had organised in the old *Verband Deutscher Arbeitervereine*, were not true socialists but adherents of bourgeois democracy; their radicalism, he said, had nothing socially progressive about it, but was inspired mainly by South German hostility to Prussia. There was much truth in these accusations, and Liebknecht's embarrassment over the Basle resolution gave Schweitzer an excellent opportunity to repeat them, assuring his followers (and the German working class in general) that the Eisenach Party stood revealed by its hesitations as a party of opportunists attentive only to peasant prejudice and the demands of 'bourgeois money-democracy'. Schweitzer appreciated the prestige of the International too well to attack it openly for allowing Liebknecht to criticise him at the Basle Congress, and contented himself with pointed references to its 'slack conditions of admission', which allowed 'all kinds of vague half-socialist organisations' to claim that they belonged to it.[2] These aspersions, coupled with the fact that Schweitzer (appealing to workers in a region of Junker estates rather than small peasant holdings) had had no difficulty in preaching land-nationalisation for some years, were enough to create violent dissatisfaction with Liebknecht's ambiguous attitude in the ranks of his own party; particularly unhappy were the members

[1] *Demokratische Korrespondenz: Organ der deutschen Volkspartei* (Stuttgart), 10 September 1869 and following numbers; Mayer, 'Die Trennung', p. 49.
[2] Mayer, *Schweitzer*, pp. 346–50.

of the Braunschweig Executive, who had only recently left
the ADAV and were especially sensitive to the charge that they
had abandoned a socialist party for a non-socialist. They put
pressure on Liebknecht in their turn, insisting that the party
must unequivocally declare its support for the Basle resolution,
and if necessary accept a breach with the People's Party in
consequence.

Liebknecht did his best to satisfy both these contradictory
demands. In his first public pronouncement on the Basle
resolution he ingeniously argued that while every individual
member of the party must make up his mind on the problem,
'the party as such' could not be expected to take sides, being
'in no way bound by the resolution, any more than the International itself is bound'. When this equivocation was publicly
denounced by Schweitzer and privately criticised by the
Braunschweig Committee, Liebknecht published an article
admitting that 'there might be different opinions in the party'
about whether the resolution was opportune or not, but
conceding that 'as it has now been passed, the party as
such cannot disavow it without betraying its basic principles'.[1]

While this produced from the People's Party press a wave of
fresh demands that the party disavow the resolution completely,
it still failed to go far enough for the Braunschweig Committee,
who insisted on its unconditional public ratification. Liebknecht
wrote repeatedly to Braunschweig, assuring his colleagues that
he was in agreement with the resolution; he urged them, however, to:

wait a little, then people will agree to march to Basle with us. But
not yet. If we start asking them now, only the best walkers will come
with us, and the rest stay behind. I don't want to let trouble break
out too soon between ourselves and the South German People's
Party. . . . The party-declaration which you propose [for the resolu-
tion] is dangerous. I have firmly refused to disavow the Basle resolutions in our party-paper for the time being . . . the People's Party

[1] *Demokratisches Wochenblatt*, 29 September 1869 (the last number under this
title); *Volksstaat* No. 4, 16 October 1869.

are demanding a disavowal. . . . Never! I am a communist, and therefore agree with the resolution in principle – I just regret on practical grounds that it was drafted in this form. The question of landed property can only gradually be made clear to the peasants.[1]

These arguments, and even a reminder from Bebel that the party owed some of its income to democrats in Switzerland who deplored the Basle resolution, failed to move the Braunschweig committee-members, who began to threaten that they would proclaim the party's agreement with the resolution themselves, if Liebknecht still refused to do so. At the same time (November 1869) the influential leaders of the People's Party were assuring Liebknecht that their alliance could only continue if the resolution were disavowed; and Bebel, on a South German speaking-tour, had to use all his diplomatic skill in order to give the impression that the Eisenach Party might after all make its choice in this direction.[2]

The tense situation lasted until late January, with Liebknecht and Bebel under pressure from both sides that would have made a decision inevitable before long, but when they finally did decide it was largely due to a new and quite unexpected factor.

Against a public declaration for the International there still spoke Liebknecht's reluctance to break with the People's Party, and his fear of frightening the peasants. The arguments on the other side were not entirely convincing: the Braunschweig Committee threatened not to support him any longer under Schweitzer's provocation—but they might be persuaded to postpone the public ratification on which they insisted; the leaders of the International themselves were disturbed at his equivocations (Engels was writing a new introduction for his *Peasants' War in Germany*, and going out of his way to stress that 'the Basle resolution... is most timely, particularly in Germany')[3]—but Liebknecht could ignore criticism from England, as he had often done before; the factor that finally made him

---

[1] Liebknecht to Bonhorst October 1869, in *Hochverratsprozess*, pp. 195–6.

[2] *Ibid.*, p. 500; Mayer, 'Die Trennung', p. 52; Bebel, *AML*, II, pp. 93–4.

[3] Engels, *Der Deutsche Baurnkrieg*, p. 16; Engels to Marx 11 February 1870, *MEB*, IV, p. 331

decide to declare himself openly for the International's resolution, and resign himself to trouble with the People's Party and the peasants, was a purely German question of party-tactics.

The socialists of Bavaria, many of whom were members of Lassalle's ADAV, had become increasingly resentful of Schweitzer's dictatorial centralisation. The nucleus of an independent social-democratic party in Bavaria, as we have seen, had already been set up in the summer of 1869, thanks partly to the initiative of Johann Philipp Becker; and when Schweitzer insisted in December that the ADAV's weekly Bavarian paper *Der Proletarier* must be suspended in favour of his *Social-Demokrat*, the local Lassalleans, including Neff, the *Proletarier*'s editor, joined with this nucleus to form a strong and independent party.[1] The final decision to constitute a separate party was taken at a congress which met in Augsburg on 23 January 1870; Bebel was there in the hope of persuading the delegates to change their minds at the last moment, and attach themselves to the Eisenach Party instead. His long speech was attentively heard, but his real arguments were too exclusively practical—he warned the Bavarians that an independent 'administrative machine' would cost money which should be used 'in fighting the bourgeoisie and reaction'—and his mission failed.[2] The Bavarians, who had not called their paper *Der Proletarier* for nothing, were extremely suspicious of the Eisenach Party's ambiguous relationship with the People's Party, and were not prepared to be suspected, as Bracke and his colleagues were suspected, of having left the outspokenly socialist ADAV for a party of 'bourgeois half-socialists'. As well as the Lassallean training which made them class-consciously denounce all existing socialist parties for 'abusing the legacy of Lassalle', they had been in prolonged correspondence with

---

[1] Mayer, *Schweitzer*, pp. 365–6; Rüll (Nürnberg) to Becker 6 October 1869 (IISG).

[2] The Augsburg Congress is described by G. Gärtner, *Die Nürnberger Arbeiterbewegung 1868–1908*, pp. 38–9; the account by Bebel (II, pp. 101–4) is kept quite separate from his discussion of the Basle resolution (*ibid.*, pp. 92–4, 106–7), so that their essential connection is obscured.

Johann Philipp Becker, and perfectly understood the Basle resolution's significance—and also that of the Eisenach Party's refusal to ratify it. One of their leaders, Conrad Rüll of Nürnberg, had written to Becker in October that the People's Party, with their violent attacks on this resolution 'have taken a great step forward towards setting up the socialists on their own feet, and convincing them that they must take ruthless measures against all elements which do not belong to them'.[1]

This interpretation of the situation made the Bavarians impervious to the arguments of Bebel, though he eloquently assured them that the Eisenach Programme contained 'the international programme in its clearest form'. They proceeded with their plan of forming a party independent of both the Eisenachers and the Lassalleans: they would not rejoin Schweitzer, and the explicit acceptance of the Basle resolution by the Eisenachers was the only thing likely to make them join Liebknecht. It was this consideration which made him finally submit to the pressure—which had now lasted nearly five months—to take sides on the resolution. Bebel's report of his failure at Augsburg made it clear that the party had most to gain by explicitly ratifying the Basle resolution, thereby silencing Schweitzer's jeers, pacifying its own Braunschweig Executive, regaining the confidence of the International's leaders, and finally enticing the high-principled Bavarians into membership—advantages for which the break with the People's Party (which must in any case come about sooner or later) seemed a price worth paying.

Once the decision was taken—taken, it must be noted, on grounds of expediency, rather than of overriding loyalty to the International—the break came quickly. In the second week of February Bebel began a series of theoretical articles in the *Volksstaat*, which answered the five-months' accumulation of attacks on the Basle resolution and 'communism' in general with a detailed statement of the socialist case against the

---

[1] Rüll to Becker 6 October 1869 (IISG); cf. Mayer, *Schweitzer*, p. 365.

laissez-faire liberalism of the People's Party.[1] This party's horrified replies showed that unity between 'proletarian and bourgeois democracy' in Germany was indeed at an end, and the symbolic confirmation of this was the People's Party's ostentatious failure—for the first time—to send a representative to the Eisenach Party's next Congress, held in Stuttgart early in June.[2] At Stuttgart, on the other hand, the decisive reason why the party had adopted the Basle resolution (which was now formally ratified) was confirmed by the adhesion of the independent Bavarian Social Democratic Party to the ranks of the Eisenachers. The party had refused to acknowledge the programme of the International during the whole winter—for its own tactical reasons; it was now once more in harmony with the International—for its own tactical reasons again.

Renewed hopes of political support in 1870

Whatever the considerations had been which brought Liebknecht back into open agreement with the International, he was determined to make the most of the new position. Even before the actual ratification of the Basle resolution he was urgently repeating a suggestion he had made at the Basle Congress itself, that the fifth Annual Congress of the International should be held in Germany.[3]

There were many reasons why Liebknecht was anxious for the Eisenach Party to be host to the International's Congress, particularly now that the party was about to proclaim its full, though belated, adhesion to the Basle resolution—for one thing, he was of course eager, as a convinced socialist,

---

[1] Mayer, 'Die Trennung', pp. 60–1. Bebel's articles of February-March 1870 later appeared as a pamphlet entitled *Unsere Ziele*. The first part of this, based on a speech in Stuttgart in November 1869, makes no mention of either the International or the Basle resolution, whereas the passages originating after the decision to ratify the resolution contain detailed exposition of this, and praise for the International in general: *Unsere Ziele, von Aug. Bebel: Eine Streitschrift gegen die Demokratische Korrespondenz. 5. unwer Auflage*, pp. 1–15, 31–44.

[2] Bebel, however, still hoped at Stuttgart for an electoral alliance with the People's Party: cf. Mayer, *Schweitzer*, p. 378.

[3] *Demokratisches Wochenblatt*, 25 September 1869; Liebknecht's letter of 6 May 1870 to Braunschweig, quoted below, in *Hochverratsprozess*, p. 330.

to show the German public that his party was now in full agreement with the Basle resolution—but his correspondence suggests that the dominant motive was to use the International to reinforce his prestige in Germany. It may be that he even relied on the holding of the Congress in Germany to sway the Bavarians (still at this stage not completely decided) into joining the Eisenach Party, though this cannot be proved. What is certain, on the other hand, is that he counted on the prestige of the International, as so often, to strengthen his position against Schweitzer: in the first place, the mere holding of the Congress under the auspices of the Eisenach Party would be a severe blow to the ADAV; and secondly, to associate the International more closely with the movement in Germany might induce its leaders to deliver the public onslaught on the Lassalleans which they were still (despite their private convictions) reluctant to make. Thus it was that Liebknecht's letter of 6 May, after urging the Braunschweig Committee to invite 'at once—today even', the holding of the Congress in Germany, went on to say 'this will give us a great boost' (*wird uns famos Wasser auf die Mühle geben*) (this was true) and added 'the International will soon open a public attack on Schweitzer' (this was *not* true, but showed clearly what kind of a 'boost' Liebknecht expected to result from the invitation).

The General Council was quite prepared to consider this proposed change in the meeting-place of the Congress. It was originally to have been held in Paris, but renewed governmental persecution of the International's French branches made this impossible; Marx, moreover, was only too glad to consider holding the Congress in Germany, because his rival Bakunin was without influence there.

Thus on 17 May the General Council resolved unanimously to accept the Braunschweig Committee's invitation (sent on 9 May) and 'to meet in Mayence on 5 September'.[1] With this decision Liebknecht had achieved his first aim—the presence of the Congress in Germany would give the Eisenach Party 'a

---

[1] Minutes, III, p. 65; Eckert, *Aus den Anfängen*, pp. 11–12.

great boost', and party propaganda duly made the most of it[1]—but the International still refused to be moved to the 'public attack on Schweitzer' which he had so confidently predicted. Marx and Engels still saw no reason to depart from the public attitude of 'strict neutrality' which they had adopted before the Eisenach Congress, or to let Liebknecht force the International into 'following all his own twists and turns with regard to Schweitzer'. They had been disgusted by Liebknecht's equivocal attitude to the Basle resolution and were amazed at his interpretation of their recent 'Confidential Communication' against Bakunin (which also contained a private attack on Schweitzer): in this, complained Marx, 'it says that the General Council reserves the right to speak "publicly" about Schweitzer *when* it seems suitable: Wilhelm changes this to read that we will "come out with a public declaration"—for Wilhelm.'[2]

By June 1870, despite this, when it was certain that the International's Congress would be held in Mainz, Liebknecht again manoeuvred for a proclamation of the kind he wanted. There were rumours that the Lassalleans planned to break up the Congress by force (their interruptions had just prevented any debates on the first day—4 June—of the Eisenach Party's Congress in Stuttgart) and Liebknecht tried to use these rumours to convince the International's authorities how necessary their intervention was. 'Tell Marx', he wrote to the party secretary Bonhorst 'to take sides for us against Schweitzer. Schweitzer's plan to disrupt the Mainz Congress offers the opportunity.'[3] Marx, when approached, firmly refused to issue any general condemnation of Schweitzer; if forcible interruption of the Congress was inevitable, he said, they must be sure in advance

[1] *Volksstaat*, May-June 1870, *passim*; Eckert, *Aus den Anfängen*, p. 13.
[2] Marx to Engels 10 May 1870, *MEB*, IV, p. 386; the 'Communication' in *Briefe an Kugelmann*, pp. 94–107.
[3] Liebknecht to Bonhorst 20 June 1870, *Hochverratsprozess*, p. 330 (Liebknecht explains that owing to 'a slight difference' with Marx—echoes of which occur in the latter's correspondence with Engels—he cannot write to London himself). On the Stuttgart Congress, cf. Mayer, *Schweitzer*, p. 377.

that articles appeared 'in the *Volksstaat, Zukunft,* and other available newspapers', putting the blame on the Prussian police, and denouncing them for planning 'to obstruct the International Congress in Mainz . . . through their agent Schweitzer's organisation'. If such warnings appeared in the German press, said Marx, 'the General Council would see to it that similar notices were published in London, Paris, etc.', but unless the Germans managed to put the blame on the government in this way the General Council would do nothing. 'The International can welcome a conflict with Herr Bismarck, but not anything that could be described as spontaneous "attacks by German patriotic workers" bearing the label of "struggles of principles".' After receiving this refusal to let the International's name be used in the Eisenach Party's quarrels, Liebknecht said no more of the Lassallean threat to the Congress, and Bonhorst even officially assured Marx that the danger was negligible.

A further attempt by the Braunschweig Executive to adapt the International to its own concerns—the not unreasonable request that the Mainz Congress be postponed from September to October to leave the party free for the German elections fixed for September—was firmly rejected by Marx; and the Congress programme, requesting 'the delegates . . . to assemble on Monday, 5 September, at nine-o'clock in the forenoon' was published on 12 July.[1]

For a year the German leaders had looked to the International to give them political support and financial help; but they had equivocated over its programme, and then invited its Congress to Germany, in accordance with their own tactical preoccupations—their alliance with the People's Party, their need to impress the Bavarians, and their feud with Schweitzer. This had been their attitude during a year of European peace which now came abruptly to an end.

---

[1] Handbill, *The Fifth Annual Congress of the International Working Men's Association* (IISG); correspondence of mid-June between Braunschweig and the General Council in Eckert, *op. cit.,* pp. 14–16.

THE SECOND ATTITUDE: FROM THE
OUTBREAK OF WAR TO THE COMMUNE OF PARIS
(JULY 1870–MAY 1871)

The last item on the agenda for the Mainz Congress, published on 12 July, read: 'reconsideration by the Congress of the means to suppress war'. In a Europe which had seen no serious threat to peace since the Luxemburg crisis of 1867, the suppression of war seemed almost an abstract subject for debate, included as an afterthought along with the more familiar economic and social problems; yet on this same 12 July the French Ambassador in Berlin received the intransigent directions for his interview with King Wilhelm on the 13th which gave Bismarck the opportunity to distort the Ems telegram, and led directly to the Franco-Prussian War.[1]

By 5 September, when the Mainz Congress should have met, the Second Empire was in ruins and the political landscape of Europe was utterly changed. Hundreds of the International's French and German supporters were dispersed on the battle-fields of the Somme or the Loire; correspondence between the Sections and the General Council was largely interrupted; and the power of the whole organisation seemed broken for ever. It had indeed lost its influence as the directing centre of European socialism—an influence which it never regained; its public proclamations, now calling less for socialism than for a constructive political settlement, went almost unnoticed in the mighty tide of events; and its rival 'Marxist' and 'Bakuninist' factions might have been left to fight out their struggle in complete obscurity, if the International had not been suddenly and firmly associated with the Commune of Paris.

Although the International's French branches had little or nothing to do with the establishment of the Commune,[2] some

[1] A. J. P. Taylor, *The Struggle for Mastery in Europe*, p. 205.
[2] R. W. Postgate, *Revolution from 1789 to 1906*, p. 281; F. Jellinek, *The Paris Commune of 1871*, pp. 39, 124; G. D. H. Cole, *Marxism and Anarchism*, pp. 159–60; G. Bourgin, *La Commune*, p. 14; N. Lukin, 'Protokolle des Generalrats . . . als Quelle für die Geschichte der Pariser Commune', in *Unter dem Banner des Marxismus*, Vol. VI, p. 103 fn.

of their leading members played a large part in directing it; and this led the governments and the press of all Europe to denounce the Commune as the first step in the International's plot to subvert the whole existing order of society. It was the violence and unanimity of these denunciations which provoked public defence of the Commune from all the International's spokesmen who could give it: from Bebel in the German *Reichstag* as well as from Marx in London and Becker in Geneva.

In these troubled circumstances there could be no question of the Eisenach Party's fulfilling its nominal obligations to act as part of the International's organisation: the organisation simply collapsed, and its original purposes—trade-union activity, the development of co-operatives, and conventional propaganda for socialism—were laid aside in the turmoil of war and revolution. A study of the Germans' attitude to the International during this period has simply to consider how far they took account of its leaders' public or private views in deciding their own line on urgent problems—in other words, how important they thought the International was.

The urgent problems were, of course, those of war-aims and peace-terms. Until the war of 1870, the International had been, in Germany, mainly a symbol of socialism. German nationalism during the 1860s had of course been very pronounced, but it had signified the idea of national unity, which socialists could under certain circumstances accept, not that of aggression against other nations. In this period when national rivalries, although far from absent, were at least relatively unobtrusive, internationalism was an attitude which could be taken more or less for granted among socialists; and thus the resolutions asserting the 'international character of the labour movement', which had been passed by all the major German socialist congresses since 1868, paid tribute to the International as the symbol of socialism, rather than of internationalism. With the sudden conflict of nationalisms inflamed by the war, the internationalist significance of the International Working Men's

Association stood out in a new light. How far was that significance recognised by its German adherents?

The beginning of the war

In the first days of the crisis, when there still seemed to be a chance of avoiding war, German socialists all acknowledged a responsibility to the International. On 12 July its members in Paris had published a proclamation (reprinted in the General Council's first address on the 23rd), which appealed to the 'workers of France, Germany and Spain' to 'unite their voices in a cry of horror against war'; and the response of Bonhorst, the Braunschweig Committee's secretary, was to draft a reply calling for 'no more war, no more fratricide' in the 'personal interests of dynasties'—'no more war, except the last, the war for liberty, equality and fraternity!' Bracke, another member of the Committee, had a different conception of its responsibilities to the International: convinced that the party would be banned at once for a manifesto as inflammatory as this, he vetoed its publication until a policy had been decided 'in consultation with Marx, Geib and Liebknecht', and on 14 July consoled Bonhorst with the thought: 'Our supreme authority (*unsere Oberleitung*) is international, and will soon decide when the time for action has come. Our task in the meantime is to remain silent, and at the right moment to obey without question.'[1]

Liebknecht and Bebel also affirmed the party's opposition to war; on 17 July (between the French Chamber's approval of military credits and the formal declaration of war) they got a mass-meeting in Chemnitz to pass a resolution 'declaring the present war purely dynastic', 'grasping with joy the hand extended by the workers of France', and promising: 'true to the motto of the International Working Men's Association, "Workers of the World, unite", we will never forget that the

---

[1] Marx, *Der Bürgerkrieg in Frankreich*, pp. 26–7; Bonhorst's draft in W. Bracke, *Der Braunschweiger Ausschuss . . . vor dem Gericht*, p. 156; Bracke to Bonhorst 14 July 1870, *ibid.*, pp. 83–4 and in *Hochverratsprozess*, pp. 327–8.

workers of all countries are our friends, and the despots of all countries our enemies'.[1]

These declarations of the Eisenach Party's opposition to war were courageous and honourable, but had no effect on the course of events and could provide no firm basis for action; once war became inevitable, and fighting actually started, each leader of the party had to decide for himself what attitude to take, and the unanimity of the party's first reactions was quickly broken. In the first place, the members of the Braunschweig Committee swung rapidly away from their feeling that they ought to wait for instructions from an international 'supreme authority'; they were by now convinced (like the Lassallean party, and the overwhelming majority of the German people) that Napoleon was the aggressor who had wantonly forced the war on an innocent Germany. On 16 July, even, while there was still a hope of peace, they had firmly pronounced this view in a resolution passed by a Braunschweig meeting: 'Napoleon and the majority of the so-called representatives of the French people are the frivolous destroyers of the peace...of Europe; our first duty is to oppose them. The German nation...is the victim of aggression. Therefore the meeting, with great regret, must accept the defensive war as a necessary evil.'[2]

The Committee never forgot the aims of the party; Bracke was probably right in his later claim that their two main considerations at the outbreak of war had been:

(1) That democracy in France would have greater opportunities if the war was fought with the maximum of determination on the German side, and brought about the fall of the Imperial throne, and (2) that with the terrific impetus given by this war to the national idea in Germany the unification of the country would be realised, perhaps with the co-operation of the people and under the influence of the social-democratic workers, and that henceforth, 'the national

<hr />

[1] *Der Bürgerkrieg*, p. 29; the same version is given in a letter sent to Moses Hess on 17 July 1870 (printed in Berlin *Vorwärts*, 28 March 1926), but the version published by Bebel (*AML*, II, p. 157) makes no mention of the International.

[2] Full text in K. Kautsky, *Sozialisten und Krieg*, p. 190.

question' would no longer obstruct and limit the great movement of freedom and social democracy.

On 24 July, a few days after the declaration of war, the Braunschweig Committee summed up these views in a proclamation which stressed the need 'to defend German soil against Napoleonic or any other aggression', to support the creation of a united German state, and 'to work in effective co-operation at the birth of this...State, so that if possible not a dynastic state but a social democratic People's State comes into being'.

The proclamation was vague about the actual steps to be taken to transform the victorious Prussian monarchy into a socialist Germany, democratic and peace-loving; it simply warned 'those who hold power in our country' that once Napoleon was beaten, 'we would remind them what the people, in God's name and that of justice, deserve, and what they have earned by the unending sacrifices and miseries of war', and it ended unconvincingly: 'Long live Germany! Long live the international struggle of the proletariat!'[1]

By this time the earlier Braunschweig statement, the resolution of 16 July, had been sent to Liebknecht for publication in the *Volksstaat*; he found its talk of defensive wars against Napoleon so far removed from his own attitude that he delayed publishing it until on 20 July a peremptory letter from Braunschweig ordered him to do so 'without answering back'.[2] Liebknecht obeyed, but his own feelings in the first days of the war remained very different from the Executive's.

The men in Braunschweig, who had had their political training under Schweitzer (however greatly they differed from him now) regarded it as natural to use the chance offered by Napoleon's apparent provocation to create a united Germany; and even if the country seemed overawed by Bismarck and the Prussian army while the war lasted, they were prepared to speculate on the chance that radical social changes would be demanded when it was over. They recognised, in any case, that

---

[1] Bracke's preface to *Der Braunschweiger Ausschuss* . . ., pp. 2–5.
[2] Eckert, *Aus den Anfängen*, p. 20.

German public opinion was overwhelmingly in favour of the war, and that the party could only oppose it at the cost of 'estranging from us . . . the hearts of the people'.[1]

Liebknecht was unable to calculate in this way. Since 1848 he had regarded Prussian militarism as the main enemy, and he could never bring himself to welcome German unifaction as the result of a Prussian war, even a war fought against Napoleon III. He also deluded himself gravely about the weakness of the North German Confederation built in 1866. Still moving in particularist and federalist circles which dreamed of 'undoing the work of 1866', he seems to have believed that a French threat to Prussia would be enough in Saxony to set off a determined movement for 'liberation' from the Prussian yoke, and that once the power of the Hohenzollern dynasty was broken, it would be the turn of the French to overthrow the Bonapartes, so that Europe would live under a regime of socialist democracies.

The reaction of Liebknecht's comrades to these fantasies varied from furious dissent by Bracke to sceptical agreement by Bebel. Bracke's views were expressed in his letter to Geib on 29 July, already quoted: 'if Liebknecht goes on like this, all we shall have at the end of the war will be a dozen well-trained social-republicans and a few Saxons whose particularism makes them prefer the distant international ideal to the national one which is nearer, but which has been spoilt for them since 1866 by its black and white [i.e. Prussian] colouring'.[2]

As for Bebel, although he failed to share Liebknecht's optimistic view of the situation in its entirety, he did agree that no support whatever should be given to Bismarck's war against France, and when the *Reichstag* was summoned on 21 July to provide war-credits, both Liebknecht and Bebel showed their disapproval by abstaining from voting. This courageous attitude provoked furious anger in the *Reichstag*—the government received the votes of the Lassalleans, and also of the

---

[1] Bracke to Geib 29 July 1870, *Der Braunschweiger Ausschuss*, p. 5.

[2] *Ibid.*; on Liebknecht's views, Mayer, *Schweitzer*, pp. 384–5.

former Lassallean Fritzsche, now a member of the Eisenach Party—but Liebknecht and Bebel held firm.

'As opponents on principle of all wars,' they declared, 'as social republicans and members of the International Working Men's Association, which opposes all oppressors, and aims to unite all the oppressed into one great league of brotherhood, we cannot declare ourselves either directly or indirectly in favour of the present war and therefore abstain from voting, expressing the confident hope that the people of Europe, having learnt from the present tragic events, will make every effort to achieve their right of self-determination and will overthrow the present domination of sabre and of class, the cause of all public and social evil.'[1]

The German branch of the International was thus split into two camps by the coming of the war. The first question that may be asked: 'which of the two pursued a policy closer to that of the International?' has been much discussed by Marxist historians, but has only a theoretical interest, since the General Council had even less influence on events than the German Social Democrats. The more important question, to which a partial answer has already been attempted, is therefore 'what were the actual views of the two German factions, and for what reasons were they held?'. The General Council's Manifesto of 23 July did in fact incline towards the standpoint of the Braunschweig Committee in accepting the need for Germany to fight a defensive war against Napoleon, but it pointedly refrained from remarking on the possible benefits for German socialists if they acquiesced in a Prussian victory, and it ended with a vision, like Liebknecht's, of 'a brighter future' in which 'a new society will arise, whose international principle will be peace, because inside every nation the same principle will rule —Labour!'.[2]

In their private letters Marx and Engels, when they examined the disagreement in Germany, condemned what Engels

[1] Bebel, *AML*, II, pp. 158–60.
[2] *Der Bürgerkrieg in Frankreich*, pp. 29–30.

described on 15 August as 'total obstruction à la Wilhelm' as much as the 'national enthusiasm' and 'theoretical uncertainty' of Bracke and Bonhorst; so that neither Braunschweig nor Leipzig could justly claim the International's approval for its views. Bebel did in fact claim in a letter to the Executive on 13 August that 'Marx has declared himself for us', but Marx made it clear to Engels four days later that his approval for Liebknecht's and Bebel's stand in the Reichstag did not imply agreement with their view of the situation.[1]

The fact was that both groups in Germany had really made up their minds on considerations which had nothing to do with the International—Bracke and his friends on their view of the threat from Napoleon and of the party's chances of profiting from national unification, Liebknecht and Bebel on their absolute refusal to accept alignment with Bismarck and their hope (in Liebknecht's case a conviction) that a popular rising in Germany would sweep away 'the work of 1866'.

The International played only a small part in the German leaders' thoughts at this stage. The Executive corresponded with Marx on questions of organisation like the postponement of the 1870 Congress, and took up with him minor points like the need for propaganda warning the German people against a threat from Russia;[2] but when they told him in mid-August of their major disagreement about the war, it was really, as Bracke said later, 'to have the opinion of someone who was highly esteemed by us all'[3] rather than to submit the dispute to the binding arbitration of an acknowledged *Oberleitung*—despite what Bracke had said in July. The attitudes which the German

[1] *Hochverratsprozess*, pp. 312–13; *MEB*, IV, pp. 438–40, 443. Engels' comment to Marx, 'Du bist natürlich auf Wilhelms Seite' (*ibid.*, p. 441) is of course merely a sarcastic allusion to Liebknecht's own claims.

[2] Eckert, *op. cit.*, pp. 16–19; Jaeckh, *Die Internationale*, pp. 228–9; Marx and Engels, *Briefe an A. Bebel, W. Liebknecht*, p. 489.

[3] *Hochverratsprozess*, p. 515 (Bracke's evidence); Marx to Natalie Liebknecht 2 March 1871 (in *Einheit: Zeitschrift für Theorie und Praxis des Wissenschaftlichen Sozialismus*, VIII, 1953, pp. 575–7): 'The letter I sent to the Braunschweigers was *not* sent in the name or on behalf of the General Council . . . it contains only my personal opinion.' Marx's argument, meant as a legal defence for the accused Braunschweigers, was in fact the truth.

factions had taken up at the beginning of the war were based in fact on such firm convictions that even a judgment from Marx would have done nothing to alter them, if the situation had remained the same. Marx's comments, however (which reached Braunschweig shortly before the French defeat at Sedan) arrived when the situation was decisively changing.

The war's end and the Commune

In the first stage of the war, when all Germany was convinced of the aggressive designs of Napoleon, the Braunschweig Committee had had a case for supporting a defensive war, and for postponing pressure on the German government until the danger was over; Liebknecht and Bebel, on the other hand, had been justified in their grave mistrust of Bismarck, and in warning Bracke and his colleagues, as Bebel did on 13 August, that no good could come if the movement let itself be carried away in 'a sort of national paroxysm'. Throughout August the two factions stuck to their original attitudes, reproaching each other bitterly but recognising that mutual tolerance was the most they could hope for: as Liebknecht had told the Braunschweig Committee on 26 July, the atmosphere of nationalist excitement in Northern Germany was so great that 'I ought not to reproach you too much for your patriotic zeal. But' he continued, 'be tolerant on your side too. Even if you disagree with Bebel's and my stand in the *Reichstag*, this disagreement must be overcome at all costs, or at least prevented from coming out into the open.'[1]

It was only when a French defeat became certain that unity could be restored. The Prussian victory of Sedan on 2 September destroyed the Second Empire, to the joy of every socialist in Germany; its results, however, showed Bracke and his colleagues to their horror that the Prussian government did not regard the war as defensive at all, and that the future German state would scarcely, as they had anticipated, 'bear the stamp of their ideas'. They saw on the contrary that the Prussian

---

[1] Letters of Bebel and Liebknecht in *Hochverratsprozess*, pp. 197, 312.

Government, far from regarding its war-aims as fulfilled by the disappearance of Napoleon, was turning the war into 'a war of aggression against the French people' with the aim of establishing the European hegemony of a Prussianised Germany, and of consolidating it by the annexation of Alsace-Lorraine.

Liebknecht, on hearing that the Republic had been proclaimed in France, wept tears of joy; the Braunschweig Committee may not have shared his emotions to the same degree, but the party was now united in demanding that Prussia should include 'an honourable peace with France', and that the annexation of Alsace-Lorraine (which, Marx predicted, would inevitably lead France to seek a Russian alliance against Germany) should not take place.[1]

The Braunschweig Committee's new proclamation of 5 September, in which these demands were eloquently voiced on behalf of the re-united party, incorporated long extracts from a letter of Marx (to his great annoyance, since this tactlessly revealed his satisfaction at the prospective 'shifting of the centre of the European Labour movement' from France to Germany through the latter's victory): the proclamation was thus not unnaturally in harmony with the manifesto which Marx drafted for the General Council a few days later. This realignment with the International of both sections of the German party has been interpreted as signifying that their basic attitude from the beginning had been inspired by 'internationalist Marxist thinking';[2] it is clear, however, that their alignment with the International in September, just as much as their various deviations in July, was a matter of circumstances and calculation. Both Bracke and Liebknecht chose their lines of policy on grounds which had nothing to do with the International, and although both of them were anxious to feel that they had the support of Marx, they only accepted his point of view because the new situation had already changed their own.

[1] Bebel, *AML*, II, p. 164; Kautsky, *Sozialisten und Krieg*, pp. 192, 197; Marx, *Der Bürgerkrieg in Frankreich*, p. 37
[2] Kautsky, *op. cit.*, p. 200.

The manifesto in which the Braunschweig Committee opposed the continuance of the war and the annexation of Alsace-Lorraine was published on 5 September. On 9 September all five members of the Committee were arrested by the orders of the Military Governor of North Germany, and transported in chains to the East Prussian fortress of Lötzen; Bismarck, with the victorious German armies near Paris, sent orders to Berlin on 18 September that similar steps should be taken 'wherever treasonable manifestations of the same kind' came to light, and within a few days the Military Governor had forbidden 'all meetings of the socialists, whether these call themselves by the name of social-democrats or People's Party', and had banned the circulation of the party-paper *Volksstaat* throughout North Germany. The functions of the arrested Executive were taken over by the party's Supervisory Board in Hamburg, but by the end of the month its leader, Geib, had joined the Braunschweig committee-members in prison, and the party's viewpoint could be expressed only in the curtailed *Volksstaat*, and by its representatives in the *Reichstag*.[1]

When the *Reichstag* was summoned in November to approve financial means for the continuation of the war, Liebknecht and Bebel lifted their voices against the overwhelming majority of the assembly in a courageous protest against annexation. (The Lassalleans under Schweitzer voted against the government this time, but remained silent in the debate.) Certain newspapers had already demanded the arrest of the two 'traitors' in October; and a few days after the *Reichstag* session ended they were arrested, to be charged with 'undertaking a forcible attack on...the state constitution...and preparing an enterprise of High Treason'. It was not until March 1871, after the peace treaty with France had been signed, that the prisoners were released (though still awaiting trial) and the party could speak with a stronger voice. In the meantime, however, the peace-treaty had been immediately followed by a general

---

[1] *Ibid.*, p. 202; Prussian *Ministerium des Innern* Rep. 77 Abt. II Sekt. 11D, Vol. I, pp. 26, 28, 33; Bebel, *AML*, II, p. 166.

election, in which a wave of nationalist enthusiasm swept away every socialist candidate except Bebel, now the party's only representative in the *Reichstag*.[1]

The government lawyers charged with investigating the masses of party correspondence seized at the time of the Braunschweig and Leipzig arrests had by this time come to the conclusion—natural but erroneous—that the party's spokesman had been acting on the direct orders of the International, particularly in proclaiming their new line after the beginning of September. There was indeed no doubt that the party's attitude throughout the war had been based partly on internationalist sentiments; the indignant words of the report which the Counsel Heppenstedt sent to the Prussian government on the Braunschweig documents, at the end of October, reflect his horrified reaction to modes of thought completely alien to his own:

The Social Democratic Party [he concludes] persistently describes itself as exclusively international and denies every national interest . . . the socialists have no feeling for the unity, greatness, and prestige of the German fatherland. At the beginning of the war they issue orders for the French declaration of war to be opposed: without any expression of patriotism, however, but because the war is regarded as one exclusively between princes . . . in which the people can have no interest. The letters of Bebel, Hepner, Liebknecht and others utter no hope of success for the German arms at the beginning of the war, and later no satisfaction at the victories won.[2]

This was a fair summary of part of the story (its author conceded that the Braunschweig Committee's attitude, early in the war, had been less 'treasonable' than Liebknecht's), but the authorities were wrong to conclude that the party was 'no more and no less than the German Section of the International based on London',[3] or that the discussion with Marx during August had implied a recognition of his supreme author-

[1] Mayer, *Schweitzer*, pp. 397, 401; Bebel, *AML*, II, p. 167; *Hochverratsprozess*, p. 89.
[2] Prussian *Ministerium des Innern* Rep. 77 Abt. II Sekt. 11D, Vol. I, p. 145.
[3] Regierungsrat Goltz to Graf Eulenburg (Minister of the Interior) 18 September 1870, *ibid.*, p. 47.

ity; these accusations formed part of the charge against the party leaders when they were brought to trial (the Braunschweig Committee in November 1871, Liebknecht and Bebel in March 1872) but could not be proved and were finally withdrawn. The German socialists had in fact realised that the International, which most of them had taken seriously before the war, did not count for much in the wartime situation, and had ignored it in deciding their lines of action.

The coming of the war had destroyed the International's influence as a centre of socialism, and turned it for a time into a symbol of internationalism. The passions let loose during the second half of the brief war, however (it was perhaps a 'war of cabinets' until Sedan; thereafter it became a 'peoples' war',[1] inevitably reduced the general popularity of any internationalist organisation, and by the time the war was over the Social Democrats in Germany were unable to look up to the International with the respect and admiration which they had felt in the later 1860s. Bebel's moving defence of the Commune, between March and May 1871, marked in fact the transition to a new outlook on the International; the Germans came to realise that the International's prestige depended entirely on the support it received from its members or sympathisers in the various countries, and although they were prepared to stand up for it in its hour of need, the relationship was not what it had been before the war. For one thing, the Germans had realised that they, almost alone among the International's supporters, had a relatively well-organised national party of their own.

When the Commune was proclaimed on 18 March, Bebel —though he was still in prison—had just heard of his election (as the only socialist) to the *Reichstag* of the new German Empire. By the end of the month he had been released in order to take his seat, and he soon spoke to defend the Commune against its critic. His first speech was made in April, when the Commune was still firmly in control of Paris; he admitted to disagreement with some of its policies, simply praising it in a brief speech for

[1] F. Fischer, *Geschichte in Ueberblick*, p. 187.

'acting with the greatest moderation', but even this was enough to provoke the *Reichstag* to 'loud and continuing interruptions'. An even more courageous gesture was Bebel's speech of 25 May; the Commune, now defeated, had been execrated throughout Europe as a regime subversive of religion, property, order and morality, and the news that its members and supporters were being massacred by the troops of Thiers was being received with relief and satisfaction. In the face of a savagely hostile *Reichstag*, Bebel defiantly proclaimed: 'the whole European proletariat, and all who still have any feeling for freedom and independence, have their eyes fixed on Paris... and even if Paris is overthrown today, I warn you that the battle in Paris is only a skirmish, that the main battle in Europe is still to come, and that before many decades pass the battle-cry of the proletariat of Paris...will become that of the whole proletariat of Europe!'[1]

Such a gratuitous identification of his party with the Commune, in its hour of violent defeat and universal denunciation, could bring Bebel and his friends no immediate popularity; on the contrary, it made the public authorities of Germany more determined than ever to suppress 'the revolutionary goings-on' of the Social Democrats, and the dossiers of police reports circulating in government departments rapidly began to thicken. In the General Council of the International, however, now that 'International' and 'Commune' were regarded throughout Europe as synonymous, Bebel's gesture of solidarity, which was followed by meetings of sympathy in various German towns, made a great impression.[2]

The war, it transpired, had weakened the International— already split internally by the rivalry between Marx and Bakunin—relatively more than it had weakened the Eisenach Party, and a situation had now arisen where the International was more than ever in need of help and encouragement from

---

[1] Bebel, *AML*, II, pp. 194–7; Jellinek, *The Paris Commune of 1871*, pp. 411–12; S. Bernstein, *Essays in Political and Intellectual History*, pp. 166, 175–6.

[2] Minutes (IISG) 18 April, 30 May, 11 July 1871; Engels to Liebknecht 22 June 1871 in Marx and Engels, *Briefe an A. Bebel, W. Liebknecht*, pp. 28–9.

all its branches, including the German. This situation continued during the period of a year and a half until the International moved its headquarters to New York after the Hague Congress.

THE THIRD ATTITUDE: FROM THE COMMUNE TO THE HAGUE CONGRESS (MAY 1871 — SEPTEMBER 1872)

At the end of May 1871, when European society was applauding the suppression of the Commune, the International's General Council approved an *Address on the Civil War* drafted by Marx; it proudly associated the International with the defunct Commune, and accepted as 'naturally correct' the verdict of a neutral journalist that 'most of the Commune's members were the most active, far-sighted and energetic members of the International Working Men's Association'.[1] From this moment the International, more than communism in 1848, was a spectre haunting the dreams of civilised society; what *The Tablet* called 'the ominous, the ubiquitous International Association of Workmen' was represented by the French foreign minister as an all-powerful conspiracy, bent on the immediate destruction of 'family, religion, order and property', and possessed of the means to encompass it.[2] Despite this, scarcely more than a year was to pass before the leaders of the International—either despairing of its very survival and expecting it to die a natural death, or at least convinced that to survive at all it would have to be removed from the influence of its Bakuninist members—transferred its headquarters to the remoteness of New York. In 1871, in fact, the International, though the Commune had made it seem more powerful than ever and its total membership may actually have risen, was only a shadow of what it had been in the 1860s. How had this come about?

[1] *Der Bürgerkrieg in Frankreich*, p. 103.

[2] Jules Favre's circular of 6 June 1871, reprinted in *International Review for Social History*, Vol. IV, pp. 50–6; *Tablet*, 15 July 1871, quoted by Henry Collins in *Essays in Labour History*, edited by A. Briggs and J. Saville, p. 242.

In 1871 and 1872 the International was gravely hampered both by incessant persecution from the governments of Europe and by the irreconcilable feud between its rival leaders. Almost every government in continental Europe took measures to repress and destroy the International, acting with a thoroughness which only the universal horror at the alleged excesses of the Commune could explain:[1] in France and some other countries the International was expressly outlawed; Bismarck assured his Emperor that he would have the provisions of German law amended so that any preparation by the International of 'a forcible attack' might be 'not only spied upon and discovered, but best of all, crushed'; and hundreds of notes were despatched from one capital to another, passing on 'news' of the International's alleged activities, suggesting methods of spying on it, and recommending ways of deterring workers from joining it.[2]

These external hindrances to the International's work, though they had existed ever since 1864, created serious difficulties only from 1870 onwards; the explosive tension between Marx's followers and Bakunin's, on the other hand, had been accumulating dangerously for some years. Even before the war of 1870 Marx and Engels had decided that their relations with 'the intriguer Bakunin' could be nothing but a prolonged (and even then interrupted) armistice; if the war had not supervened the issue might have been fought out in 1870. No full Congress could be held until 1872, however, and it dragged on unsettled. This meant that the rival factions concentrated on gathering support for the final struggle. The International's British and German adherents, if they could be persuaded to interest themselves in the dispute, were on the whole likely to side with Marx, and those in Italy and Switzerland (the main centre of the struggle in 1870 and 1871) with

---

[1] The British government's refusal even to discuss collective measures is described and documented by J. Braunthal, *Geschichte der Internationale*, Vol. I, pp. 173-4.

[2] *Ibid.*, pp. 167-73 *passim*; Bismarck to the Kaiser 4 April 1872 in Deutsches Zentralarchiv, Merseburg, *Acta des Königlichen Civil-Kabinets* I. Abthl. Rep. 89H, Abthl. XXI Nr. 18, *Polizei-Sachen*, I, pp. 3-5.

Bakunin; both leaders, however, realised that active canvassing was necessary to rally their followers, and they accordingly came to devote much of their energy to seeking support not for the International as a whole but for their own faction inside it.[1] With the International thus in danger of succumbing to governmental molestation and internal rivalry, what attitude to it were the leaders of the Eisenach Party to take? In the first place, they had to direct their main attention to the problems of their own seriously weakened party: the *Volksstaat* had lost half its subscribers during the war; all but one of the Social Democrat deputies in the *Reichstag* had lost their seats at the victory-election of March 1871; almost every prominent party leader was in prison; and the party faced the certainty of further legal reprisals if its activities attracted too much attention from the police. It continued to undertake public demonstrations— protest-meetings against social, fiscal, or constitutional injustices, speeches by Bebel in the *Reichstag*, and even a party congress (held at Dresden in August 1871) when speakers paid tribute to the Commune despite warnings not to do so from the police; in time, the atmosphere of repression even began to help the party's propaganda and thus to strengthen it, but the process was slow and the difficulties were enormous.[2]

After the March elections were over, the prisoners from Leipzig and Braunschweig were released, but only while the charges against them were being elaborated: in November 1871 the members of the Braunschweig Committee received prison sentences varying from five to sixteen months (though these were later reduced), and in March 1872 came the sensational trial for High Treason of Liebknecht and Bebel, who were sentenced to two years' imprisonment each, and re-entered prison in July—two months before the International's Hague Congress.[3]

[1] Mayer, *Engels*, II, pp. 221 *et seq.*, 233–7; J. Ragaz, *Geschichte der Arbeiterbewegung in der Westschweiz*, pp. 108–23; Marx's appeals to Germany are discussed below.
[2] P. Kampffmeyer and B. Altmann, *Vor dem Sozialistengesetz, passim*; Bebel, *AML*, II, pp. 200–6; *Volksstaat*.
[3] Bebel, *op. cit.*, II, pp. 191, 216–23; Braunschweig and Leipzig trial-reports.

These circumstances made the German leaders only too aware of the risks to their party if it appeared to have close links with the International. One incident after another reminded them of these risks. From 1871 to 1873, for instance, a wave of strikes took place throughout Germany; their ultimate cause was post-war inflation, but employers and administrators attributed them to 'the agitation of Trade Unions which mostly belong... to the International Working Men's Association',[1] and called for government action to protect society from 'the abyss' opened before it by the International's machinations. A strike in the Cologne railway-workshops in October 1871 for instance, according to an employers' publication, was 'fomented by an agent of the so-called International'; a few weeks later the press of Silesia was full of 'authentic' news of the London General Council's plots for a general strike in the coal-pits, which the ministers in Berlin were only too ready to believe; and a detailed report of thirty pages, presented to the Saxon Ministry of the Interior by a committee of burgomasters and police-authorities from Saxony's industrial towns, concluded that 'the strikes are clearly nothing but the feelers put out by the International... to judge the force at its disposal'.[2] These rumours increased the interest of the police in the Eisenach Party. Its leaders could hardly deny that they had baptised their Trade Unions 'international'; but now that 'internationalism' was taken to imply full agreement with the aims and methods of the Paris Commune (as construed by a fanatically hostile press) the party leaders could only regard their alleged connection with the International, publicised by the strike-movement, as a source of embarrassment.

Again, a rumour originating in France, which alleged that

[1] *Amtliche Mitteilung des Deutschen Handelstages: Die Arbeitseinstellungen in Deutschland...*, pp. 45 *et seq.*; Mehring, *Geschichte der deutschen Sozialdemokratie*, Vol. IV, pp. 39–42.
[2] *Amtliche Mitteilung des Deutschen Handelstages*, pp. 15, 45; *Schlesische Zeitung*, 3 December 1871; copy of Saxon report in Prussian *Ministerium für Handel und Gewerbe*, Rep. 120, BB VII, Fach 1, Nr. 2: *Acta betr. die Massregeln gegen die Bestrebungen der Internationale*, Vol. I, pp. 120–35.

the Eisenach Party's Dresden Congress of August 1871 was 'a Congress of the International', was enough to make the rulers of Germany redouble their police precautions; in an atmosphere like this, the party's leaders could not afford, as Liebknecht told Engels at the end of the year 'to gamble with the existence of our organisation' for the sake of mentioning the International and its ideals too insistently in public.[1]

Systematic propaganda for the International could clearly not be thought of; but what did the Eisenach Party's leaders feel about it in private, and what part did it play in their political considerations? Briefly, the respect, even enthusiasm which they had felt for it before 1870 were by now reduced to habitual loyalty and mere sympathy. The Germans sensed that the International (or rather the 'Marxist' General Council with which they were in contact) needed them more than they needed it; and they could hardly regard it with their former reverence when Marx and Engels, preoccupied with attempts to overawe Bakunin by exaggerating the General Council's popularity in Germany, allowed its dependence on their party to become so obvious. In the winter of 1871–2 Marx and Engels wrote imploring them repeatedly to ensure an impressive German representation to defeat Bakunin at the Hague Congress, scolding them for having revealed the International's low German membership-figures even to save themselves from imprisonment, and telling them in detail how the General Council was 'busy drafting a circular to be printed for private circulation, containing revelations on the goings-on of Bakunin . . .'.[2]

The repeated appeals for help from London made the Germans realise as never before how far the International depended on the support of its adherents in each country. After the Com-

[1] Kampffmeyer & Altmann, *op. cit.*, p. 82; Bismarck to Eulenburg, 18 July 1871 in *Ministerium des Innern* Rep. 77 Abt. II, Sekt. 11D Gen, Vol. II, p. 178; Liebknecht to Engels late 1871 in Mayer, *Schweitzer*, p. 440.
[2] Marx to Berlin 1 February 1872 in *Die Gesellschaft*, 1933, p. 262; Marx and Engels, *Briefe an A. Bebel, W. Liebknecht*, pp. 47, 56, 60, 70–1; *Der Braunschweiger Ausschuss*, pp. 151–2; Eckert, *Wilhelm Bracke und die Anfänge der Braunschweiger Arbeiterbewegung*, pp. 12–13.

mune, Germany had replaced France as the main centre of European socialism; if the General Council, however, appeared to the Germans no longer as an inspiration but as an organisation whose usefulness was at the best marginal, and which was always appealing to them to keep it alive, they would hesitate before using in its interests the power they possessed. This power, after all, despite its relative impressiveness inside the international labour movement, was in real terms negligible, and was not to be wasted.

The Germans agreed with the General Council on the main theoretical issue involved in the International's dissensions: the need for the socialist movement to engage in political action. 'Political action' seemed so unquestionably necessary to German socialists, whether they had been trained in the Lassallean agitation for the right to vote or in the 'greater-German democratic' atmosphere of the People's Party, that the very existence in the International of so many Bakuninists and others arguing for 'purely economic' propaganda must have helped to prevent them from taking the organisation altogether seriously. On the other hand, if Marx and Engels asked them to publish the London Conference resolutions of 1871, or to come and vote against Bakunin at the Hague Congress of 1872, they were prepared to do so, partly because they agreed that the advocates of 'purely economic action' ought to be taught a lesson and partly because of their personal attachment to Marx and Engels. (It should not be forgotten that the prestige of Marx and Engels was continually increasing at this period through the occasional reprinting of one or another of their older writings in the *Volksstaat*, or the appearance of a new edition of Volume I of *Das Kapital* in 1872—even though the extent to which these publications made their admirers into 'Marxists' is highly debatable.)[1]

Admiration for Marx and Engels was certainly one motive disposing the Eisenach Party's leaders to take a considerable

[1] An anonymous review by Engels of the new edition of *Das Kapital* is printed by B. Andreas in *Archiv für Sozialgeschichte*, Vol. II, p. 284.

interest in the International; but what other motives did they have, which could help to outweigh their powerful reasons for ignoring it? The main motive for which they had emphasised their connection with the International before the war—that it increased their prestige in Germany *vis-à-vis* their Lassallean rivals—was now less powerful. This was partly because the Lassalleans, now that 'the International' inevitably suggested 'the Commune', were less likely to lose ground to an adversary claiming to belong to it; and partly because the rivalry between the two parties, though still extremely bitter, was at last beginning to show signs of diminishing.

The drastic loss of socialist *Reichstag* seats at the election of March 1871 had shown the penalty paid by unpatriotic unwillingness to welcome the new German Empire with proper jubilation, and any attempt to swim against the nationalistic tide would obviously continue to incur unpopularity of the same kind. The Lassalleans thus had every motive for retreating from the internationalist line which had led them into denouncing the annexation of Alsace-Lorraine (and which had caused even Schweitzer to speak in defence of the Commune), and for returning instead to an explicitly patriotic outlook; far from seeking close relations with the International as Schweitzer had done in 1868, his successors in 1871–2 (Schweitzer himself had left political life in May 1871) fitted the ADAV so well into 'the existing order of state and society' that the Prussian government considered 'keeping it alive as an opponent of the Bebel-Liebknecht party'.[1] Bismarck and his advisers were fundamentally right in thinking that 'the ADAV places the *national* aspect of the labour movement in the foreground, and claims to be indifferent to the International';[2] and this meant that a connection with it, which both Lassalleans and Eisenachers had eagerly sought before the war, would no longer be regarded as a claim to superiority.

[1] Kampffmeyer & Altmann, *op. cit.*, p. 134; Mayer, *Schweitzer*, pp. 399–401.
[2] Tessendorff to the Magdeburg Chief of Police 10 December 1871, in Prussian *Ministerium des Innern*, Rep. 77, Abt. II, Sekt. 11D Gen, Vol. VI, p. 98.

Contact with the International was thus no longer needed as a weapon in the struggle between Lassalleans and Eisenachers, and in fact this struggle itself was beginning very gradually to abate. One observer noticed this within a few weeks of Schweitzer's retirement in May 1871,[1] and from now on the two parties (though their opposition sometimes flared up with all the old bitterness, and their unification was delayed until 1875) began to lay stress on their common attitudes and common problems, and to avoid issues which still divided them. They had, after all, joined in opposing the annexation of Alsace-Lorraine and in protesting at the authoritarian structure of the new German *Reich*—for which reason the government, despite occasional toyings with the sort of pro-Lassallean tactics just mentioned, determinedly persecuted them both; and a gradually increasing desire for reconciliation led the two parties to emphasise these common features, and to refer less often to the International, which was associated—among many other things—with their past divisions.

Just as considerations of party finance and party tactics (combined with admiration for Marx) had made the Eisenach Party leaders insist on their connection with the International before the war, so considerations of finance and tactics were predominant now in making them (despite their continued admiration for Marx) wish to play this connection down. A further example of this desire to minimise contact with the International occurred in September 1871, when the General Council arranged a small Conference in London—the International's first representative gathering since the Basle Congress in 1869. Germany was not represented, though a year earlier Liebknecht had actually suggested the Conference himself. He now excused his absence and Bebel's by the charge of High Treason already hanging over their heads and making it dangerous for them to leave Germany; but when Marx and Engels reprimanded him for failing to send other German delegates instead, he produced the lame excuse that Marx's letters had

---

[1] C. Hillmann, *Die Internationale Arbeiterassociation*, p. 9.

implied a wish 'to hold the Congress in complete privacy'.[1] He had apparently not even informed his German colleagues that the Conference was being held; this was part of a systematic policy—understandable in the circumstances, though not to Marx and Engels—of minimising the party's contact with the International.

It was the party-leadership's indifference to the London Conference which determined Marx to make his direct approach (already mentioned) to the Eisenach Party's branch in Berlin. His letters certainly impressed the Berliners (just as certainly as they infuriated Liebknecht),[2] and his advice seems on one occasion to have been taken: a meeting organised by the Berlin Eisenachers in December, to protest against measures taken against the party by the Leipzig police, was apparently inspired by a suggestion of Marx. The meeting, however, was not a success (it was 'captured' by the Lassalleans, and turned into a protest against their own party's maltreatment), and it led to the increased police-interference with the party's activities.[3] When Liebknecht made up his mind to

[1] Adoratski, *op. cit.*, pp. 34, 43, 45; Liebknecht's suggestion of a conference in August 1870, *Hochverratsprozess*, p. 331; the suggestion was transmitted from Braunschweig to London on 19 August 1870, *Ministerium des Innern*, Rep. 77, Abt. II, Sekt. 11D Gen, Vol. II, p. 143. It is noteworthy that Marx, despite his unwillingness to accede to Liebknecht's request for a public condemnation of Schweitzer, denounced him in the privacy of the London Conference as a paid agent of Bismarck: Freymond, ed., *La Première Internationale*, Vol. II, pp. 195–6.

[2] Marx to Liebknecht 17 November 1871, in Adoratski, pp. 39–40.

[3] On 6 November 1871 Marx suggested to a Berlin member of the Eisenach Party (perhaps Metzner) that meetings should be called 'to make the most of occasions possessing general significance and public interest'—for instance the forthcoming Braunschweig trial (*Die Gesellschaft*, 1933, p. 261). On 11 December 1871 Metzner called a meeting in Berlin to debate 'measures taken by the police against social democrats, particularly the recent affair in Leipzig'. The thirty Eisenachers present, however, were outnumbered by 450 Lassalleans, who elected their President Hasenclever as chairman for the evening, and used the meeting to protest against their own party's maltreatment by the police in Schleswig-Holstein. They also made speeches attacking the Eisenach Party (one of them described 'the internationalists of Bebel's faction' as 'old washerwomen'), and the meeting, far from being the 'coup' which Metzner and Karl Hirsch were said to have expected, was a serious setback for the Eisenach Party. The full police report of the meeting was sent to the Minister of the Interior himself (*Ministerium des Innern, loc. cit.*, Vol. II, pp. 404–7), and resulted in increased police-surveillance of the International's Berlin 'Section'. One of its members, F. Milke, wrote to Marx on 4 July 1872

THE GERMAN SOCIAL DEMOCRATS

publish the resolutions of the London Conference and the International's new statutes in the *Volksstaat* (15 November 1871 and 10 February 1872 respectively), the result was to convince the authorities even more firmly that the Eisenach party was completely subordinated to the International, and it inevitably confirmed the unwisdom of making any public reference to the International at all.

By the time of the Hague Congress in September 1872, the situation of the German party was more difficult than ever: Liebknecht and Bebel had just entered on their two-year imprisonment for 'High Treason', the members of the former Braunschweig Committee were under such close police observation that they could take little active part in the movement, and the party's organisation and activities were being sustained, with much difficulty, by a team of substitute leaders. (After the arrest of the Braunschweig and Hamburg Executive members, the seat of the party's organisation was moved in 1871–2 successively to Dresden and Leipzig, then back to Hamburg; the Supervisory Board was reconstituted in 1871 in Berlin.)

Despite their problems, however, the Germans sent a large delegation to the Hague in response to urgent appeals from London—the General Council had even been ready to fix the date of the Congress so as not to clash with that of the German party's own Congress;[1] a group of nine German delegates attended the Congress as supporters of the General Council, and although the division-lists show that Marx might just have succeeded in expelling Bakunin and his lieutenant Guillaume

that he had no meetings on which to report, except for a business meeting held in May, at which he had been entrusted with the Section's affairs (original in IISG, Marx-*Nachlass*). He devoted most of his letter to the difficulties of any public demonstration in Berlin. Despite the evidence of activity produced in the article by Gemkow, *loc. cit.*, the impression that the Berlin Section of the International was relatively inconspicuous is confirmed by the well-qualified observer Rudolf Meyer, *Der Emancipationskampf des Vierten Standes*, Vol. I (2nd edition, Berlin 1882), p. 151.

[1] Marx to Milke 24 February 1872 (*Die Gesellschaft*, 1933); Engels to Liebknecht May 1872 (Marx and Engels, *Briefe an A. Bebel, W. Liebknecht*, p. 71); Liebknecht to Engels June (Mayer, *Schweitzer*, p. 440).

without their help, their presence naturally strengthened his position.[1]

Once the expulsion of Bakunin and Guillaume was secured, the other important matter before the Congress was the proposal to transfer the General Council's headquarters to New York. Some thought that this move would be unwelcome to Marx,[2] but in fact the idea, and the resolution in favour of the move, were his own. The German delegates obediently voted for his proposal; they may have reflected as they did so that the new and distant General Council would be much less exacting than Marx had been. On their way home to Germany (they had left the Hague Congress early in order to be in time for their own party-congress in Mainz),[3] the delegates may have been glad to think that they would be able to devote themselves to the daunting problem of building up a socialist party in the new German Empire, with no more than a nominal allegiance to any international authority.[4]

For some years after the Hague Congress the International's former leaders argued over the reasons for its disruption. The basic reason why it had 'been such an ignominious fiasco', as Liebknecht bluntly put it in a letter to Engels, was that the problems of the labour movement in the different countries of Europe varied so much that any form of centralised international direction was impossible.[5] As far as Germany was concerned, this had been true from the beginning: here, nationally-organised workers' parties had been created earlier than in any

---

[1] Lists of delegates in R. Meyer, *op. cit.*, Vol. I, pp. 151–2, and Guillaume, *L'Internationale*, Vol. II, p. 322; voting-results in Cole, *Marxism and Anarchism*, p. 200. The risks incurred by the Germans in even attending the Congress are illustrated by the fate of the *Volksstaat*'s acting editor Hepner, whose visit to the Hague was made the pretext for his expulsion from Leipzig by the local Chief of Police, Cf. A. Hepner, *Meine 3 1/2-jährige Polizei-Campagne*, pp. 26–9.

[2] H. Oberwinder, *Sozialismus und Sozialpolitik*, p. 56.

[3] H. H. Gerth, ed., *The First International: Minutes of the Hague Congress*, pp. 55–6.

[4] W. Liebknecht, *Karl Marx zum Gedächtnis*, p. v, claims that he personally was opposed to the move to New York.

[5] Liebknecht to Engels, early 1875, quoted by Mayer, *Schweitzer*, p. 424; H. Jung to W. Liebknecht 9 August 1874 (original in IISG, Liebknecht-*Nachlass*) proposes an exchange of views on 'the causes that led to the disruption' of the International.

other country, and socialists, like everyone else, had been forced to concentrate on the specifically German problem of national unification.

The prestige of the International had helped to make German Social Democrats willingly declare that their movement, though 'national in form', was 'international in reality', or that every member of the Eisenach Party was 'certainly in spirit a member of the International Working Men's Association as well'—as a German delegate expressed it to the International's Geneva Congress of 1873.[1] In terms of practical organisation, however, the 'international...reality' had had to be subordinated to the 'national...form'; and the International had inevitably been not the supreme authority of German labour, but a source of prestige utilised (and strictly controlled) by a party whose centre of gravity was firmly national. The original conceptions of Marx or those of Johann Philipp Becker had been overcome by those of Schweitzer, Liebknecht or Bebel.

By 1872 the problems of the German labour movement were more serious than ever; the motives which had made its leaders acclaim the International before the war were no longer valid, and when they learned of Marx's plan to remove its headquarters from Europe, they had many good reasons for welcoming it.

[1] Quoted by R. Meyer, *op. cit.*, Vol. II, p. 187.

CHAPTER VII

CONCLUSION: THE SIGNIFICANCE OF THE INTERNATIONAL IN GERMANY

The hesitations of the Eisenachers towards the International from 1869 to 1872 had the same main causes as those of the Lassalleans in 1864-6: fear of governmental persecution, and preoccupation with the party's own problems in Germany.

These were the periods—at the beginning and the end of the International's existence—when its prestige was so low that German party-leaders had no motive for disregarding these powerful considerations and seeking close contact with it.

In the intervening period—above all in 1868 and 1869—the Germans were attracted by the International's prestige, but were mainly concerned (naturally enough) to apply this to the solution of their own domestic problems, particularly those caused by the enmity between Liebknecht's movement and Schweitzer's.

The one systematic attempt to establish a close organic link between the German labour movement and the International— the work of Johann Philipp Becker—had little chance of success, because an effective organisation for Germany could scarcely be based for any length of time on Geneva.

The International's failure to establish organised relations with Germany, however, does not mean that it had no influence on the development of German socialism.[1] Contact with the International did in fact strengthen the German labour movement's belief in four fundamental ideas, and thus left a legacy whose effects were felt after the International, as an organisation, had disappeared. The four ideas were these:

(1) that 'the emancipation of labour is neither a local

---

[1] F. Borkenau, *Socialism: National or International*, p. 106, is much too sweeping in saying that the International's influence in Germany was 'nil'.

problem nor a national one, but a social one embracing all countries . . .', and that German proletarians, having more in common with workers abroad than with their own non-proletarian compatriots, therefore owed loyalty to the international labour movement rather than to the national State;

(2) that 'the emancipation of the working classes must be achieved by the working classes themselves', and that they therefore needed a political movement representing the interests of their own class contradistinction to all others;

(3) that 'the worker's economic dependence on the monopolist of the means of production' was inseparable from the capitalist system, and that the aims of the working-class movement must therefore be specifically socialist rather than merely reformist;

(4) that the truth of socialist doctrines, as well as the certainty of the socialist movement's ultimate victory, had been conclusively proved by the works of Marx.[1]

These four components of the social-democratic creed—internationalism, class-consciousness, socialist politics and Marxist philosophy—were of course interrelated, though not totally inseparable from each other. They were also ideas which were already present in German socialist thinking, and which the labour movement might have embraced by the end of the 1870s, even if the International had never existed; they were ideas, in any case, which were attractive to the movement because of the position of permanent opposition into which it was forced by the German political system.

Internationalism, for instance, was a natural reaction of progressive thinkers to the strident nationalism accompanying the Prussian victory of 1870; proletarian class-consciousness was inevitably heightened by the rapid industrialisation of Germany, and by the readiness of a *Reich* dominated by aristocracy and bourgeoisie to legislate savagely against the labour movement; the same tendencies naturally encouraged workers

[1] Extracts from the International's Statutes, re-translated from the German version adopted at Nürnberg, *Hochverratsprozess*, pp. 782–3.

to turn to socialism as an alternative to the existing economic order; and the Marxist philosophy was gladly accepted as an impressive theoretical justification of all these attitudes of opposition.[1]

Closer examination of these four doctrines—internationalism, class-consciousness, socialism and Marxism—indicates that the role of the International was to confirm and perhaps to hasten the adoption of convictions already gaining ground in Germany, rather than to make any specific doctrinal contribution of its own.

First, the internationalism of the Eisenach Party was not inspired exclusively by the party's connection with the International Working Men's Association. As we have seen, Bebel and Liebknecht, in giving the most impressive example of this internationalism when they opposed the war-credits in July 1870, did indeed declare their repudiation of 'all dynastic wars, as social republicans and members of the International Working Men's Association, which opposes all oppressors, regardless of nationality'.[2] It is clear, however, that this attitude was motivated less by Marxist theories of the superiority of class loyalties to national ones, than by the Eisenach party-leaders' consistent and deep-rooted hostility to Prussia. Liebknecht hated Bismarck not only as an enemy of socialism, but mainly as a representative of those forces of despotism, Junkerdom and militarism which had defeated the Revolution of 1848.[3] This defeat had condemned Liebknecht to more than a decade of exile, which in turn had contributed much—certainly more than the teachings of Marx—to his freedom from the emotions

---

[1] The attitude of permanent opposition was of course strengthened—and with it the 'reception' of Marxism—by the Exceptional Law of 1878. Professor Schieder remarks that 'the gradual penetration of purely Marxist ideas' in the German social-democratic movement has still not been thoroughly studied: *The State and Society in our Time* (Eng. trans. 1962), p. 122.

[2] Bebel, *AML*, II, p. 159.

[3] Cf. Chapter IV above, and two articles by Sinclair W. Armstrong, 'The Social-Democrats and the Unification of Germany' in *Journal of Modern History* XII (1940), pp. 485–509, and 'The Internationalism of the Early Social Democrats in Germany' in *American Historical Review*, XLVII (1942), pp. 245–58.

of patriotism.[1] It is against this background that his internationalism must be seen: as it was based on hatred of Prussia, it
found expression in bitter opposition to Bismarck's 'work of
1866', in the hope even that foreign intervention would destroy
this 'work', and in passionate protest against Bismarck's
completion of it in 1870.[2]

Opposition to Prussia led the 'internationalists' into sympathy
with all her enemies, including the particularist forces of rival
German states. Thus, during the war of 1870, Wilhelm Bracke
complained that his comrades Liebknecht and Bebel represented
Saxon patriots 'who prefer the far-off international ideal to the
national one, repugnant to them since 1866...because of their
particularism';[3] in this he was much nearer the truth than the
modern historian of ideas who attributes the Eisenach Party's
'completely unreal internationalism' and 'total repudiation of
the Prussian and the German state' to 'Marx's foundation of
the International Working Men's Association in 1864'.[4]

Secondly, the notion of proletarian class-consciousness was
certainly encouraged in Germany by the International's
slogans 'Workers of the world, unite!' and 'the emancipation
of the working classes must be achieved by the working classes
themselves'. The sharpening of class conflicts, however, was in
any case being brought about by the rapid industrialisation of
Germany in the 1860s and 1870s, and the International was of
course not alone in recognising its significance: a celebrated
book on social problems bore the title *The Fourth Estate's Struggle
For Emancipation*, and a fundamental dogma of the Lassallean
party was that all classes except the proletariat formed 'only

[1] On the connection between exile and internationalism cf. O. Blum, 'Zur
Psychologie der Emigration' in *Grünbergs Archiv*, VII (1917), pp. 413–30.
[2] Kurt Brandis, *Die Deutsche Sozialdemokratie bis zum Falle des Sozialistengesetzes*,
p. 28.
[3] Bracke to Geib 29 July 1870, printed by Kautsky, *Sozialisten und Krieg*, p.
191; for a fuller quotation, cf. Chapter VI above.
[4] Hermann Heidegger, *Die Deutsche Sozialdemokratie und der Nationale Staat
1870–1920*, pp. 19–20. The superficial nature of the Eisenachers' 'internationalism'
is further indicated by their readiness in 1875 to discard even the simple statement
of proletarian internationalism contained in the 1869 programme, for the sake of
unity with the Lassalleans; the disgust of Marx and Engels at this ('after the efforts
of the International') can be seen in their *Kritik des Gothaer Programms*, pp. 23–5, 39.

one reactionary mass '.[1] The representatives of the International, indeed, were not wholly consistent in their encouragement of proletarian class-consciousness. The nominal adoption of parts of the International's programme in 1868 and 1869 signified at least a potential division between 'bourgeois democracy' and 'proletarian democracy' (as Liebknecht said, 'the workers' interests demand that they separate themselves politically from those who are their enemies socially'), but in practice Liebknecht himself fought very hard to preserve the alliance of these two forms of democracy for as long as possible.[2]

The problem of whether the social-democratic party ought to be a purely proletarian 'class-party' or a broad 'people's party' representing all progressive elements of the population, was to assume great importance at the turn of the century.[3] During the period of the First International the problem was in some ways simpler, but the instinctive solution of the Eisenach Party's leaders was the same—to attempt a combination of radical class-conscious phraseology and reformist 'people's party' practice: as a recent writer has summed it up, 'the separation between social democracy and bourgeois democracy remained a sociological and organisational one, while the ideology of the workers' party continued to be decisively influenced by bourgeois-democratic modes of thought'.[4]

[1] R. Meyer, *Der Emancipationskampf des Vierten Standes*, 2 vols., Berlin 1874–5. On the Lassallean slogan (which was incorporated in the Gotha Programme), cf. Mehring, 'Zur Geschichte eines Schlagwortes' in *Neue Zeit*, Vol. XV/2, pp. 515 ff.

[2] Liebknecht at Nürnberg in 1868, *Hochverratsprozess*, p. 781; his efforts in 1869–70 to keep together 'proletarian' and 'bourgeois' democracy are described in Chapter VI above. For similar reasons Bebel attempted at Eisenach in 1869 to leave the word 'workers' out of the new party's title, as it would offend some of the members (Leidigkeit, *Wilhelm Liebknecht und August Bebel*, pp. 185, 192). Significantly, it was in each case former members of the Lassallean party who insisted on a purely proletarian party-line.

[3] Brandis, *Die Deutsche Sozialdemokratie, passim*; Siegfried Marck, *Sozial-Demokratie*, pp. 15–19; A. Rosenberg, *Democracy and Socialism*, pp. 293–5, 314–15; Carl E. Schorske, *German Social Democracy, 1905–1917*, Chapter I. On the problem as it presented itself in the 1860s, cf. Mayer, *Schweitzer*, pp. 338–9, 367–72, and Ludwig Pollnau's introduction to Mehring's *Gesammelte Schriften und Aufsätze in Einzelausgaben*, Vol. V, pp. 17–26.

[4] Erich Matthias, 'Kautsky und der Kautskyanismus', in *Marxismusstudien*, 2. Folge, p. 155.

233

It could be said that the idea of proletarian class-consciousness was encouraged in Germany by the International, but that the antecedents of the Eisenach Party (despite its self-proclaimed affinity with the International) prevented the idea from having its full effect in practice. In any case, class-consciousness, like internationalism, owed its growth to many factors besides the influence of the International.

On the third and fourth aspects of the legacy, finally (they are best considered together), how far did the International lead the German labour movement towards socialism, and more specifically, towards Marxism? The evidence that Marxism was widely understood in Germany during the period of the International is slight enough to make Professor Matthias conclude that 'Marxism as a theoretical system played no role' in the German labour movement's separation from 'bourgeois democracy' at this period.[1] Popular understanding of Marxism in Germany seems, in fact, to have been limited to acceptance of two simple ideas: that Marx's insight into the historical process had proved the inevitable ultimate victory of socialism, and that the working class must hasten this victory by creating its own political organisation, separating itself from all other classes.[2]

These doctrines were such as to encourage the socialist movement in the line it was already taking, and they were in no way contradictory to the main source of German socialism, which continued to be Lassallean. Lassalle's ideas, as well as his personal prestige, had an enormous influence, even on the adherents of the International: this was illustrated in 1868, when Liebknecht, editing an article by Engels, removed the passages derogatory to Lassalle;[3] it was illustrated again from 1870 onwards, when Bebel's much-reprinted pamphlet *Unsere Ziele*, after a brief reference to the International, propounded the socialist case with arguments and lengthy quotations from

[1] *Ibid.*, p. 155.
[2] Cf. Schweichel's and Liebknecht's speeches at Nürnberg, quoted in Chapter V above.
[3] Mayer, *Engels*, II, p. 542.

Lassalle;[1] and it was again shown by the way in which Lassalle's demand for state-aided co-operatives, after figuring even in the allegedly anti-Lassallean Eisenach Programme of 1869, was reaffirmed—despite strong private opposition from Marx—in the Gotha Programme of 1875.[2] Marx and his followers argued that Lassalle's ideas were no more than a debased plagiarisation of Marxism, which would thus still count as the original inspiration of German socialism; the force of this argument, however, is blunted by the Marxists' violent criticism of most of what Lassalle actually said.

The correspondence of German members of the International confirms the impression that although Marx was highly respected as an adviser on tactical problems, Marxism as such was virtually unknown. This was partly, as Professor Eckert has observed, because certain of Marx's fundamental writings remained unpublished until long after his death,[3] and partly because Marx himself preferred during the period of the International to present his ideas in the vague and tactful form of the *Inaugural Address* (or in the relatively inaccessible form of *Das Kapital*), rather than republish the comprehensive but inflammatory *Communist Manifesto*.[4] In any case, the German socialists who sought Marx's advice at this time usually asked for his views on topical questions such as the tactics of Schweitzer, their own propaganda, the organisation of trade unions, or the problems raised by the war of 1870; only very few were interested in his theoretical writings.[5]

[1] Bebel, *Unsere Ziele: Eine Streitscrift gegen die Demokratische Korrespondenz*, pp. 20–31, 44, where both Marx and Lassalle are included in the recommended reading.

[2] Marx, *Kritik des Gothaer Programms*, esp. pp. 27–8, 40, 47, 151–2. Bracke criticised this point of the programme in his book *Der Lassalle'sche Vorschlag*, discussed and quoted by G. Eckert, *Aus den Anfängen der Braunschweiger Arbeiterbewegung*, pp. 44–8. Bracke remarks in the preface to his book that he had expected the gradually increasing knowledge of Marx's works in the party to sweep away this Lassallean idea, but had been 'disappointed'.

[3] G. Eckert, *Wilhelm Bracke und die Anfänge der Braunschweiger Arbeiterbewegung*, p. 15.

[4] On the limited effects of the 1866 reprint of the *Manifesto*, cf. Appendix IV.

[5] Cf. letters to Johann Philipp Becker from Reimann (Berlin) 12 February 1869 ('I would like to know what you think of Dr Schweitzer, and what Karl Marx's

It is true that some party-members were aware of a distinction between Marx's ideas and Lassalle's, but, as was illustrated in the Eisenach Programme of 1869, they seem to have felt that the two 'schools', though distinct, were not incompatible: one speaker in 1869, after reviewing 'the different schools of socialism which have appeared in Germany', did insist that 'real social-democracy is the school of Marx, which has found its expression in the International Working Men's Association', but occasional insights of this kind were very far from making the Eisenach Party, in any serious sense, Marxist.[1] Much more typical was the simultaneous respect for both Marx and Lassalle shown in the Eisenach Programme itself, in the early writings of Bebel, or in the frontispiece of a party publication of 1872, where photographs of Marx and Lassalle appear together, one on each side of Wilhelm Liebknecht.[2] The strength of Lassalleanism was again shown in the Gotha Programme of 1875, when Liebknecht abandoned without much hesitation the Marxist formulae nominally 'received' at Eisenach in 1869; and the first serious challenge to Lassalle's

opinion of him is'); from Stumpf (Mainz) 21 September 1869 (on an opinion expressed on Stumpf's article in the *Demokratisches Wochenblatt* by 'Carl Marx, who was travelling through here'). Cf. Marx's conversation with J. Hamonn on Trade Union organisation (September 1869), in a *Volksstaat* article reprinted by Eckert, *Aus den Anfängen*, pp. 24–5; and Marx's advice during the war of 1870, quoted in Chapter VI above. References to Marx's published writings occur only rarely in the numerous letters from German members of the International to Becker: Urbach (Cologne) wrote on 10 March 1866 that Lassalle had clearly been no more than 'a pupil' of Marx, and Münze (Magdeburg) asked on 24 January 1867 whether he was right in thinking that Marx had written 'books'. Specific enquiries about the *Communist Manifesto* occur only in the letters of F. Meincke (a Hamburg businessman), 20 February 1866, and C. Boruttau (a Leipzig doctor), 20 February 1869; the letters to Becker give no indication that 'Marxism', in any sense, was important to the German members of the International.

[1] Speech reported in *Demokratisches Wochenblatt* 31 July 1869, quoted by Benser, *Zur Herausbildung der Eisenacher Partei*, p. 87. There is much truth in the argument of Robert Michels that the 'Marxism' and 'Lassalleanism' of the rival parties consisted largely of personal admiration for their respective leaders: *Zur Soziologie des Parteiwesens in der modernen Demokratie*, p. 61.

[2] Frontispiece to Bracke's *Der Braunschweiger Ausschuss . . . in Lötzen und vor dem Gericht*. Cf. unpublished letter (IISG) from Fritz Moll (Solingen) to Johann Philipp Becker, 12 April 1869: 'wir haben von Marx auch sein Portrai erhalten, und hängt dein und Marx' Portrai sowie Lassalle's und mehrerer unserer Parteigenossen auf unserem Versammlungszimmer. . . .'

influence in the party, which began to develop at about the same time, came not from Marx but from Eugen Dühring.[1]

The International, it could be said, increased the readiness of German socialists to turn to Marx for advice (though Liebknecht in 1875, like Schweitzer in 1865, was prepared to disregard this advice if it seemed unsuitable to German conditions);[2] on the other hand, German socialism in the 1860s and 1870s drew its inspiration from such diverse sources that it is a serious over-simplification to describe even the adherents of the International as 'the Marxists under Liebknecht and Bebel'.[3]

With these reservations, the International made a positive contribution to the doctrinal development of German socialism. Even so, however, its contribution was by no means due to any systematic exposition of its ideas by social-democratic leaders. These leaders—notably Liebknecht and Bebel—tended to present one or another aspect of the International's significance to the German public, according to the tactical needs of their changing political situation, rather than attempting a complete picture.

Thus Bebel in 1868 presented the International as a *working-class* organisation—its precise programme being relatively immaterial—whose name would consolidate the *Verband Deutscher Arbeitervereine* and separate it from the Liberal democrats; Liebknecht in 1869 represented it as a *democratic* organisation, which would as a matter of course share his opposition to the dictatorial power of Schweitzer; both Bebel and Liebknecht, though only under considerable pressure, admitted early in

---

[1] Dühring's influence in the 1870s is thoroughly studied and documented by Riasanov, '50 Jahre Anti-Dühring', in *Unter dem Banner des Marxismus*, II. Jrg. 1928, pp. 266–87.

[2] Marx and Engels, in letters to Bracke and Bebel, often criticised Liebknecht for ignoring their advice in his eagerness to achieve unity with the Lassalleans 'at any price': Adoratski, *loc. cit.*, pp. 106, 119; Mayer, *Schweitzer*, pp. 421–7.

[3] D. G. Macrae, *Ideology and Society*, p. 161; cf. Z. A. B. Zeman's statement in L. Labedz, ed., *Revisionism: Essays on the History of Marxist Ideas*, p. 103, that by Marx's death in 1883 his 'philosophical system came to dominate German socialism', and H. Lademacher's conclusion that 'the idea of the International became ever firmer' (*immer mehr Fuss fasste*) from the time of the Nürnberg Congress (*International Review of Social History*, IV, 1959, p. 390).

1870 that it had become a *socialist* organisation, whose pro-gramme included the nationalisation of the land; during the Franco-Prussian War they laid stress on its *international* ideals, arguing that its members were 'opponents on principle of any dynastic war'; and after 1870 they represented it, when they did so at all, as an organisation in which broadly *Marxist* ideas should be defended against those of Bakunin.

These fragmentary interpretations of the International's message by the leaders of the Eisenach Party can be compared to the general insight into its significance afforded to members of the ADAV by Schweitzer's manoeuvres of 1868. The only systematic exposition of its principles published in Germany during its life-time was the pamphlet written by Wilhelm Eichhoff. Apart from this, their propagation in Germany was carried on by exiles: by Marx (partly in his anonymous contributions to Eichhoff's pamphlet), by Engels, and by Johann Philipp Becker.

To the leaders of the social-democratic movement inside Germany, whatever their personal enthusiasm for the Inter-national's ideals, the organisation itself was on the whole either something to be discreetly ignored (when its prestige was low at the beginning and end of its existence), or a source of strength which could be valuable if used with care (during the years when its prestige seemed to make it an asset in internal German struggles).

That was its significance during its lifetime, and these were the obstacles which prevented its role from being larger: this role, after all, was by no means negligible.

THE PUBLISHED AND UNPUBLISHED PAPERS

OF JOHANN PHILIPP BECKER

Before his death in 1886, Johann Philipp Becker sorted and arranged the thousands of letters he had received during fifty years as a revolutionary, and presented them to the archives of the *Sozialistische Arbeiterpartei Deutschlands*. The exact number of letters he handed over is uncertain,[1] but some indication is given by his carefully-kept records of his own letters to his various correspondents. As early as 1867 he sent a letter to Sorge which was, he said, his 2,886th since 1861, and on the business of the International alone he wrote 4,300 between 1864 and the end of 1871.[2] Becker perhaps received fewer letters than he sent, and he will scarcely have kept them all, but the collection which he presented to the party, and which was in the SPD's archives in Berlin until 1933, may originally have been one of at least two thousand. During this time some of the letters, written by Becker's more important correspondents, were published, and others, which were removed without being printed, have now disappeared. The surviving letters are in the International Institute for Social History, Amsterdam, either with Becker's *Nachlass* or elsewhere in the former SPD *Partei-Archiv*.

The first publication of items from Becker's bequest, in 1888, was made by his friend the Swiss radical journalist Rüegg, who included in a series of three *Neue Zeit* articles selected extracts from letters of Marx and his wife, Borkheim, Eccarius, the Countess Hatzfeldt, Bernhard Becker, Rüstow, Herwegh,

---

[1] I am indebted to Mr B. Andréas for the information that detailed lists, compiled by Becker himself, appeared in the *Sozialdemokrat* (Zürich) from 1884 to 1888, but I have been unable to check their contents.

[2] *Briefe u. Auszüge aus Briefen von John. Ph. Becker, Jos. Dietzgen, Karl Marx u. Andere an F. A. Sorge u. Andere*, p. 1; cf. F. Berghoff-Ising, *Die Socialistische Arbeiterbewegung in der Schweiz*, p. 33, which follows *Vorbote*, December 1871.

Ladendorf, and Ludwig Büchner.[1] In the years before 1914 new work on Becker's papers was undertaken by the Marxist scholar Riazanov. He published Becker's own account of his career up to the year 1856, using the unpublished letters of Marx to Becker to show how this document had come to be written;[2] and a few months later, in the SPD's central organ the Berlin *Vorwärts*, he printed most of the thirty-six extant letters of Engels to Becker as an accompaniment to the third volume of Bebel's memoirs, published early in 1914.[3] In the following year Riazanov published the eight letters received by Becker from Bakunin (between 1868 and 1870),[4] and in 1920 the letters of Engels to Becker, printed in instalments in the *Vorwärts* of 1914, were re-published in book-form by the former USPD Chief of the Berlin police, Emil Eichhorn.[5]

In the mid-1920s the SPD historian Paul Kampffmeyer used four letters from Liebknecht (dated 1866–7), and a similar number from Bebel, in short articles on their connection with the First International published in the Berlin *Vorwärts*.[6] The eleven letters of Marx to Becker, finally, have been published

[1] R. Rüegg, 'Aus Briefe an Joh. Ph. Becker,' in *Neue Zeit*, VI. Jrg. 1888, pp. 449–63, 505–18, 558–69.

[2] N. Rjasanoff, 'Zur Biographie Joh. Ph. Becker's: Sein Curriculum Vitae bis 1856', in *Grünbergs Archiv für die Geschichte des Sozialismus und der Arbeiterbewegung*, IV. Jrg. 1914, pp. 313–29.

[3] (N. Rjasanoff), 'Johann Philipp Becker', in *Vorwärts* (Berlin), 1914, Nos. 151–2 (June 6 & 7), followed by 'Aus Friedrich Engels' Briefen an J. Ph. Becker', in *ibid*. Nos. 153, 160, 167, 174, 181, 188, 195, 202 (8 June–27 July).

[4] In *Grünbergs Archiv*, V. Jrg. 1915, pp. 185, 189–95.

[5] Friedrich Engels, *Vergessene Briefe (Briefe Engels an Joh. Ph. Becker)* ... *Eingeleitet von Emil Eichhorn*. The letters can hardly have been 'forgotten' between 1914 and 1920, at least by Riazanov, whose notes are unceremoniously copied by Eichhorn, with only minor additions.

[6] 'Liebknecht und die Internationale. Aus Seinem Briefwechsel mit Joh. Ph. Becker', in *Vorwärts*, 28 March 1926; 'Bebel und die Internationale. Nach Briefen von Bebel an Joh. Ph. Becker', *ibid*. 1 January 1927. One letter each from Liebknecht and Bebel had already been published by Riazanov in *Vorwärts* in 1914 (No. 202 of 27 July 1914) and Bebel had also quoted extracts from his letters in his *Aus Meinem Leben* (new edition 1953, Vol. I, pp. 169, 183; Vol. II, pp. 74, 82–3) (cf. Chapter V above). The originals of Liebknecht's letters have apparently not survived.

only in a Russian translation;[1] the originals are still in the Amsterdam Institute.

So much for the published letters from Becker's collection, in some cases letters whose publication has mitigated the loss caused by their subsequent disappearance; others have vanished without leaving traces of this kind. What remains is a collection of many hundreds of letters (from Germany alone, about 700 in the eight years—1864 to 1872—covered by the present study) whose authorship was not illustrious enough, in most cases, to expose them either to publication or to theft, but whose historical value is none the less great: the surviving letters from Becker's more eminent correspondents (including Bebel, Fritzsche, James Guillaume, Greulich, Hofstetten and the Countess Hatzfeldt) will be found in the *Partei-Archiv* collection in IISG. A list is here appended of the letters from other correspondents in Germany used in the present study, which will be found in Becker's *Nachlass* in IISG.

(The following list is divided into two parts, according to the date of the earliest surviving letter from the correspondent concerned; each list is further subdivided on a regional basis which illustrates, however crudely, the geographical distribution of Becker's influence.)

LIST 1. LETTERS FROM CORRESPONDENTS WHO FIRST WROTE BEFORE 1870

(1) Ruhr
Solingen. *Willms* 8 Dec 64; *C. v. Giessen* 7 Oct 69; *Klein* 22 letters, April 1866–Nov 71; *Moll* letters, Nov 66–March 71; Balance of Steel-*Genossenschaft*, 1868/69; *Denkschrift* ditto, June 71.
Barmen. *Walter, G.* 13 letters, 1869–72; *Kotter* 2 Dec 66; *Hülsiep, R.* 2 letters, Jan 68, May 70; *Kröttker*, 30 Sept 66; *König* 17 June 68; *Werth, H.* 22 Nov 68; *Werth, G.* 11 April 69; 7 June 69; *Gräser, B.* 22 June 69.
(2) North Rhine
Cologne. *G. Heinrichs* 19 letters, March 66–Jan 71; *H. Schob*, Nov 68, April 69; *M. F. Urbach*, Jan, March 66.
Bayenthal. *Kallen* July 66, Nov 67.
Kalk. *A. Kalter* May, July 68; *H. Thiemann* 4 letters, Feb 67–Feb 68.

---

[1] Marx-Engels, *Sochineniya*, Vols. XXV, XXVI, and XXVII. The two letters—of January 1866 and August 1870—which have the greatest importance for the history of the International will be found in Vol. XXV, pp. 460–2 and Vol. XXVI pp. 64–7 respectively.

APPENDIX I

Rheinfelden. *B. Bang* July, Aug 68; *M. Vogel* 3 letters, Aug-Sep 66.
Siegburg. *J. Dietzgen* 2 letters, 6 Nov 68, 10 Jan 69.
Uckerath. *F. Ellinger* 28 April 70 (cf. Dietzgen's first letter).
Iserlohn. *F. Kaiser* 11 Feb 69.
Wilheim. *P. Bilstein* 12 Nov 67.

(3) Saxony
Dresden. *Kratsch* 19 Feb 68; *Jacoby* 30 May 68; *Grumpelt* 24 June 69.
Leipzig. *W. Lange* Sept, Nov 65; *F. E. Welsch* Dec 65; *Graihanger?* May 68; *Demokratisches Wochenblatt* 15 Oct 68; *E. Werner,* 5–7 letters, April-Sept 1869; *C. Boruttau* 10 letters, Aug? 1868–72.
Chemnitz. *Schelle* 1 June 68.
Wechselburg. 1 letter Nov 70.
Mühlhausen? *Pfaff* 3 letters, 1867–9.

(4) Prussia
Berlin. *Röttger* 18 letters, 1861–9 (mainly from outside Germany); *Koennecke* 6 letters, 1868–77; *Arndt & Schilling* 18 March 65; *A. Vogt* 29 Jan, 8 April, 18 Aug 66, 30 Ap 67; *Reimann* 13 letters, June 67–Jan 72; *J. Haug* 24 March 67; *Liebkert* Feb, May 69; *W. Eichhoff* 24 Sept 68; *F. W. Fritzsche* 8 Aug 68 (2 more letters from Fr. in *Partei-Archiv*); *Saony?* 4 April 69.
Kaukehmen (later Danzig). *Martini* 4 letters, Sept 66–March 79.
Peterswaldau. *F. Paul* 3 letters Jan 66–68.
Luckenwalde. 2 collective letters, 22 July 69 & 22 Feb 71.

(5) Central German towns
Braunschweig (earlier Wiesbaden). *Bonhorst* 16 letters, May 67–Aug 70.
Wolfenbüttel. *Schömers* 12 Jan 69.
Hildesheim. *Kirchner* 3 letters, Jan–May 68.
Minden. *Vogel* 3 letters, Sept 68–Jan 69.
Hanover. *C. Brandes* 3 letters, Aug 68–Feb 72; *Kugelmann* 11 letters, June 66–Dec 77; *Borchers* 21 Aug 68.
Magdeburg. *J. Münze* 15 letters, Jan 66–Dec 67; *Uhlich* 5 Feb 68; *Wellner* 19 May 68; *J. H. Gaede* 25 Nov 68; *Probst* 14 Dec 69; *Bremer* 15 letters, Jan 69–Dec 71.

(6) Württemberg and Baden
Göppingen. *Bronnenmaier* 7 letters, 1866–70; *Bostel* 3 Nov 66, Oct 67.
Tübingen. *Ph. Reiter* 16 letters, 1867–74 (incl. S. Francisco).
Gelnshausen. *Hempel,* 10 June 67.
Worms. *Schroeder* 22 Aug 67.
Schwenningen. *C. Manthe* 19 Oct 67.
Cannstatt. *Thorst* 26 Feb 68.
Pforzheim. *M. Müller* 5 Aug 68.
Villingen. *Hauser* Nov–Dec 68.
Esslingen (Eislingen?) *Baser* 4 letters 1867–73; *Bonzhof* April 68, Jan 69; *Weber-association* 6 letters, March 69–Nov 71.
Stuttgart. *J. Kochendörfer* 9 letters, Dec 65–Sept 66; *Steiss* July, Aug 66; *Gutscher* Oct 66, March 67; *Bütter* 20 Sept 68.

(7) Rhine towns
Coburg. *Schweigert* Feb 64; *H. Heyn* 5 letters, Ap 65–March
Darmstadt. *Büchner* 28 Aug 67.
Frankfurt. *Hoff* Nov 63, Oct 68.
Mannheim. *Kinzel* 22 May 68.
Offenbach. *Sauer* 20 Nov 67.
Wiesbaden. *Habich* 23 April 67; *Braubach* 12 Feb 68.

APPENDIX I

Mainz. *Stumpf* 31 letters, 1866–71; *Klein* etc. 11 Jan 68; *Göbel* 6 Jan 69; *Schot* 2 Aug 68; *Schoeppler* 8 Oct 68, 3/5 May 70.

(8) Bavaria
Augsburg *Schmieding* 20 Aug 66; *Arbeiter-Bildungsverein* 1 Sept 67; *Steinbacher* 3 letters, June 68–May 73.
Bamberg. *Titus* 10 letters, 8 July 67–12 Aug 68.
Fürth. *Löwenstein* March, April 1869.
Hof. *Vollrath*, 10 July 70.
München. *Heyriger* 3 Aug 66.
Nürnberg. *Weller* 9 letters, Nov 68–March 71; *C. Rüll* 5 letters, Nov 60–Oct 69; *H. Seichab*? May 69, March 71; *Böhm* 2 letters, June 69; *Faaz* 2 Aug 69 (another letter fr. Faaz in 1869 coll.).
(9) North Germany
Pinneberg. *Fahl* 24 April 66.
Bremen. *Heinemann* 3 letters July, Aug, Oct 68.
Hamburg. *Martens* 1841 (Paris), then July 68, then 1874–5; *Bruhn* 23 letters, 1864–6, then 21 Nov 68; *Siebold* 13 letters, 1863–March 1871; *Meincke* 21 letters, Jan 66–March 74; *Isaacsen* May, Aug 68; *Meissner* 24 Aug 68; *Scholmeyer* 12 Aug 69.

LIST 2. LETTERS FROM CORRESPONDENTS
WHO FIRST WROTE IN 1870 OR LATER

(1) Ruhr
Barmen. *G. Wahl* 4 Aug 70; *H. Marwitz* 5, 24 March 71; *A. Herbst* 8 July 70.
(2) North Rhine
Cologne. *J. Sauer* 25 Jan 71.
(3) Saxony, etc.
Leipzig. *Ufert* Aug 71; *Fink*? Sept 71; *Seifert* March, Jun 70; *Röthing* July 70; *Volksstaat Exped.* 12 Nov 72; *Genossenschafts-Druckerei* Oct 73, April 75 (w. note by *Liebknecht*); *C. Moor* June 74; *Motteler* Aug 77.
Chemnitz. *Kiehaupt* (Unter-red. *Freie Presse*) 27 Nov 71.
Dresden. *J. A. Hempel* 8 May 70; *M. Kobitsch* 28 June 70.
Hubertusburg (!). *P. A. Rüdt* 1 May 70. *A. Müller* 17 Jan 1885.
(4) Prussia
Berlin. *N. Lebiny*? 2 March 70; *L. Simion* 28 Dec 71; *R. Schlingmann* Feb, April 72; *Red. der Zukunft* 21 Aug 77; *Fr. Milke* 15 Aug 73.
Sechansen. *C. Niemann* 19 Aug 71.
Neustadt. *Arnold* 20 Aug 71.
Hessen-Preussen. *Lampmann* 3 letters, Aug-Sept 70.
Bromberg. *Jolewicz* 15 Feb 71.
(5) Central German towns
Braunschweig. *C. Ludecke* 3 Aug 70 and (from Strasbourg) 21 Feb 73.
Wolfenbüttel. *Spier* 11 Jan 70.
(6) Württemberg & Baden
Stuttgart. *G. F. Krauss* 8 May 70; *A. Mühlberger* 21 Oct 70 (another letter fr. *Muhlberger-*, Tübingen-, in IISG, general collection); *H. Moser* Sept. 73, June 79.
Tübingen. *E. Kurz* 3 letters, 1 undated, others Jan 71, Nov 72.
(7) Rhine towns
Coblenz. *A. Ellner* 14 March 71.

243

Mannheim. *Allg. Dtsche. Unterstutzungsverband* 19 March 72; *F. Lingemann* 1874.
Wiesbaden. *F. Nauert* 28 March 75.
Heidelberg. *Krankenhaus* 28 Sept 70; *Nook?* 29 Feb 72.
Frankfurt. *Fr. Ellner* 29 June 71; *Exped. Arbeitgeber* May 72; *A. Saber* 12 June 72.
Mainz. *Komite des Soz. Dem. Arbeitervereins* 17 Oct 71; *Ph. Müller* 24 Nov 74.
(8) Bavaria
Augsburg. *F. Steinbacher* 30 Jan 70; *B. Thomas* 27 March 71.
Nürnberg. *A. Stark* 6 Dec 70; *J. Gier* 4 March 71.
München. *Sadlemayr?* 10 Sept 70; *Cuno* (telegram) 5 April 72 (6 letters from Cuno in IISG general collection).
(9) North Germany
Hamburg. *Th. Mencke* 15 Sept 71; *Th. Yorck* 26 March 73; *Gustav Rathenau* c/o Geib 10 Oct 73, then Friedrichshagen bei Berlin 30 October 74.

Figures for the number of letters written in each year, which show how Becker's influence rose to its maximum in 1868–9 and then declined, are given in note 2 on p. 151.

APPENDIX II

BECKER'S FINANCIAL RECEIPTS FROM GERMANY

(*See* Note 1, p. 83)

The records made by Becker of his receipts from Germany are naturally an important source of information on the extent of his influence. Almost every month from September 1866 onwards he acknowledged in the *Vorbote* the subscriptions and donations received, and the frequent concurrence of these acknowledgements with references to payments in the surviving letters addressed to him (IISG) suggests that they form virtually a complete record of the Geneva Committee's income; certainly no cases can be found in which Becker exaggerated in the *Vorbote* the sums he actually received, and he is most unlikely, for the sake of the International's prestige, to have minimised them either.

On two occasions, early in the existence of the Group of German-speaking Sections, Becker published accounts covering periods of several months, and by comparing these with the monthly acknowledgements for the periods concerned it is possible to calculate the proportion of his total income which came from Germany. Thus his accounts for the nineteen months from January 1866 to July 1867 (published in *Vorbote* October 1867, pp. 159–60), compared with the records of receipts in *Vorbote* (1866, pp. 121, 140, 176, 192; 1867, pp. 16–32, 63, 80, 96, 112), show that out of total receipts of 2,544 francs roughly 441 francs, or between one-fifth and one-sixth, came from Germany. In the succeeding twelve months (August 1867 to July 1868) the growth of Becker's influence in Germany can be measured by the fact that it sent him over one-third of his income, roughly 596 francs out of 1,766 (*Vorbote* 1867, pp. 144, 160, 176, 192; 1868, pp. 16, 32, 48, 96, 112; accounts for 1867–8, *ibid.* 1869, pp. 88–9).

For the period after July 1868 calculations of this kind

245

are impossible, because Becker published no further balance-sheets, only the monthly acknowledgements of sums received; a second complicating factor is that his correspondents in Germany, although usually less willing than before to subscribe to the International as such, after the Nürnberg Congress of 1868 had turned the *Verband Deutscher Arbeitervereine* into an informal German branch of it, still responded generously to Becker's appeals on behalf of several important strikes in Switzerland (listed in *Vorbote* August 1869, p. 118). Becker's monthly records of receipts (other than donations for strike-funds) show that his actual income from Germany continued to rise steadily, even after his power there was undermined in 1868-9: his income from Germany in 1866-7, as shown, was 441 francs, a monthly average of about 23 francs or £1 15s., and in 1867-8 rose to 596 francs, a monthly average of 49 francs or £3 15s.; in 1868-9 the monthly average remained the same, though this was due to exceptionally heavy receipts in August and September 1868, before the Nürnberg Congress reduced them; in 1869-70, 1870-1, and the last five months of 1871, finally, Becker's average monthly income from Germany rose respectively to £4 15s., £4 17s., and £6 9s. It must be noted, however, that after 1869 the proportion contributed in individual donations (from Martini in Danzig, Meincke in Hamburg, or Stumpf in Mainz) was much greater, and the amounts raised from rank-and-file members (except in the two Sections of Magdeburg and Barmen) was significantly less than before. At this point the declining figures for Becker's correspondence with Germany (given in Note 2, p. 151) become a more direct guide to the extent of his influence; the known facts about the sources of his financial support, however, confirm rather than contradict the impression given by this correspondence.

(The above calculations, expressing Becker's receipts in Swiss francs and £ sterling, instead of the original Prussian, Austrian, and South German currencies, are based on his own figures announcing the subscription-rates to the *Vorbote*, which are printed on the front page of each number: 15 cents = $4\frac{1}{2}$ Kreuzer = $1\frac{1}{2}$ silver Groschen; 1 franc = 35 Kreuzer = 10 silver Groschen = 1s. 6d.)

APPENDIX III

THE CORRESPONDENCE BETWEEN MARX AND ENGELS

There have been four editions of the correspondence between
Marx and Engels, each in four volumes:
(1) *Der Briefwechsel zwischen Friedrich Engels und Karl Marx*,
ed. by August Bebel & Eduard Bernstein, Stuttgart 1913;
(2) *Karl Marx, Friedrich Engels: Briefwechsel*, forming Volumes I–IV of Abteilung IV of the Marx-Engels *Gesamtausgabe*,
Berlin 1929–31;
(3) *Karl Marx, Friedrich Engels: Briefwechsel*, Herausgegeben
vom Marx-Engels-Lenin Institut, Moskau, 1935–7;
(4) *Karl Marx, Friedrich Engels: Briefwechsel*, Berlin 1949–50.

All but the first of these editions probably contain the full
texts of all surviving letters exchanged by Marx and Engels
(the third and fourth editions reprint the text of the *Gesamtausgabe*—here to be referred to as *MEGA*—omitting only the
valuable indexes to subjects and publications); the first edition,
on the other hand, despite its editors' claims to have omitted
nothing important in publishing it, is a thoroughly dishonest
compilation, designed to mislead, and worthless for any serious
historical purpose.

Despite this, the edition of 1913 is still widely used, either in
the original or in the partial French translation by Molitor.[1]
There may be relatively less cause for regret when this edition
is used or recommended by the authors of general histories of
socialism,[2] but when it is used in the writing of specialised
monographs,[3] or worse still, included in impressive biblio-

---

[1] Nine volumes; Paris (Costes), 1931–4.
[2] Cf. for instance, M. Drachkovitch, *De Karl Marx à Léon Blum; la Crise de la
Social-Democratie*, p. 169; G. D. H. Cole, *Marxism and Anarchism 1850–90*, p. 446;
R. N. Carew Hunt, *The Theory and Practice of Communism*, p. 273.
[3] Cf. W. Mühlbradt, *Wilhelm Liebknecht und die Gründung der deutschen Sozialdemokratie*, Göttingen 1950 (unpublished dissertion), where the 1913 edition is
used as well as the later one.

graphies,[1] the results must seem deplorable to anyone who has compared it with the unexpurgated edition.

The motives for which Bernstein and his colleagues in the preparation of the first edition made several hundred cuts and alterations (only a few of which were indicated as such) varied from a desire to moderate the frequently coarse language of the originals to a concern lest Marx's and Engels' outspoken criticisms of most of their contemporaries should offend any survivors or relatives, but the main motive was political. The editors were guided by the principles expressed by Victor Adler in a letter of 28 May 1913 to the publisher Dietz; on reading the proofs, even after extensive cuts had already been made, Adler declared himself alarmed because 'this publication in this form and at this time *would do the party more harm than good*', and strongly urged the publication only of 'what is personally and historically important, and *not compromising for the memory of our great leaders* in the eyes of the masses'.[2] On nearly every occasion when the editors had to decide whether a passage should be published as being 'personally or historically important' or suppressed as 'compromising', they chose to suppress it, and the resulting version of the original correspondence makes astounding the editors' claim to have published the correspondence 'unabridged with the exception only of passages of an unimportant or private character, possessing no interest for wider circles'.[3]

---

[1] Cf. Dolléans & Crozier, *Mouvements ouvrier et socialiste: Chronologie et Bibliographie*, p. 92. The authors do mention the existence of the *MEGA* in another section of their book (p. 126), but without indicating the differences between it and the edition of 1913.

[2] *Victor Adler: Briefwechsel mit August Bebel und Karl Kautsky . . . Gesammelt und erläutert von Friedrich Adler*, pp. 567–8 (underlining by the present writer). Adler's correspondence (*op. cit.* pp. 524–88 *passim*) gives a revealing account of how the leading intellectuals of the SPD—including Kautsky and Mehring—conspired together over the publication of the Marx-Engels letters. Further important details are given by W. Blumenberg, 'Ein Unbekanntes Kapitel aus Marx' Leben', in *International Review of Social History*, Vol. I, Amsterdam 1956, p. 55, where one of the individuals concerned is reported as saying that the SPD would do better to destroy the whole correspondence than to publish it.

[3] *Briefwechsel*, 1913, Vol. I, *Vorwort*, V. For the editors' agreement on the wording of this mendacious formula, see *Adler, Briefwechsel*, p. 571.

APPENDIX III

One aim pursued by the editors of 1913 was to avoid giving the impression that Marx and Engels had misunderstood or despised Lassalle, whose name was still revered in the SPD to such an extent that the revelation of the abuse of him exchanged by Marx and Engels might have caused grave disunity.[1] Their other main object, in fact a more important one, was to preserve the reputation of Wilhelm Liebknecht (who had died in 1900) as a life-long and respected confidant and collaborator of Marx and Engels. If their often outrageously cruel comments on his personal and political capacities were now to be made public, serious damage would be done to the morale of the party's rank and file: as an apologist of the editorial procedure has put it, 'at the time of the first edition, large circles in German Social Democrary regarded Wilhelm Liebknecht in no sense as a *historical* personage...his living image was still present to the eyes of the masses';[2] and as Victor Adler asked, after reading the proofs, 'why should the old man (*der Alte*, i.e. Liebknecht), whose failings we all knew about anyway, be exhumed and attacked as a superficial ignoramus and so on?'.[3] The picture of Marx's and Engels' judgment of Liebknecht which emerged after the suppression or amendment of scores of insults was far removed from the original reality, and it is not even the case, as a recent writer on Liebknecht has suggested, that the mutilated correspondence occurs mostly in the last of the four volumes (which covers the period from 1868 to 1883): the omissions and alterations begin earlier, and are extremely important precisely where the writers' opinion of Liebknecht's political acumen is concerned.[4]

The falsifications had their desired effect in perpetuating

[1] Cf. Thilo Ramm, *Ferdinand Lassalle als Rechts- und Sozialphilosoph*, p. 19. *Adler, Briefwechsel*, p. 575 fn., describes how Mehring attempted to foil this aim of the editors by publishing long extracts from the relevant letters in July 1913, three months before the official volumes appeared.

[2] Dr Benedikt Kautsky in *Die Gesellschaft*, Vol. X, Nr. 3 (March 1930), p. 266.

[3] *Loc. cit*, p. 568.

[4] Mühlbradt, *Wilhelm Liebknecht*, pp. 352–3. To give only one example from the third volume of the correspondence, the derogatory references to Liebknecht on p. 284 of *MEGA* IV/3 are completely omitted in the edition of 1913, Vol. III, pp. 271–2.

ignorance of the letters' full significance: even such a specialist as Professor Gustav Mayer (though he knew that cuts had been made in the correspondence, and suspected that they would tend to preserve the legend that Liebknecht had enjoyed the confidence of Marx and Engels in the 1860s), overlooked what he was meant to overlook.[1] The reviews written by the conspirators themselves, meanwhile, multiplied fresh perjuries about the 'completeness' of the published letters.[2]

The editors of 1913, with their calculations and their fears, need be discussed no further (though the episode sheds a certain revealing light on the SPD's history in particular and on the problems of publishing controversial documents in general): Bernstein and his colleagues have been denounced, with very little sympathy for their problems, by Riazanov[3] and defended,

[1] Gustav Mayer, 'Marx und Engels in ihrem Briefwechsel', in *Zeitschrift für Politik*, Vol. VII, 1914, Heft 3, pp. 428–44; see especially pp. 442–3. Professor Hermann Oncken (*Preussische Jahrbücher*, February 1914, pp. 209 *et seq.*, summarised by Mehring in *Grünberg Archiv*, V, 1915, p. 5) was also thinking more of Marx's and Engels' opinion of Lassalle than of their views on Liebknecht when he said that the correspondence made necessary a 'revision of accepted values'.

[2] Mehring, 'Engels und Marx', in *Grünbergs Archiv*, V (1915), pp. 1–38, speaks on p. 2 of the letters being published 'untouched in all essentials'; Victor Adler's review in *Der Kampf* (October 1, 1913; reprinted in Victor Adler's *Aufsätze, Reden, und Briefe*, Vol. I, 1922, pp. 178–87) starts by saying that the letters are published 'as far as they have survived', which may indeed conceal a conscience-saving double meaning!

[3] A revealing letter published by Blumenberg (*loc. cit.* p. 55) shows that Riazanov was in agreement with the expurgation of the correspondence before it was published. In his review of 1914, however, he uttered his misgivings about the omissions ('Der Briefwechsel zwischen Marx und Engels', in *Neue Zeit*, XXXII/2, esp. pp. 568–9), and his report of 1923 ('Neueste Mitteilungen über den literarischen Nachlass von Karl Marx und Friedrich Engels', in *Grünbergs Archiv*, XI, pp. 385–400) seems a classic *cri du coeur* of an academic *Gelehrte*, distraught at the betrayal of truth by the opportunistic calculations of party-politicians: he deals with the old edition of the correspondence on pp. 396–8, describing it as 'beneath all criticism', and its editors as 'philistine and *spiessbürgerlich*'. Riazanov returned to the attack, discussing in detail the differences between Bernstein's edition and his own, in the introductions to Volumes I and III of the latter (*MEGA*, IV/1, 1929, esp. pp. ix–xviii, and *ibid.* IV/3, 1930, pp. ix–x, xii–xiii). The charge of Riazanov's successor Adoratski (*MEGA* IV/4, 1931, p. XI) that Bernstein and Mehring, in cutting out Marx's and Engels' worst criticism of Liebknecht, wanted to make their opinion of him appear *lower* than it really was, is an example of what can be done, with a little ingenuity and a lot of prejudice, to sustain even the most unpromising party-line. In the *MEGA*, however, as Bernstein so finely, and so utterly falsely, said of the 1913 edition (*ibid.* Vol. IV, p. vii), 'the word is with the writers of the letters themselves'.

with perhaps too much sympathy, by Dr Benedikt Kautsky.[1] What is important now is that the 1913 edition, prepared (as Kautsky puts it) 'to bring the ideas of Marx and Engels to the members of a fighting political party', many of them too unsophisticated or uninstructed to be offered a complete edition,[2] should be denied the scholarly value which it claimed in addition to its primary purpose; and that it should finally cease to be regarded (as the later editions may be) as a reliable source of information on Marx and Engels.

[1] Kautsky reviewed the successive instalments of the *MEGA* in *Die Gesellschaft* (Berlin): Vol. V (1927), pp. 174 *et seq.*, Vol. VII (1930), pp. 260 *et seq.*, Vol. VIII (1931), pp. 456 *et seq.*, and Vol. X (1933), pp. 265 *et seq.* His observations in defence of Bernstein and his colleagues will be found in the last three of these articles, which deal with the four volumes of the Marx-Engels correspondence.

[2] *Die Gesellschaft*, VII (1930), p. 268.

APPENDIX IV

THE BERLIN SECTION OF THE INTERNATIONAL,
1865 TO 1866

(*Cf. Note* 1, p. 78, *and Note* 3, p. 103. *Further details are given in* H. *Gemkow's article on this subject, cited in the bibliography, and in the recent book by H. Hümmler,* Opposition gegen Lassalle, *Berlin, 1963*).

Meyer, Metzner and Vogt wrote to Marx in November 1865 (original in IISG, summarised in *Marx-Chronik*, p. 247 and reprinted by Gemkow, *loc. cit.* pp. 530–1) assuring him that his writings were widely read and admired in Berlin, and begging him to come and lead or advise the anti-Lassallean labour movement, since 'we lack intellectual leadership here since the departure of Liebknecht, who understood splendidly how to arouse the revolutionary spirit'. (Engels' comment on this was that the letter was 'obviously written by a chap with more go in him than Liebknecht, and who seems to refer to the latter not without a certain irony': *MEB*, III, p. 352.) Marx could not consider visiting the socialists of Berlin (cf. *MEB*, III, p. 353), but wrote a reply (now lost) telling them to join the International: this is clear not so much from Metzner's answer of 4 December (IISG) as from Marx's report to the General Council (Minutes, I, pp. 83–4) and from Vogt's letter to Johann Philipp Becker of 29 January 1866 (cf. Chapter III above). Liebknecht himself contributed something to founding this Berlin Section of the International, but not much: I am indebted to Mr Boris Nicolaevsky for informing me (in a letter of 23 December 1957) that Liebknecht wrote to Becker on 6 February 1866, commending Vogt to him as 'ein Prachtbursche von der alten Garde', who would shortly be writing to him; Liebknecht's delay (Vogt and Becker were by this time already in correspondence) seems to confirm that he gave the work of the International a low priority among his many preoccupations, which is also indicated by Marx's instructions to the Berliners to write to Becker (the implication was that he, rather than Liebknecht, should be regarded as the International's agent, although Meyer's letter to Liebknecht of 25 October 65—printed by Leidigkeit, *op. cit.* p. 93 (see bibliography)—shows that on other matters they remained in close contact with him). Meyer had in the meantime received Marx's authorisation to reprint the *Communist Manifesto* (cf. Jenny Marx to Meyer, early February 66, IISG), and brought out in Berlin the first German edition since 1848. The edition (to which Mr B. Andréas kindly drew my attention) must have been very small: only two copies of it are now known to exist, and although one copy was apparently seized by the police in 1870 and read in evidence at the trial of Liebknecht and others in 1872 (cf. *Hochverratsprozess*, pp. 166, 206), there is no other evidence of this edition's influence, which must have been extremely slight. A very full report on 'the literature of the International', sent to Bismarck by the Munich police early in 1874 (DZA Merseburg, Prussian *Ministerium des Innern,* Rep 77, Abt. II, Sekt 11D Gen, Vol. 5, pp. 89–92) mentions only two editions of the *Manifesto*, that of 1847 and the well-known reprint of 1872. Later in 1866 Meyer emigrated to America (*Marx-Chronik*, p. 447), being followed in May 1867 by Vogt (Vogt to Becker 15 May 1867, IISG); they were both active in the German-American labour movement and in the International (cf. Becker to Sorge 3 August 1867, in Sozialarchiv, Zürich, and Bebel to Meyer 8 February 1870, printed by Leidigkeit, *Wilhelm Liebknecht und August Bebel*, pp. 202–3). Metzner stayed in Berlin and remained active in the ADAV as an opponent of Schweitzer (cf. Bernstein, *Die Geschichte der Berliner Arbeiter-Bewegung*, Vol. I, pp. 155, 161, and Vahlteich to Metzner 6 September 1866, in IISG, Liebknecht *Nachlass*). He later joined the Eisenach Party, and in 1871 played a prominent part in rebuilding its organisation after the war, as well as in the new Berlin Section of the International (cf. Bebel, *AML*, I, p. 193, and Nicolaevsky in *Die Gesellschaft*, 1933, p. 258–9, as well as Chapter VI above).

BIBLIOGRAPHY

I. UNPUBLISHED CORRESPONDENCE AND OTHER SOURCES

International Institute for Social History, Amsterdam (IISG):

(a) *Nachlässe* of Johann Philipp Becker, Hermann Jung, Wilhelm Liebknecht, Karl Marx and Friedrich Engels, and letters of August Bebel, F. W. Fritzsche, James Guillaume and others, in former SPD *Partei-Archiv*;

(b) MS. Minute-books of the General Council of the International Working Men's Association. (See below, IIIa, for the recently published edition of the minutes for 1864–6.)

Schweizerisches Sozialarchiv, Zürich:

Letters from Johann Philipp Becker to F. A. Sorge.

II. STATE ARCHIVES

Deutsches Zentralarchiv, Abteilung Potsdam:

Reichsamt des Innern: Handel und Verkehr, Gen. Nr 31, Adhib. I: *Acta betr. Statistische Erhebungen über den Umfang, die Organisation und die Folgen der Arbeitseinstellungen*, Vol. I, 1873–4.

Deutsches Zentralarchiv, Abteilung Merseburg (formerly Geheimes Preussisches Staatsarchiv):

Ministerium des Innern: Rep 77, Ab II, Sekt 11D (Volksaufstände und Tumulte) Gen: *Acta betr. die Massregeln gegen die in unserer Zeit in Deutschland hervorgetretenen sozial-demokratischen Umtriebe sowie gegen die Bestrebungen der sogenannten Internationale*, Vols. 1–9, 1870–8.

Ibid. Rep 77, Tit 509, Nr 31: *Acta betr. das Revolutionäre Treiben und die Volksaufstände in der Schweiz*, Vol. 1, 1867.

Ibid. Rep 77, Tit 865; *Acta betr. Vereine*, Vols. 1–2, 1862–6.

Acta des Königlichen Zivil-Kabinets, I. Abthl, Rep 89H, Abthl XXI, Nr 18, Polizei-Sachen, Gen: *Acta betr. die Sozialdemokraten unp Anarchisten*, Vol. 1, 1872–82.

Ministerium für Handel und Gewerbe, Rep 120, BB VII, 1, 2: *Akten betr. die Massregeln gegen die Bestrebungen der Internationale*, Vols. 1–3, 1871–8.

Ibid. Rep 120, BB VII, 1, 1: *Die gewerbliche Arbeiter im Allgemeinen, deren Lohn- und Arbeitsverhältnisse sowie die Agitation für Erziehung höher Arbeitslöhnen, Herabsetzung der Arbeitszeit, usw.*, Vol. 1, 1865–75.

Brandenburgisches Landeshauptarchiv, Potsdam:

Polizeipräsidium Berlin Rep 30, C Tit 94, Lit A, Nr 100: *Die Arbeitervereine* (1850–67).

Rep 30, C Tit 94, Lit A, Nr 258: *die hiesige Arbeiterverhältnisse, insbes. die Entlassungen und Neueinstellungen von Arbeitern . . .*, Vol. 1 (1859–66).

Rep 30, C Tit 94, Lit B Nr 869: *Der Kaufmann Wilhelm Bracke* (1873–80).

Rep 30, C Tit 94, Lit E Nr 166: *betr. den Literaten Karl Ludwig Wilhelm Eichhoff* (1850–95).

Rep 30, C Tit 94, Lit S, Nr 1206: *betr. die Sozialdemokratische Liedersammlungen* (1873–96).

Rep 30, C Tit 94, Lit S Nr 1217: *betr. die Sozialdemokratische Arbeiterpartei Deutschlands* (sic), Vol. 1 (1875–7).

Rep 30, C Tit 95, Sekt 4, Nr 319: *Die Koburger 'Allgemeine Deutsche Arbeiterzeitung'* (1863–5).

Rep 30, C Tit 95, Sekt 4, Nr 378: *Der 'Social-Demokrat' zu Berlin* (1864–7).

Rep 30, C Tit 95, Sekt 5, Nr A. 33: *Der Sozialdemokratische Arbeiterverein zu Berlin* (1866–7).

Rep 30, C Tit 95, Sekt 5, Nr A. 37: *Der Sozialdemokratische Arbeiterverein zu Berlin* (1868–75).

Rep 30, C Tit 95, Sekt 5, Nr M. 53: *Die Internationale Gewerkschaft der Manufaktur-, Fabrik-, und Handarbeiter* (1872–8).

Badisches Generallandesarchiv, Karlsruhe (cf. Note 2, p. 154):

Zugang 1924, Nr 56: *Die Internationale Arbeiter-association betreffend*.

III. REPORTS OF CONGRESSES, TRIALS AND PARLIAMENTARY DEBATES

(a) Congresses

MINS, L. E. (ed.). *Founding of the First International (September–November 1864). A Documentary Record*, London, 1939.

BIBLIOGRAPHY

The General Council of the First International 1864–1866. The London Conference 1865. Minutes, Moscow, n.d. (1963).

Congrès ouvrier de l'Association internationale des Travailleurs, Genève, 1866.

Procès-verbaux du Congrès de l'Association internationale des Travailleurs réuni à Lausanne du 2 au 8 septembre 1867, La Chaux-de-Fonds, 1867.

Congrès de l'Association internationale des Travailleurs, Bruxelles, 1868.

Report on the Fourth Annual Congress of the International Working Men's Association . . . Basle 1869, London, 1869.

Report of the 5th Annual Congress of the International Working Men's Association, held at the Hague, Holland, Sept 2–9, 1872 . . . by Maltman Barry . . . London, 1872.

FREYMOND, J. (ed). *La Première Internationale. Receuil de Documents,* 2 Vols., Geneva, 1962.

GERTH, H. H. (ed). *The First International: Minutes of the Hague Congress of 1872, with Related Documents,* University of Wisconsin Press, 1958.

Protokolle über die General-Versammlungen des Allgemeinen Deutschen Arbeitervereins: Frankfurt a.M., 1865, Leipzig, 1866, Berlin, 1870, 1871, 1872.

Bericht über den fünften Vereinstag deutscher Arbeitervereine am 5., 6. & 7. Sept. 1868 in Nürnberg.

Protokoll über die Verhandlungun des Allgemeinen Deutschen Sozialdemokratischen Arbeiterkongresses zu Eisenach am 7., 8. & 9 August 1869.

Protokoll über den ersten Congress der Sozialdemokratischen Arbeiterpartei zu Stuttgart am. 4., 5., 6. & 7. Juni 1870.

Protokoll über den zweiten Congress der Sozialdemokratischen Arbeiterpartei zu Dresden am. 12., 13. & 14. August 1871.

(b) *Trials*

Der Braunschweiger Ausschuss der Sozialdemokratischen Arbeiterpartei in Lötzen und vor dem Gericht, von W. Bracke, Jun., Braunschweig, 1872.

Der Hochverraths-prozess wider Liebknecht, Bebel, Hepner, vor dem Schwurgericht zu Leipzig vom 11. bis 26. März 1872. Mit einer Einleitung von W. Liebknecht, Berlin, 1894. (New edition, including the Eisenach Congress *Protokoll: Der Leipziger Hochverratsprozess vom Jahre 1872,* Berlin, 1960.)

Der Wiener Hochverratsprozess. Bericht über die Schwurgerichts-Verhandlung gegen Andreas Scheu, Heinrich Oberwinder, Johann Most und Genossen (1870). Neu Herausgegeben von Heinrich Scheu, Wien, 1911.

BIBLIOGRAPHY

Procès de l'Association internationale des Travailleurs. Première et Deuxième Commissions du Bureau de Paris, Paris, 1870 (June).
Troisième Procès de l'Association internationale des Travailleurs, Paris, 1870 (July).

(c) Parliamentary Debates

Stenographische Berichte über die Verhandlungen des Reichstages im Norddeutschen Bunde, Berlin, 1867–70.

IV. NEWSPAPERS, ETC.

Arbeiter-Zeitung: Organ der Württembergischen Arbeiterbildungsvereine, Göppingen, 1867–8.

The Bee-Hive, London, 1865.

Demokratische Korrespondenz: Organ der deutschen Volkspartei, Stuttgart, 1868–70.

Demokratisches Wochenblatt: Organ der deutschen Volkspartei (& from Dec. 1868 *Organ des Verbandes Deutscher Arbeitervereine*), Leipzig, 1868–9.

Deutsche Arbeiterhalle, Flugblätter, im Auftrage des ständigen Ausschusses deutscher Arbeitervereine herausgegeben . . ., Mannheim, 1867–8.

Gewerkverein der Holzarbeiter (Internationale Genossenschaft); *Circulair des Direktoriums . . .*, Hamburg, 1870, 1873.

Hermann: Deutsches Wochenblatt aus London, 1861.

The Miner, and Workman's Advocate (later *The Commonwealth*), London, 1865–6.

Der Nordstern, Hamburg 1864–6.

Social-Demokrat, Organ des Allgemeinen deutschen Arbeitervereins (from 1866 *Organ der Sozialdemokratischen Partei*), Berlin, 1864–9.

Die Tagwacht, Zürich, 1870.

Der Volksstaat, Organ der Sozialdemokratischen Arbeiterpartei und der Gewerksgenossenschaften, Leipzig, 1869–72.

Der Vorbote, politische und sozialökonomische Monatsschrift, Zentralorgan der Sektionsgruppe deutscher Sprache der Internationalen Arbeiterassociation, Geneva, 1866–71 (reprinted, Zürich, 1963).

V. BIBLIOGRAPHIES, ETC.

Comité International des Sciences historiques. 'Répertoire des Sources pour l'Etude des Mouvements Sociaux aux XIXᵉ et XXᵉ Siècles', *La Première Internationale*, Vols. I, II & III. Paris, 1958, 1961, 1963.

DOLLÉANS, E. and CROZIER, M. *Mouvements ouvrier et socialiste, Chronologie et Bibliographie: Angleterre, France, Allemagne, Etats-Unis*, Paris, 1950.

BIBLIOGRAPHY

GULICK, C. A., and others. *History and Theory of Working-class Movements: A Select Bibliography*, Berkeley, Calif., n.d. (1954?).

RUBEL, M. *Bibliographie des Oeuvres de Karl Marx avec, en appendice, un répertoire des Oeuvres de Friedrich Engels*, Paris, 1956.

SNELL, J. L. 'Some German Socialist Newspapers in European Archives', *Journal of Modern History*, Vol. XXIV, 1952.

STAMMHAMMER, J. *Bibliographie des Socialismus und Communismus*, 3 vols., Jena, 1897, 1900, 1911.

VI. REVIEWS, ETC., CONTAINING HISTORICAL ARTICLES OR DOCUMENTS

(The more important articles are also listed separately below, under 'secondary works'.)

Archiv für Sozialgeschichte, Vol. II, Hanover, 1962.

Archiv für Sozialwissenschaft und Sozialpolitik, Jena. Vols. for 1907, 1913, 1922, 1927.

Beiträge zur Geschichte der deutschen Arbeiterbewegung, Berlin. Vols. for 1959, 1962.

Braunschweigisches Jahrbuch, Braunschweig. Vol. for 1962.

Dokumente des Sozialismus, 5 Vols., Berlin, 1902–6.

Einheit: Zeitschrift für Theorie und Praxis des Wissenschaftlichen Sozialismus, Berlin. Vol. for 1953.

Die Gesellschaft, Internationale Revue für Sozialismus und Politik, Berlin, 1924–33.

Grünbergs Archiv für die Geschichte des Sozialismus und der Arbeiterbewegung, Leipzig, 1911–30.

Hamburger Echo, Hamburg. Vol. for 1926.

International Affairs, London. Vol. for 1935.

International Review of Social History, Amsterdam, 1936–9 and since 1956.

Der Kampf, Sozialdemokratische Monatsschrift, Wien, 1907–38.

Marx-Engels Archiv, 2 Vols., Frankfurt a.M., 1926–7.

Die Neue Zeit, Wochenschrift der deutschen Sozialdemokratie, Stuttgart, 1883–1923, esp. Vols. for 1888–1916.

Socialist International Information, London. Vol. for 1954.

Unter dem Banner des Marxismus, Berlin-Wien. Vols. for 1928, 1932.

Vierteljahrschrift für Sozial- und Wirtschaftsgeschichte. Vol. for 1954.

Vorwärts, Berlin. Vols. for 1914, 1926, 1927.

Der Wahre Jakob, politisch-satirische Zeitschrift der deutschen Sozialdemokratie, Stuttgart. Vol. for 1900.

Die Waage, Wochenblatt für Politik und Literatur, Berlin. Vol. for 1877.

Zeitschrift für Geschichtswissenschaft, Berlin. Vol. for 1954.

VII. PUBLISHED CORRESPONDENCE

ADLER, VICTOR. *Briefwechsel mit August Bebel und Karl Kautsky*. Ed. Friedrich Adler. Wien, 1954.

Bismarck und Lassalle: Ihr Briefwechsel und Ihre Gespräche. Ed. Gustav Mayer. Berlin, 1928.

Aus den Anfängen der Braunschweiger Arbeiterbewegung. Unveröffentlichte Bracke-Briefe. Ed. Georg Eckert. Braunschweig, 1955.

'Briefe und Dokumente der Familie Marx aus den Jahren 1862–1873'. Ed. Bert Andréas. *Archiv für Sozialgeschichte*, Vol. II, 1962, pp. 167–293.

Friedrich Engels' Briefwechsel mit Karl Kautsky. Ed. Benedikt Kautsky. Wien, 1955.

ENGELS, FRIEDRICH. *Vergessene Briefe*. Ed. Emil Eichhorn. Berlin n.d. (1920).

Frédéric Engels, Paul et Laura Lafargue: Correspondance. Vol. I, 1868–86. Ed. E. Bottigelli. Paris 1956.

HESS, MOSES. *Briefwechsel*. Ed. E. Silberner and W. Blumenberg. S'Gravenhage, 1959.

LASSALLE, FERDINAND. *Nachgelassene Briefe und Schriften*. Ed. Gustav Mayer. 6 vols. Stuttgart-Berlin, 1920–5.

LIEBKNECHT, WILHELM. *Briefwechsel mit Karl Marx und Friedrich Engels*. Ed. Georg Eckert. S'Gravenhage, 1962.

Briefe und Auszüge aus Briefen von Joh. Phil. Becker. Jos. Dietzgen, Karl Marx u. Andere an F. A. Sorge u. Andere, Stuttgart, 1906.

Die Briefe von Karl Marx und Friedrich Engels an Danielson (Nikolai-on). Ed. Kurt Mandelbaum, intro. by Gustav Mayer. Leipzig, 1929.

Der Briefwechsel zwischen Friedrich Engels und Karl Marx, Vols. III & IV. Stuttgart, 1913.

MARX, KARL, and ENGELS, FRIEDRICH. *Ausgewählte Briefe*. Berlin, 1953.

——. *Briefwechsel*, Vols. III & IV. Berlin, 1950.

——. *Briefe über Das Kapital*. Berlin, 1954.

——. *Briefe an A. Bebel, W. Liebknecht, K. Kautsky und Andere: Teil I 1870–1886*. Ed. W. Adoratski. Moscow, 1933.

——. *Letters to Americans 1848–1895* . . . . New York, 1953.

——. *Sochineniya*, Vols. XXV–XXVII. Moscow, 1930–46.

MARX, KARL. *Briefe an Kugelmann*. Berlin, 1952.

——. *Kritik des Gothaer Programms*. Berlin, 1946.

VIII. PAMPHLETS, SPEECHES, MEMOIRS, ETC.

ADLER, VICTOR. *Aufsätze, Reden und Briefe*, Vol. I. Vienna, 1922.

BIBLIOGRAPHY

ANON. *Amtliche Mitteilung des deutschen Handelstages: Die Arbeitsein-stellungen in Deutschland. Bericht auf Grund des dem Handelstag zugegenen Materials* . . . n.p., n.d. (Berlin, 1873?).

——. *Ein Complott gegen die Internationale Arbeiter-Association: im Auf-trage des Haager Congresses verfasster Bericht über das Treiben Bakunin's und der Alliance der sozialistischen Demokratie.* Übersetzt von C. Kokosky. Braunschweig, 1874.

——. *Correspondence between the British and Spanish Governments respecting the International Society: Presented to both Houses of Parliament by Command of Her Majesty.* London, 1872.

——. *Generalstatuten, zugefugte Reglemente und Zentral-Statuten der Sectionsgruppe deutscher Sprache der Internationalen Arbeiter-Genossen-schaft.* Geneva, 1867.

——. *Die Geschichte der sozialdemokratischen Partei in Deutschland seit dem Tode Ferdinand Lassalle's* (by Bernhard Becker?). Berlin, 1865.

——. *Zur Geschichte der Internationale* ('von M.B.'). Leipzig, 1872.

——. *Die Handwerker-, Arbeiter-, und ähnlichen Vereine in Preussen.* Herausgegeben vom Centralverein in Preussen für das Wohl der arbeitenden Klassen. Berlin, 1865.

——. *Ferdinand Lassalle: Dokumentarische Darstellung seiner letzten Lebenstage, von Augenzeugen und Freunden.* Verlag von Reinhold Schlingmann. Berlin, 1865.

——. *Verhandlungen der zur Berathung der Coalitionsfrage berufenen Kommission, nach den amtlichen Protokollen und stenographischen Aufnahmen.* Berlin, 1865.

BEBEL, AUGUST. *Aus Meinem Leben,* 3 Vols. New ed. Berlin, 1953.

——. *Unsere Ziele. Eine Streitschrift gegen die 'Demokratische Korres-pondenz'.* 5. unveränd. Auflage. Leipzig, 1875.

——. *'Wilhelm Liebknecht'. Der Wahre Jakob,* No. 368. Berlin, 1900.

BECKER, BERNHARD. *Geschichte der Arbeiter-Agitation Ferdinand Las-salle's nach authentischen Aktenstücken.* Braunschweig, 1874.

——. *Der Grosser Arbeiter-Agitator Ferdinand Lassalle: Denkschrift für die Totenfeier des Jahres 1865.* (Frankfurt?)

BECKER, JOHANN PHILIPP. *Offener Brief an die Arbeiter über Schultze-Delitsch und Lassalle* . . . . Geneva, 1863.

ANON (JOHANN PHILIPP BECKER). *Die Letzten Tagen von Ferdinand Lassalle: ein Wahrheitsgetreuer Bericht von einem Augenzeugen.* Hamburg, 1864.

——. *Mahnruf an die deutschen Arbeiter.* Geneva, 1868.

——. *Die Internationale Arbeiterassociation und die Arbeitseinstellungen in Genf* . . . . 1868.

261

BIBLIOGRAPHY

ANON (JOHANN PHILIPP BECKER). *Die Internationale Arbeiterassociation und die Arbeiterbewegung in Basel....* Geneva, 1869?
(*see also: Biographie des alten Veterans der Freiheit Johann Philipp Becker.* Hrsg. vom Zentral-komite Genfs zur Denkmal-Enthüllung am 17.3.1889. Zürich, 1889).

BERNSTEIN, EDUARD. *Sozialdemokratische Lehrjahre.* Berlin, 1928.

BLOS, WILHELM. *Denkwürdigkeiten eines Sozialdemokraten,* Vol. I. München, 1914.

BRACKE, W. *Der Lassalle'sche Vorschlag: Ein Wort an den 4. Congress der Sozialdemokratischen Arbeiterpartei.* Braunschweig, 1873.

BUSCH, M. *Tagebuchblätter,* Vol. III. Leipzig, 1899.

EICHHOFF, WILHELM. *Die Internationale Arbeiter-Association.* Berlin, 1868.

ENGELS, FRIEDRICH. *Der deutsche Baurnkrieg.* Zürich, 1946.

——. *Internationales aus dem Volksstaat.* Berlin, 1894.

——. *Die Preussische Militärfrage und die deutsche Arbeiterpartei.* Hamburg, 1865.

FRIBOURG, E. *L'Internationale.* Paris, 1871.

GUILLAUME, JAMES. *L'Internationale, Documents et Souvenirs,* 4 Vols. Paris, 1905–10.

HELD, A. *Die deutsche Arbeiterpresse der Gegenwart.* Leipzig, 1873.

HEPNER, A. *Mein 3 1/2-jährige Leipziger Polizeicampagne....* Braunschweig, 1874.

HILLMANN, C. *Die Internationale Arbeiterassociation....* Hamburg, 1872.

ANON (K. HIRSCH). *Die deutsche Arbeiterpartei: Ihre Prinzipien und Ihr Programm.* Berlin, 1868.

HIRSCH, KARL. *Die Organisation der deutschen Arbeiterpartei.* Berlin, 1869.

LASSALLE, FERDINAND. *Reden und Schriften,* Vol. III. Berlin, 1892.

LIEBKNECHT, WILHELM. *Karl Marx zum Gedächtnis.* Nürnberg, 1896.

——. *Über die politische Stellung der Sozialdemokratie, insbesondere mit Bezug auf den Reichstag.* Leipzig, 1869.

——. 'Zwei Pionere', in *Neue Welt,* 1900, Nr. 17.

LIESE, AD. *Zur Arbeiterfrage: Beleuchtung des in der Volksversammlung vom 20. März gehaltenen Vortrages des Abgeordneten Bebel.* Luckenwalde, n.d. (1869?).

MARX, KARL. *Der Bürgerkrieg in Frankreich.* Berlin, 1952.

MARX, KARL, and ENGELS, FRIEDRICH. *Über die Gewerkschaften.* Berlin, 1953.

Marx-Engels-Lenin-Stalin. Zur Deutschen Geschichte, Vol. II. Berlin, 1954.

BIBLIOGRAPHY

MEINER, F. (ed.). *Die Volkswirtschaftslehre der Gegenwart in Selbstdarstellungen* (article by Bernstein). Berlin, 1924.

MILKE, F. *Notwendige und Berechtigte Forderungen der Arbeiter.* Berlin, 1869.

SCHILLING, C. *Die Ausstossung des Präsidenten Bernhard Beckers aus dem Allgemeinen deutschen Arbeiterverein.* Berlin, 1865.

SCHWEITZER, J. B. V. *Politische Aufsätze und Reden.* Ed. F. Mehring. Berlin, 1912.

TESTUT, C. *L'internationale,* 3rd ed. Versailles, 1871.

——. *Le Livre Bleu de l'Internationale.* 1871 (on Testut's employment as a spy by the French government, cf. G. del Bo in *Movimento Operaio,* Nov-Dec 1952, pp. 954–970).

TÖLCKE, C. *Zweck, Mittel und Organisation des Allgemeinen deutschen Arbeitervereins.* Berlin, 1873.

VAHLTEICH, J. *Der Parteikampf zwischen den Sozialisten in deutschland.* Chemnitz, n.d. [1873].

——. *Ferdinand Lassalle und die Anfänge der deutschen Arbeiterbewegung.* München, n.d. [1904].

——. (with Bebel, Mehring & Jaeckh): *Die Gründung der deutschen Sozialdemokratie; Eine Festschrift der Leipziger Arbeiter zum 23 Mai 1863.* Leipzig, 1903.

IX. SECONDARY WORKS

ARMSTRONG, SINCLAIR W. 'The Internationalism of the early Social Democrats in Germany', *American Historical Review,* Vol. XLVII (1942), pp. 245–58.

——. 'The Social Democrats and the Unification of Germany, 1863–71', *Journal of Modern History,* Vol. XII (1940), pp. 485–509.

BABEL, ANTONY. 'La Première Internationale, ses débuts et son activité à Genève, 1864–70', *Mélanges d'Etudes Economiques et Sociales offerts à William E. Rappard,* pp. 225–364. Geneva, 1944.

BAUMANN, J. (ed.). *Das Hambacher Fest.* Speyer, 1957.

BENSER, GUNTER. *Zur Herausbildung der Eisenacher Partei.* Berlin, 1956.

BERGHOFF-ISING, F. *Die Socialistische Arbeiterbewegung in der Schweiz.* Leipzig, 1895.

BERGSTRÄSSER, LUDWIG. *Geschichte der Politischen Parteien in Deutschland,* Seventh edition. München, 1952.

BERNSTEIN, EDUARD. *Die Geschichte der Berliner Arbeiter-Bewegung,* Vol. I. Berlin, 1907.

BERNSTEIN, SAMUEL. *Essays in Political and Intellectual History.* New York, 1955.

BOESE, FRANZ. *Geschichte des Vereins für Sozialpolitik 1872–1932.* Berlin, 1939.

BORKENAU, FRANZ. *Socialism, National or International.* London, 1942.

BOURGIN, GEORGES. 'La lutte du Gouvernement Français contre la Première Internationale', *International Review of Social History,* 1939, pp. 39–137.

——. 'Une entente franco-allemande; Bismarck, Thiers, Jules Favre et la Répression de la Commune de Paris', *Ibid.* 1956, pp. 41–53.

——. *La Commune.* Paris, 1953.

BRANDIS, KURT. *Die deutsche Sozialdemokratie bis zum Falle des Sozialistengesetzes.* Leipzig, 1931. (This is identical with the dissertation submitted at Frankfurt a.M. under the same title in 1930, the author's name here being given as Karl F. Brockschmidt.)

BRAUNTHAL, JULIUS. 'The First International; an Appraisal of its Significance', *Socialist International Information,* Vol. IV, No. 35. London, 1954.

——. *Geschichte der Internationale,* Vol. I. Hanover, 1960.

BRIGGS, A. and SAVILLE, J. (eds.). *Studies in Labour History.* London, 1960.

BRÜGEL, L. *Geschichte der Oesterreichischen Sozialdemokratie,* 5 Vols. Vienna, 1922–5.

BRUPBACHER, F. *Marx und Bakunin: ein Beitrag zur Geschichte der Internationalen Arbeiter-Association.* München, 1913; Berlin, 1922.

CAREW HUNT, R. N. *The Theory and Practice of Communism,* Fifth edition. London, 1957.

CARR, E. H. *Karl Marx; a Study in Fanaticism.* London, 1934.

——. 'The League of Peace and Freedom, an Episode in the Quest for Collective Security', *International Affairs,* Vol. XIV, 1935, pp. 837–44.

——. *Michael Bakunin.* London, 1937.

——. *The Romantic Exiles.* London, 1933; Penguin Books, 1949.

——. *Studies in Revolution.* London, 1950.

COLE, G. D. H. *Marxism and Anarchism 1850–1890.* London, 1954.

COMMONS, J. R. and ANDREWS, K. *A Documentary History of American Industrial Society,* Vol. IX. Cleveland, 1910.

CONZE, WERNER. 'Vom "Pöbel" zum "Proletariat"', *Vierteljahrschrift für Wirtschafts- und Sozialgeschichte,* Vol. XLI, 1954, pp. 332–64.

DAUN, MICHAEL. 'Skizze der Geschichte der I. Internationale'. Unpublished dissertation. Cologne, 1923.

BIBLIOGRAPHY

DLUBEK, ROLF, and HERRMANN, URSULA. 'Die Magdeburger Sektion der I. Internationale und der Kampf um die Schaffung einer revolutionären Massenpartei der deutschen Arbeiterklasse', *Beiträge zur Geschichte der deutschen Arbeiterbewegung*, IV. Jg., 1962, Sonderheft, pp. 189–218.

DOLLÉANS, EDOUARD. *Histoire du Mouvement Ouvrier*, Vol. I. Paris, 1936.

DRACHKOVITCH, M. *De Karl Marx à Léon Blum; la Crise de la Social-Démocratie*. Geneva, 1954.

ECKERT, GEORG. 'Die Flugschriften der lassalleanischen Gemeinde in Braunschweig', *Archiv für Sozialgeschichte*, Vol. II, 1962, pp. 295–358.

———. *Wilhelm Bracke und die Anfänge der Braunschweiger Arbeiterbewegung*. Braunschweig, 1957.

———. 'Zur Geschichte der Braunschweiger Sektion der I. Internationale', *Braunschweigisches Jahrbuch*, Vol. 43, 1962, pp. 131–72.

EISNER, KURT. *Wilhelm Liebknecht. Sein Leben und Wirken*, Second edition. Berlin, 1906.

ENGELBERG, ERNST. 'Die Rolle von Marx und Engels bei der Herausbildung einer selbständigen deutschen Arbeiterpartei (1864–9)', *Zeitschrift für Geschichtswissenschaft*, Vol. II. Berlin, 1954, pp. 509–37, 637–65.

EYCK, ERICH. *Der Verband Deutscher Arbeitervereine. Ein Beitrag zur Entstehungsgeschichte der deutschen Arbeiterbewegung*. Berlin, 1904.

———. *Bismarck*, Vol. II. Zürich, 1943.

FISCHER, FRITZ, et al. *Geschichte in Ueberblick*, Vol. III. Oldenburg, n.d.

FOOTMAN, DAVID. *The Primrose Path, a Life of Ferdinand Lassalle*. Guild Books edition, Vienna, 1947.

GÄRTNER, GEORG. *Die Nürnberger Arbeiterbewegung 1868–1908*. Nürnberg (?), 1908.

GAY, PETER. *The Dilemma of Democratic Socialism; Eduard Bernstein's Challenge to Marx*. New York, 1954.

GEMKOW, H. 'Zür Tätigkeit der Berliner Sektion der I. Internationale', in *Beiträge zur Geschichte der deutschen Arbeiterbewegung*, Vol. I, 1959, pp. 515–31.

HALÉVY, ELIE. *Histoire du Socialisme Européen*. Paris, 1948.

HEIDEGGER, HERMANN. *Die deutsche Sozialdemokratie und der nationale Staat, 1870–1920*. Göttingen-Berlin-Frankfurt, 1956.

HUMMLER, HEINZ. *Opposition gegen Lassalle*. Berlin, 1963.

HUNTER, ROBERT. *Violence and the Labor Movement*. New York, 1916.

BIBLIOGRAPHY

JAECKH, GUSTAV. *Die Internationale; eine Denkschrift zur 40-jähriger Gründung der Internationalen Arbeiter-Association.* Leipzig, 1904.

JANTKE, CARL. *Der Vierte Stand; die gestaltenden Kräfte der deutschen Arbeiterbewegung im XIX. Jahrhundert.* Freiburg, 1955.

JELLINEK, F. *The Paris Commune of 1871.* London, 1937.

JOHANNSEN, HARRO. 'Der Revisionismus in der deutschen Sozial-Demokratie, 1890 bis 1914'. Unpublished dissertation, Hamburg, 1954.

JOLL, JAMES. *The Second International.* London, 1955.

KAMPFFMEYER, PAUL. 'Bebel und die Erste Internationale, nach Briefen von Bebel an Joh. Ph. Becker', in *Vorwärts.* Berlin, 18 Jan. 1927.

——. 'Liebknecht und die Internationale. Aus seinem Briefwechsel mit Joh. Ph. Becker', in *Vorwärts.* Berlin, 28 March 1926.

——. *Die Sozialdemokratie im Lichte der Kulturentwicklung,* 4th edition. Berlin, 1913.

——. *Die Sozialdemokratie in der deutschen Geschichte bis zur Reichsgründung.* München, 1926.

——, and ALTMANN, B. *Ver dem Sozialistengesetz.* Berlin, 1928.

KAUTSKY, KARL. *Sozialisten und Krieg; ein Beitrag zur Ideengeschichte des Sozialismus von den Hussiten bis zum Völkerbund.* Prague, 1937.

KLÜHS, FR. *Der Aufstieg,* Third edition. Berlin, 1930.

KORSCH, KARL. 'Der Marxismus der Ersten Internationale', in *Die Internationale,* Jrg. 7, Berlin 1924, pp. 573–5.

——. *Die Materialistische Geschichtauffassung: Eine Auseinandersetzung mit Karl Kautsky.* Leipzig n.d. (1929).

LABEDZ, L., (ed.). *Revisionism: Essays on the History of Marxist Ideas.* London, 1962.

LADEMACHER, HORST. 'Zu den Anfängen der deutschen Sozialdemokratie 1863–78', in *International Review of Social History,* Vol. IV, 1959, pp. 239–60, 367–93.

LANGHARD, A. *Die anarchistische Bewegung in der Schweiz* Berlin, 1903.

LAUFENBERG, H. *Geschichte der Arbeiterbewegung in Hamburg, Altona u. Umgebung,* Vol. I. Hamburg, 1911.

——. 'Die Politik J. B. von Schweitzers und die Sozialdemokratie', in *Neue Zeit,* Vol. XXX, 1911–12.

LEIDIGKEIT, KARL-HEINZ. *Wilhelm Liebknecht und August Bebel in der deutschen Arbeiterbewegung 1862–1869.* Berlin, 1957.

LICHTHEIM, GEORGE. *Marxism, an Historical and Critical Study.* London, 1961.

LÖSCHNER, HARALD. 'August Bebels Politische Entwicklung während seiner Leipziger Jahre'. Unpublished dissertation, Leipzig, 1952.

BIBLIOGRAPHY

LUKACS, GEORG. *Geschichte und Klassenbewusstsein.* Berlin, 1923.

LUKIN, N. 'Protokolle des Generalrats der Internationalen Arbeiter-Association als Quelle für die Geschichte der Pariser Kommune', *Unter dem Banner des Marxismus,* Vol. VI, Wien/Berlin, 1932, pp. 79–105.

MACRAE, D. G. *Ideology and Society.* London, 1961.

MARCK, SIEGFRIED. *Sozial-demokratie.* Berlin, 1931.

Marx, Karl: Chronik seines Lebens in Einzeldaten. Moscow, 1934.

MATTHIAS, ERICH. 'Kautsky und der Kautskyanismus; Die Funktion der Ideologie in der deutschen Sozialdemokratie vor dem ersten Weltkriege', in *Marxismusstudien,* 2. Folge. Tübingen, 1956.

———. *Sozialdemokratie und Nation. Ein Beitrag zur Ideengeschichte der sozialdemokratischen Emigration in der Prager Zeit des Parteivorstandes, 1933–1938.* Stuttgart, 1952.

MAYER, GUSTAV. 'Die Lösung der deutschen Frage im Jahre 1866 und die Arbeiterbewegung', *Festgabe für Wilhelm Lexis.* Jena, 1907, pp. 223–68.

———. *J. B. v. Schweitzer und die Sozialdemokratie.* Jena, 1909.

———. 'Die Trennung der proletarischen von der bürgerlichen Demokratie in Deutschland, 1863–70', *Grünbergs Archiv* ..., 2. Jrg. Leipzig, 1911, pp. 1–67.

———. 'Der Allgemeiner Deutscher Arbeiterverein und die Krisis 1866', *Archiv fur Sozialwissenschaft und Sozialpolitik,* Vol. 57. Jena, 1927, pp. 167–75.

———. *Friedrich Engels: Eine Biographie,* 2 Vols. The Hague, 1934.

———. *Erinnerungen.* Wien, 1949.

———. and others. *Geschichte der Frankfurter Zeitung, Volksausgabe.* Frankfurt a.M., 1911.

MEHRING, FRANZ. *Zur Geschichte der deutschen Sozialdemokratie.* Bremen, 1877.

———. *Die deutsche Sozialdemokratie: ihre Geschichte und ihre Lehre,* Third edition. Bremen, 1879.

———. *Geschichte der deutschen Sozialdemokratie,* 4 Vols., 10th edition. Stuttgart, 1922.

———. (ed.). *Politische Aufsätze und Reden von J. B. v. Schweitzer.* Berlin, 1912.

———. *Karl Marx,* 5th edition, mit Einleitung von Ed. Fuchs. Berlin, 1933. (English translation, London 1936.)

———. *Gesammelte Schriften und Aufsätze in Einzelausgaben.* Hrsg. Ed. Fuchs; Bd. V. *Zur Deutschen Geschichte,* mit Einleitung von Ludwig Pollnau. Berlin, 1931.

BIBLIOGRAPHY

MEYER, RUDOLF. *Der Emancipationskampf des Vierten Standes*, Vol. I, 2nd edition, Berlin, 1882; Vol. II, Berlin, 1875.

MICHELS, ROBERT. 'Die deutsche Sozialdemokratie im internationalen Verbande', *Archiv für Sozialwissenschaft und Sozialpolitik*, Vol. 27, 1907, pp. 148–231.

——. *Zur Soziologie des Parteiwesens in der Modernen Demokratie.* Stuttgart, 1958.

MILHAUD, EDGAR. *La Social-démocratie allemande.* Paris, 1903.

MOMMSEN, WILHELM. *Deutsche Parteiprogramme: eine Auswahl vom Vormärz bis zur Gegenwart.* München, 1952.

MORGAN, ROGER. 'Travaux effectués dans les deux Allemagnes sur l'Histoire du Mouvement Ouvrier', *L'Actualité de l'Histoire. Bulletin trimestriel de l'Institut français d'Histoire sociale*, No. 19, October, 1957, pp. 28–35.

MÜHLBRADT, WERNER. 'Wilhelm Liebknecht und die Gründung de, deutschen Sozialdemokratie, 1862–1875'. Unpublished dissertation, Göttingen, 1950.

MÜLLER, HERMANN. *Die Geschichte der Lithographen, Steindrücker und Verwandten Berufe*, Vol. I. *Allgemeine Gewerkschaftsgeschichte.* Berlin, 1917.

NETTLAU, MAX. *Der Anarchismus von Proudhon zu Kropotkin.* Berlin, 1927.

NICOLAEVSKY, BORIS. 'Aus der Geschichte der I. Internationale', *Die Gesellschaft.* Berlin, 1925, pp. 445–75.

——. 'Karl Marx und die Berliner Sektion der I. Internationale', *Die Gesellschaft.* Berlin, 1933, pp. 252–64.

——. and MAENCHEN-HELFEN, O. *Karl und Jenny Marx: Ein Lebensweg.* Berlin, 1933.

——. *Karl Marx: Man and Fighter.* London, 1936.

OBERWINDER, HEINRICH. *Sozialismus und Sozialpolitik. Ein Beitrag zur Geschichte der Socialpolitischen Kämpfe unserer Zeit.* Berlin, 1887.

ONCKEN, HERMANN. *Ferdinand Lassalle, Eine Politische Biographie*, 4th ed. Stuttgart, 1923.

OSTERROTH, F. *Biographisches Lexikon des Sozialismus*, Vol. I. Hanover, 1960.

PLAMENATZ, JOHN P. *German Marxism and Russian Bolshevism.* London, 1954.

POSTGATE, RAYMOND W. *Revolution from 1789 to 1914.* London, 1920.

——. *The Workers' International.* Swarthmore, 1921.

RAGAZ, JACOB. *Geschichte der Arbeiterbewegung in der Westschweiz.* Aarau, 1938.

RAMM, THILO. *Ferdinand Lassalle als Rechts- und Sozialphilosoph.* Maisenheim-Wien, 1953.

RJASANOV, N. 'Sozialdemokratische Flagge und Anarchistische Ware: ein Beitrag zur Parteigeschichte', *Neue Zeit*, Vol. 32. Stuttgart, 1913–14, pp. 150–61, 226–39, 265–72, 320–33, 360–76.

——. 'Die Entstehung der Internationalen Arbeiterassociation', *Marx-Engels Archiv*, Vol. I. Frankfurt a.M., 1926, pp. 119–202.

——. '50 Jahre Anti-Dühring,' *Unter dem Banner des Marxismus*, Vol. II. Vienna/Berlin, 1928, pp. 266–87.

ROSENBERG, ARTHUR. *Die Entstehung der Deutschen Republik.* Berlin, 1928; New ed. Frankfurt a.M., 1961.

——. *Democracy and Socialism; A Contribution to the Political History of the Past 150 Years.* English translation, London, 1939.

RUSSELL, BERTRAND. *German Social Democracy.* London, 1896.

SAUERBREY, MANFRED. 'Bebel und die Grundfragen der deutschen Politik im Zeitalter Bismarcks'. Unpublished dissertation, Cologne, 1951.

SCHÄFER, JOHANN. 'Das politische Verhalten der Internationale zum Deutschfranzösischen Kriege und zur Kommune (1870–1871)'. Unpublished dissertation, Heidelberg, 1921.

SCHIEDER, THEODOR. *The State and Society in our Times.* English translation, London, 1962.

SCHORSKE, CARL, E. *German Social Democracy 1905–1917.* Cambridge, Mass., 1955.

SCHRÖDER, WILHELM. *Handbuch der sozialdemokratischen Parteitage von 1863–1909.* München, 1910.

——. *Geschichte der sozialdemokratischen Parteiorganisation in Deutschland.* Dresden, 1912.

SOMBART, WERNER. *Sozialismus und Soziale Bewegung.*, 8th ed. Jena, 1919.

——. *Der proletarische Sozialismus* ('*Marxismus*'), 2 Vols. Jena, 1924.

STEINER, HERBERT. *Zur Geschichte der österreichischen Arbeiterbewegung 1867–1888.* Vienna, 1962.

STEINIGER, P. A., and KLENNER, H. *Die Ueberwindung der Lassalleschen Staatsideologie; Eine Voraussetzung für die Demokratische Lösung der Deutschen Frage in den 60er Jahren des 19. Jahrhunderts.* Berlin, 1955.

STEKLOFF, G. M. *History of the First International.* London, 1928.

STERN, LEO (ed.). *Archivalische Forschungen zur Geschichte der Deutschen Arbeiterbewegung*, Vol. I. Berlin, 1954.

STOLTENBERG, GERHARD. *Der Deutsche Reichstag 1871–1873.* Düsseldorf, 1955.

BIBLIOGRAPHY

STRAUSS, R., and FINSTERBUSCH, K. *Die Chemnitzer Arbeiterbewegung unter dem Sozialistengesetz*. Berlin, 1954.

TREUE, WILHELM. *Deutsche Parteiprogramme 1861–1954*. Göttingen-Frankfurt-Berlin, 1954.

VALIANI, LEO. *Storia del Movimento Socialista*, Vol. I. *L'Epoca della Prima Internazionale*. Firenze, 1951.

WECKERLE, EDUARD. *Hermann Greulich; Ein Sohn des Volkes*. Zürich, 1947.

WURM, EMANUEL (ed.). *Volks-Lexikon: Nachschlagsbuch für sämtliche Wissenszweigen* . . ., Vol. IV. Nürnberg, 1897.

ZLOCISTI, THEODOR. *Moses Hess, der Vorkämpfer des Sozialismus und Zionismus, Eine Biographie*, 2nd ed. Berlin, 1921.

INDEX

(Note that the Appendices are not indexed; see Table of Contents)

271

INDEX

273

unwillingness of Eccarius to leave, 105
see also International
Lörrach, 121, 154
Lötzen, fortress of, 182, 213
Löwenstein, 156n
Lüdecke, 153
Lugau, 115, 149, 150
Lukin, N., 203n
Luscher, J., 42

Macrae, D. G., 237n
Magdeburg, 28, 168
support for International in, 76, 92n
see also International; Workers' Educational Clubs
Mainz, 83, 88f, 93, 109, 152
Carpenters' Union of, 152
Social-democratic Club of, 192, 152
International's planned congress in (1870), see International; Eisenach Party's Congress in (1872)
see also Sozialdemokratische Arbeiterpartie; International
Maenchen-Helfen, O., 59n
Mannheim, 15, 18, 93, 193
Marck, S., 233
Martini, Solicitor, 151
Marx, Karl
relations with Germany and German labour movement, ix, 8, 29, 31–3, 38f, 42, 45, 47, 57, 62, 80, 105, 184, 222, 230ff
relations with Lassalle, 6, 45f
relations with Liebknecht, 7, 27, 44, 49–51, 53, 55–9, 98–128, 132, 136, 140–1, 148–50, 160–72, 201n, 210–12
as Corresponding Secretary of the International for Germany, 23, 44f, 57, 80, 101, 104, 108–10, 128, 149–50, 171–2, 183–4,
relations with Schweitzer, 23–5, 38–62, 100–2, 128–31, 135–41, 160–7
Das Kapital, 23, 46f, 89, 94, 116, 120ff, 132f, 135f, 139, 222, 235
Communist Manifesto, 38, 104, 123, 169, 235f
relations with J. Ph. Becker and attitude to Group of German-speaking

sections, 66–7, 74–5, 80, 86, 172–3, 176–9
Herr Vogt, 104
Confidential Communication, 201; Inaugural Address, see International
Matthias, E., 233n, 234
Mayer, G.,
Friedrich Engels, xiv, 19n, 113n, 118n, 123n, 124n, 125n, 128n, 132n, 137n, 138n, 149n, 162n, 169n, 219n, 234n
J. B. von Schweitzer, passim (note in Mayer's own copy of, 71n).
Bismarck and Lassalle, 9n
"Die Trennung der proletarischen von der bürgerlichen Demokratie in Deutschland", 12n, 16n, 20n, 87, 107n, 111n, 113n, 118n, 119n, 125n, 194n, 196n
Ferdinand Lassalle, Nachgelassene Briefe und Schriften, xiv, 40n, 46n, 67n
"Die Lösung der deutschen Frage im Jahre 1866", 79n, 98n, 108n, 109n
Meerane, 117
Mehring, F., 12n, 33n, 37n, 53n, 58n, 59n, 60n, 89n, 98, 165n, 220n, 233n
Meincke, K., 76n, 151, 236n
Mende, F., 28, 167
Metzner, Th., 42, 77, 84n, 103, 110n, 112n, 225n
Meyer, R., 226n, 227n, 228n, 233n
Meyer, S., 30, 42, 77, 103, 104, 109
Michels, R., 236n
Milke, F., 225n–6n
Mins, L. E., 45n
Mitteldeutsche Volkszeitung, 113, 114, 122, 145n
Moll, F., 77, 80n, 82n, 153n, 236n
Mommsen, W., 7n
Mühlbradt, W., 17n, 45n, 100n, 104n, 108, 111n, 115n, 123n, 167n
Müller, H., 11n, 91n, 101n, 163n
Müller (Stuttgart), 82n
Müller, M., 90
München, 80n, 93
Münze, J., 79, 80n, 89, 92n, 236n

Napoleon III, Emperor of France, 31, 52, 206–9
Nationalverein (National Association), 4, 5, 109

For EU product safety concerns, contact us at Calle de José Abascal, 56–1°, 28003 Madrid, Spain or eugpsr@cambridge.org.

www.ingramcontent.com/pod-product-compliance
Ingram Content Group UK Ltd.
Pitfield, Milton Keynes, MK11 3LW, UK
UKHW010348140625
459647UK00010B/906